The Quality Business

Quality is now a key issue in commerce and industry. This book is the first to seriously consider quality issues in small firms, based upon well-conducted research and careful theorising. Subjects covered include:

- the relevance of formal quality standards such as BS 5750 to small firms
- definitions and implementation of 'quality' in a business context, from informal methods to Total Quality Management
- interviews with a selected sample of over 150 owner-managers
- detailed case studies of small firms
- analysis of self-generated quality strategies

The Quality Business will be of interest to all those studying business and management. Its factually-based assessment of quality management strategies means that it will also be very useful for those actively involved in implementing quality strategies or promoting small businesses.

Julian North is a Researcher in the Small Business Research Centre at Kingston University. **Robert A. Blackburn** is Director of the Small Business Research Centre at Kingston University. **James Curran** is Emeritus Professor of Small Business Studies at Kingston University.

Routledge Studies in Small Business
Edited by David Storey

The Quality Business

Quality issues and smaller firms

Julian North, Robert A. Blackburn and James Curran

London and New York

First published 1998 by Routledge
11 New Fetter Lane, London EC4P 4EE

Simultaneously published in the USA and Canada
by Routledge
29 West 35th Street, New York, NY 10001

© 1998 Julian North, Robert A. Blackburn and James Curran

Typeset in Times by RefineCatch Limited, Bungay, Suffolk
Printed and bound in Great Britain by TJ International Ltd, Padstow, Cornwall

British Library Cataloguing in Publication Data
A catalogue record for this book is available from the British Library

Library of Congress Cataloguing in Publication Data
A catalogue record for this book has been requested

ISBN 0–415–14608–9

Contents

Tables

Notes on authors

Julian North is a Researcher in the Small Business Research Centre at Kingston University. He has undertaken a wide variety of research on small firms. Recently he completed a research project on small businesses and their relations with trade associations and currently is investigating entrepreneurship and the older person. In 1995 and 1996 he co-authored papers which won the prize for best paper presented at the Institute of Small Business Affairs National Small Business Policy and Research Conference.

Robert A. Blackburn is Director of the Small Business Research Centre at Kingston University. He is the Midland Bank Research Fellow in small business studies at the centre and has published widely on aspects of the small business. A recent project, sponsored by the Management Charter Initiative and the Department of Education and Employment, has been on business support networks in Denmark, Baden Württemberg and the UK. He is also responsible for several other projects being undertaken by the centre.

James Curran is Emeritus Professor of Small Business Studies at Kingston University. He established the University's Small Business Research Centre in 1987 and was Midland Bank Professor of Small Business Studies and Director of the centre until 1996. He continues to be associated with the centre and its research. He has a long record of research and publications on the small firm and is widely known in the UK and internationally. He is currently directing a study of small business owner involvement in the community and researching the possible impact of a statutory national minimum wage on UK small firms.

Preface

Quality and quality management have become the focus of much attention in recent management writing and research in the UK and other economies. Small businesses, now widely accepted as playing a key role in the UK economy, have received some of this attention particularly in relation to why so few have opted for registering for BS 5750 (now relabelled BS EN ISO 9000 or more simply ISO 9000 to denote its international application). Government and many commentators on small business have sought to encourage more small firms to adopt formal quality management strategies as a key to improving business performance, their contribution to the UK economy and to bring them into line with what many larger enterprises have been doing.

This research started as an investigation into why small business owners have been so reluctant to register for BS 5750. As the research developed, however, it became a much wider investigation of the quality management strategies used by small business owner-managers, a more fundamental issue than the adoption or non-adoption of BS 5750. The findings and the analysis put BS 5750 and similar formal quality management strategies in context, that is, as one approach to the issue of managing quality in the small enterprise. As much previous research has emphasised, small firms are a highly heterogeneous population and any analysis needs to take account of this variability. As the findings presented in the following pages demonstrate, this variability is as evident in how quality is managed as it is in so many other aspects of the small enterprise. Quality management in small firms, in other words, emerged as much more complex than it is often portrayed.

The research was funded by Kingston University as part of a policy to support new areas of business research and we are grateful for the University's backing. We are also grateful for the contributions to the project made by other members of the Small Business Research Centre as well as other friends and colleagues. We would especially like to thank John Kitching, Valerie Alsop and Madeline Swarbrick for their help and support. We would also like to thank those individuals who commented on the conference papers reporting findings and interpretations from earlier stages of the research. In parallel to the project reported in this book, a number of other research ventures on quality issues in the enterprise were undertaken by colleagues at other institutions and we benefited from the exchanges at conferences etc. where they presented their findings. Their work is acknowledged appropriately in the book.

Most important, we would also like to thank the 150 small business owners who took part in the telephone survey which provided the bulk of the data for the project. In addition, ten of the owner-managers allowed us to visit them at their businesses, interview them in depth and talk to others in the businesses. These provided the material for the case studies and were invaluable in providing insights which enabled us to develop the overall theorisation offered in the book. Their generosity with their time and views deserves an extra thank you. We hope the results not only contribute to the greater understanding of how quality is managed in the small firm but also to the development of support policies and help for those running small enterprises who have to cope every day with the problems of producing high quality goods and services for other businesses and consumers.

Julian North, Robert A. Blackburn, James Curran
Small Business Research Centre
Kingston University
March 1997

1 Small firms and quality management

INTRODUCTION

Small firms are now major contributors to employment and wealth in the British economy. Though awareness of the contribution of small enterprises is now widespread, their importance is still often underestimated. After a period of strong growth over the last two decades, small firms (those employing at least one but under 50 employees) now number over one million, accounting for over 97 per cent of *all* businesses with employees in the UK (DTI, 1996a: 9).[1] Between them, these businesses generate over a third of UK business turnover and provide almost seven million jobs (DTI, 1996a: 9).

The reasons offered for the dramatic increase in the importance of the small firm in the UK economy are varied. They range from the promotion of an 'enterprise culture' by the Conservative governments of the 1980s, to changes in technology, to increases in outsourcing by larger enterprises, to the massive economic restructuring which saw the decline in manufacturing and the expansion in services and knowledged-based economic activities (Curran, 1996: 7–25). In all likelihood, several of these influences (as well as others) have been important to a greater or lesser extent. Some of the influences such as the emergence of information technology (IT) based economic activities and the decline of older, mass production manufacturing and heavy industry, as well as the effects of globalisation, appear irreversible (Meadows, 1996).

One inference to be drawn from the above is that the increased importance of small scale enterprise in the economy is unlikely to decline (Blackburn, 1996). Quite the reverse, the indications are that the role of small businesses will increase contributing more to business turnover and employment in the future. Britain's economy is becoming more services and knowledge based and these are the kinds of activities in which small firms can often compete very effectively, often outperforming larger businesses. The precipitous decline in manufacturing's share of UK economic activity since the 1960s has probably halted, but smaller businesses have also gained a significant share of the surviving manufacturing also. Much of the new technology employed in manufacturing, for example, permits small scale production to be carried out profitably. In high technology sectors small businesses have already shown their ability to innovate by introducing new products and opening up new markets (Oakey, 1995).

MANAGEMENT SKILLS AND THE SMALL FIRM

Given the rise in the importance of small scale enterprise, much depends increasingly on the quality of management in small businesses. Up to now, management education and research, particularly in Britain's business schools, has centred on meeting the needs of larger enterprises. Yet, if small businesses continue to grow in importance, the overall performance of the UK in a more competitive world economy becomes more reliant on small businesses and the managerial abilities of those who own and run them. Any shortfall in management skills among small business owners could, in other words, seriously hurt Britain's economic future.

Fears about managerial skill levels in small firms are, in fact, already widely voiced. Commentators and researchers have long identified persistent managerial weaknesses among owner-managers of small firms (Bolton Report, 1971; Stanworth and Gray, 1991). In part, the lack of managerial skills is said to be due to the demands of the small business management role itself. Many small businesses are owned and run by one person who has to bear all the managerial responsibilities for the enterprise. Besides being responsible for the production of the firm's output, he or she also has to manage cash flow and finance, marketing and the firm's employees. All too easily, it is argued, this leads to managerial overload (Dewhurst and Burns, 1993). Even where there are two or more partners running the business their managerial performance may be poor. A major reason for this, it is believed, is that too few small business managers have any formal managerial training (DTI, 1995).

Governments have attempted to strengthen the alleged weak management of small firms by mounting a huge range of management support programmes since the early 1980s (Storey, 1994). Many argue that these initiatives have been largely ineffective (Stanworth and Gray, 1991: 188–189: Storey and Westhead, 1994). Only about a third of owner-managers take up publicly supported or privately provided training (Curran *et al.*, 1996a: 12). Besides the time constraints mentioned above, many small business owners also believe that either they do not need any outside training or the training on offer is unsuitable (Curran *et al.*, 1996a: 16). For example, much of the publicly supported training has concentrated on the needs of start-ups rather than those of the much more numerous established small businesses (Stanworth and Gray, 1991: Chapter 8).

SMALL FIRMS' MANAGEMENT AND QUALITY

'Quality' has emerged as a key management concern since the beginning of the 1980s to be added to financial management, marketing and human resource management as essential to the success and survival of any business, large or small (Tuckman, 1995: 59–74; Barad, 1996). The success of Japanese businesses, particularly in invading markets in Britain and the USA and riding out the severe economic crises and recessions of the early 1970s and 1980s, was linked closely by commentators to Japanese management strategies which made quality central to business success (see, for example, the highly influential book by Peters and Waterman, 1982; and Deming, 1986).

Inevitably with the greater importance of small firms in the economy, the quality management skills of their owner-managers have come under close scrutiny. Like their other management skills, quality management has been argued to be too haphazard and uneven, an implicit assumption of, for example, the Department of Trade and Industry's (DTI) Enterprise Initiative in the late 1980s and early 1990s (DTI, 1992). The main focus of the help offered to small firms has been on the formal quality management system currently labelled BS EN ISO 9000 but best known in the UK as BS 5750 (the latter label is used throughout this book).[2] The assumption has been that small firms typically lack rigorous, systematic approaches to achieving quality in the goods and services they produce and that the formal quality standard approach will improve their quality management. Both the British Standards Institute (BSI) and the Department of Trade and Industry have developed initiatives to help small firms implement BS 5750 (DTI, 1996b: 52).

FORMAL QUALITY STANDARD – BS 5750

BS 5750 has provoked both confusion and a great deal of debate since its original publication in 1979. It is based on formal systems for the management of production originally introduced into general manufacturing industry by the Ministry of Defence (MOD) (Sherwood, 1986: 13). Because of the need for defence products to meet exacting technical standards, emphasis was placed on how products were made and the quality management methods of component and original equipment suppliers (Ashton and Jackson, 1993). Although defence standards were intended as the basis of a complete quality management system, they were not widely adopted outside the sector. Following the recommendations of the Warner Report on 'Standards and Specifications in the Engineering Industries' (cited in Sherwood, 1986), BS 5750 was developed to provide a more general set of requirements. However, the standard, as originally published, had a strong manufacturing bias (Ashton and Jackson, 1993). Accordingly, a majority of the early registrations were achieved by engineering and manufacturing firms (O'Rourke, 1993).

In 1987 the BSI attempted to remedy the above bias by re-writing the standard and introducing a guide to implementation for service sector businesses (BSI, 1987: Part 8). Also at this time, international (ISO 9000) and European (EN 23000) equivalents were introduced, though in Britain the standard was still generally known as BS 5750. In 1988, the government began promoting BS 5750 and other quality initiatives through the Enterprise Initiative.[3] The standard then became more widely recognised and applications for registration were received from businesses in a broader array of economic sectors. For example, there was a sharp increase in the number of applications from service based organisations (O'Rourke, 1993).

The basic principle of the standard is to offer a universal framework for quality management systems within which businesses can formulate their specific needs. An additional key principle is that businesses should be assessed and registered by an approved body independent of both suppliers and customers, although in practice the latter often contribute to defining and assessing the relevant standard. It should be clear, therefore, that the standard is not itself a quality system for any particular business but rather offers a framework for a quality system which should be acceptable to customers and others with whom a business has relations.

Firms applying to 'register for', or 'certify to', BS 5750, amend their existing operating procedures to reflect those advocated in the standard's framework.[4] The process can be time-consuming and often requires the help of an expert outsider such as a consultant. The new procedures are then documented in a 'manual' which has then to be assessed against BS 5750. Assessments are usually performed by a 'third party certification body' of some kind though 'first party assessment', for example, by individual firms and 'second party assessments', for instance, by customers or suppliers, may become more common.[5]

It is estimated that there are now just above 42,000 UK BS 5750 registrations.[6] (Unlike some previous estimates, these figures are not inflated by including firms registered by non-accredited certification bodies or second party registered against BS 5750 or directly equivalent standards. However, they do include larger organisations which have registered several of their individual branches or units of operation despite being only one commercial entity.) There are indications that the adoption of BS 5750 in the UK has been faster than elsewhere in the European Union or indeed in the world. For instance, the government's *Small Firms in Britain Report, 1996* (DTI, 1996b: 52) claimed that almost half (46 per cent) of the world's ISO 9000 certificates are held by firms in Britain.

BS 5750 AND SMALL FIRMS

Given the increase in emphasis on formal quality standards generally and the government's promotion of BS 5750, it was almost inevitable that small firms would be pressured to adopt a formal standard approach to quality management. Unfortunately, there is no specific record kept of small firm registrations so nobody knows just how many small firms have adopted the standard in the UK. On the other hand, there is plenty of research to indicate that a large and increasing number of small businesses are aware of the standard. For example, a 1992 survey of small firms by Curran and Blackburn (1992) showed that nearly two thirds (63 per cent) were aware of BS 5750, and 43 per cent thought it would have an effect on their business. Similarly, research conducted at about the same time by the Small Business Research Trust (SBRT, 1992), reported that almost 41 per cent of a sample of small business owners thought it would have an effect on them and their businesses, 10 per cent had implemented, or were implementing, BS 5750, and a further 17 per cent stated they intended to do so.

Results from more recent research by the Small Business Research Trust (SBRT, 1994a) indicated that 78 per cent of the small firms sampled had 'heard' of BS 5750 and that 11 per cent were 'using' the standard, while a further 38 per cent intended to do so. However, these figures are likely to overstate the real situation. About 75 per cent of small firms with at least one employee are in services (DTI, 1996a) but, typically, samples of small firms used in research contain much higher proportions of manufacturing firms. For instance, the SBRT (1994a) sample from which findings were quoted above, contained 36 per cent of manufacturing firms but a representative sample of firms with at least 1 but under 50 employees based on the DTI (1996a) estimate, would suggest the sample should contain under 11 per cent of manufacturing firms. Because BS 5750 originated in the manufacturing sector and more firms in manufacturing are likely to be registered, any over-representation of manufacturing firms in a small firm sample will tend to overstate the proportion of all firms who have adopted BS 5750. Research by Curran, Blackburn and Woods (1993), for example, based on a carefully selected sample of small firms in a range of services, reported that only 3.4 per cent were registered for BS 5750. The DTI (1996a) estimate suggests there are just under 1.2m businesses with at least 1 but under 50 employees in the UK. If just 5 per cent of these were registered that alone would produce almost 60,000 small firm registrations which, given the earlier estimates of total BS 5750 registrations in the UK, makes it clear that the total (and proportion) of small firms who have adopted BS 5750 is likely to be low.

Clearly, though some small firms have adopted BS 5750, the vast majority have not. But many of the reactions from those involved in the small business community are of concern about the pressures on small firms to go down the formal quality standard route. For example, one of the longest established and most authoritative consultants on the role of the small firm in the UK and Europe, has argued that BS 5750 threatens the future of many small firms: 'the explosive power of BS 5750 lies in the fact that a major customer might one day inform a business that he [sic] will no longer trade with them unless they are certificated under the standard' (Bannock, 1991: 15).

However, there are also other problems linked to BS 5750 according to Bannock. Along with many other commentators he has claimed that for many small firms, BS 5750 means implementing a system which is over-complex, over-bureaucratic, costly and irrelevant to their needs. Some of the research cited above (for example, SBRT, 1994a) indicates that small business owners themselves often share some of these reservations. These are important issues where the subject is a major, government supported, national quality strategy with important implications for the UK's economic future.

If, for example, it was established that small firms were being induced to adopt BS 5750 when its relevance and effectiveness has yet to be established for smaller enterprises, then government promotion of the standard might be seen as questionable. Worse still, if it was established that the adoption of such formal standards were unsuited to the needs and performance of what amounts to a third of the private sector of the economy, then government promotion of BS 5750 could be judged wrong-headed and even harmful to Britain's long-term economic future.

QUALITY MANAGEMENT STRATEGIES AND THE MODERN BUSINESS

A first step in clarifying the debate on small firms and formal quality standards is to establish more firmly the context in which formal quality standards are linked to small businesses. Where, in other words, does the belief in the potency of formal quality systems come from and how has it affected Britain's small businesses? Given the apparent reluctance of small businesses to adopt formal quality systems, the latter question might more accurately be put in the form: why are small firms so reluctant to embrace these new quality systems?

While producing goods and services at a price which the market is prepared to pay is the basic *raison d'etre* of any firm in a market-based economy, the explicit discussion of quality as an element in this exchange emerged in the early classic US management writings of Frederick W. Taylor (1911). It developed further in the early 1930s with the greater use of statistical methods for ensuring consistency to specification in manufacturing to minimise losses through waste and poor final products (Barad, 1996). After World War II, these ideas evolved into a wider literature on quality with a number of specific themes, often linked to particular advocates whose names are now widely known including Deming, Crosby, Feigenbaum, Ishikawa, Juran, Taguchi and Porter.[7]

The main ideas or themes of the quality movement were often summed up in the catch phrases of their advocates. Among the best known are 'zero defects', 'quality circles', 'right first time', 'total quality control', 'continuous improvement' (sometimes referred to by the Japanese term '*Kaizen*') and, most widely used currently, 'total quality management' or TQM. More broadly, the overall thrust in the development of the quality strategies literature has been from simple inspection in the early literature to an all embracing, holistic approach to quality. This involves a remoulding of the entire corporate culture and accompanying structure of the business to which every member of the firm from top to bottom is urged to be totally committed. At the same time, there has been a shift to include not only mass production firms, in which the first statistical quality control techniques were used, but also services and knowledge-based enterprises and, recently and very importantly politically, the public sector (Kirkpatrick and Martinez Lucio, 1995).

It has been suggested that the influence of the quality literature on business and politics stems more from its ideological appeal than any firmly grounded empirical soundness of its strategies or results (Tuckman, 1995). Certainly, while there are studies which purport to offer empirical support for particular quality strategies, many have been criticised on the familiar grounds of the poor theorisation, design and execution of much management research (ESRC, 1994). Even the concept of 'quality', whose clear conceptualisation might be thought to be basic to discussion and research on its role in economic activities, appears blurred and fuzzy: 'the meaning of "quality" has been attached indiscriminately to a multitude of diverse practices. However, far from being viewed as a difficulty for the coherence and credibility of quality management, this promiscuity, and its attendant confusion, is embraced by some as a principal virtue (Wilkinson and Willmot, 1995: 7).

Equally, the same authors and others (see, for example, Hill, 1991) criticise the detail of the specific research offered to support various quality strategies. Often, they argue, the arguments and propositions are put in non-testable forms. For example, where strategies achieve poorer results than predicted, failure is often ascribed to the 'poor leadership' of top management or poor resourcing. Interviews are often only with selected management respondents, often the 'change champions' introducing the strategies, with no attention to the views and experiences of other employees. Where employees' responses are sought it is often through internal surveys or questionnaires. Employees may well feel wary of offering critical or negative views under these conditions for fear it will jeopardise their careers or future employment in the business. The possible effects of other influences, positive or negative, which may produce change in the business are rarely controlled for in the research design: introducing TQM with its appeal to all members of the firm to give total commitment to quality, for example, may be less than effective if it is accompanied, as has often been the case in the 1990s, with large scale redundancies.

The above critique applies to quality strategies used mainly in large businesses. Like so much of contemporary management literature and research, the authors appear to address an economy exclusively composed of large enterprises, private and public. The small enterprise is almost entirely ignored or it is assumed, as government policy apparently does, that what is good for large firms must be good for small firms. One of the central themes of this book is the testing and challenging of such propositions based on a careful research-based analysis. At this stage, it suffices to argue that, as we have suggested previously (North *et al.*, 1993) the existing large enterprise-based literature and research which is mainly concerned with medium and large firms, is inadequate for assessing the relevance and impact of BS 5750 on small firms.

SMALL FIRMS AND IMPLEMENTING BS 5750

If much of the contemporary management writing ignores the small firm, it is fair to say that this neglect is reciprocated by small business owners themselves. It is unusual to hear small business owners use any of the 'management speak' of key management texts or business schools, except perhaps as a result of coincidence where the usage of such expressions refers to common sense practices applied in everyday circumstance. Much of the quality literature discussed briefly above will be unknown to the majority of small business owners. On the other hand, as the research cited earlier showed, awareness of BS 5750 is high among small business owners.

Small business owner-managers aware of BS 5750 have to make a decision on whether it is right for their businesses. As with any other investment in the business, the standard requires resources, money and time, which could be used in other ways. The crucial question is will the pay-off for the business be worth the investment? When considering the adoption of BS 5750 or any new project, small firm owner-managers will consciously or subconsciously, employ some form of cost–benefit evaluation. The decision on whether to implement BS 5750 is, however, complicated by other issues. For instance, there may well be contradictory motivations influencing the decision and the non-financial implications of introducing the standard may not always be easy to predict. The motivations to implement or reject BS 5750 by business owners may be classified into one or a combination of the following sets of issues.

Procedural benefits

The first relates to the realisation of what are often termed *procedural benefits*, that is, any improvements to the internal operation of a firm or organisation that may, or it is believed are likely to, result from implementing BS 5750 or its equivalents. Since the standard is promoted as setting minimum requirements for a quality assurance system then it is not unfair to assume (as many have) that implementing the system will improve the quality of a firm's goods or services. However, the proponents of formal quality systems have become increasingly cautious about claiming quality benefits from adopting the standard. Rather than any simple claim to guarantee improvements in quality, promoters of the standard such as the government, now merely claim, for instance, that:

> Surveys have shown that when certification to ISO 9000 is introduced into an organisation as part of a strategy, it provides a useful and progressive tool for improving internal operations. Whilst the standard does not offer any guarantee of a company's products, it assures purchasers that specifications will be met consistently.
>
> (DTI, 1996b: 52)

Once implemented, BS 5750 requires firms to define and document customer requirements and ensure that the firm has the capability to meet these requirements. The firm must then establish product or service conformance to these requirements (BSI, 1987: Part 1). This is likely to be more suitable for firms in economic sectors where standards of quality are well known and accepted or where the customer has a precise notion about what is required (Halliday, 1993). But in other sectors, where standards of quality cannot be defined so easily or where the customer is not particularly knowledgeable about the product or service, conformance to requirements is much more problematic.

It has already been noted that there has been an increased interest in introducing BS 5750 to businesses in the service sector (Tisdall, 1991). This is almost essential if the standard is to become more significant in the UK economy if only because such a high proportion of UK economic activity – two thirds or more – are now in services and related activities. In many services there is no easily measured final 'product' and in many product and process are so integrated that their culmination only occurs at the moment of consumption by the consumer. Further, the results may be measured in several different ways depending on who is doing the measuring. Consequently, it is much more difficult to make precise judgements about what constitutes a 'quality service' than in many other kinds of economic activities where clear agreed standards are accepted by suppliers and customers.

One highly relevant area which illustrates the problems of defining service quality standards is professional services (such as legal or financial services). This area is of increasing importance in the UK's emerging knowledge-based economy and for small firms which are strongly represented in such activities. Fennel illustrates this point in the legal context:

> Most law firms pride themselves on providing high-quality services, but nobody is sure whether that means they devise ingenious solu-

tions to difficult problems, or promptly answer letters and return telephone calls . . . the ultimate arbiter of quality should be the client. The problem is . . . if the client is a lay person, he or she will be ill-placed to make an informed judgment

(Fennel, 1991: 35)

It is quite feasible, in other words, that in services of these kinds, firms could develop widely varying standards and still register for BS 5750. Two firms ostensibly providing the same kind of service could, in short, adopt very different standards and yet both display BS 5750 certificates. More generally, this may lead to situations where:

the customer would not be able to tell the difference unless he was sufficiently knowledgeable about BS 5750 to ask the right questions. This is very unlikely to be the case where customers are members of the public rather than sophisticated organisations who are them-selves familiar with quality assurance issues. There is therefore a real danger that customers will be deceived into believing that BS 5750 guarantees high quality, which it emphatically does not.

(Halliday, 1993: 98)

Since, strictly, BS 5750 only offers a way of establishing a system of consistent performance against some set of defined criteria, it is logic-ally possible that no actual increase in quality is intended or achieved by the firm or experienced by the customer. Some evidence suggests that this logical possibility actually occurs in practice (see, for example, SBRT, 1992; Holliday, 1994). Holliday, for example, cites a case where a firm implemented and registered BS 5750 and though they were subject to periodic third party assessment to ensure conformity to the original standard as registered, no meaningful attempt to improve the quality of the final product or service was made. The firm chose instead to use BS 5750 almost solely as a marketing tool. It was used, in short, mainly to gain market credibility for the firm's range of products which remained substantially the same as before the adoption of the standard.

It is also possible, however, that the adoption of BS 5750 may lead to improved quality even if the improvement is not always dramatic. The procedure of preparing for and achieving registration may well be accompanied by an assessment (even as an involuntary byproduct of exploring the possible benefits of registration) of the way the firm pro-duces its goods or services. This may result in a genuine and successful attempt to improve quality or, at the very least, achieve greater quality consistency. Most firms, like most individuals, easily fall into inefficient or unsystematic ways of doing things. Standing back and attempting to look critically at how activities are performed is very likely to suggest improvements extending to the final products and services themselves.

Fox (1991) offers another view which again claims that implementing BS 5750 to address quality issues may be secondary to other procedural benefits it can give to businesses. He suggests 'cost-effective quality management ... is the only valid objective for seeking BS 5750 approval' (Fox, 1991: 2). In other words, by implementing the standard, owner-managers have a greater understanding and control over the internal processes of the business but this need not itself lead to any automatic increase in the quality level of the product or service as experienced by the customer. For example, it is argued that BS 5750 enables firms to quickly trace the source of defects which saves time and other costs associated with making corrective adjustments. In turn, this may have implications for wastage.[8] So there is no absolute increase in quality of the final product or service even if there is a significant fall in poorly produced outputs.

The literature often seizes on procedural benefits of the above kinds, stressing the direct benefits for reducing operational costs from adopting a formal quality standard. One common result of such emphases is absurdly unrealistic estimates of potential cost saving from implementation of the standard (see, for example, Tickit, 1992: section 1.3.2; Harland in Bailey, 1992). An obvious point to make in relation to cost savings claims is that small business owner-managers are often physically very close to the production process and volumes are generally lower than in larger enterprises. Waste through poor employee performance has the potential to be spotted much more quickly than in larger enterprises where managerial oversight is hampered by the greater complexity and volume of the production process and the key managers' physical distance from it. The scope for savings in small firms, therefore, may be much lower than in larger enterprises and this must be offset against the costs of implementation.

The savings and other benefits associated with BS 5750 in the long term cannot be considered independently of costs incurred in the short term. In small firms, it could be argued, much will depend upon their ability to digest the costs of implementation, registration and the periodic formal monitoring to retain registration (North *et al.*, 1993: 5). But the standard may incur long term problems also. Increases in bureaucracy and paperwork can make cost reductions unattainable or actually increase costs. Some support exists for this kind of contention. A survey by Blackham (1992) for instance, found 33 per cent of respondents reported increases in costs, with only 6.1 per cent experiencing cost reductions.

Implementing BS 5750, it is argued, may also have other procedural benefits. For example, the standard requires firms to 'establish and maintain procedures for identifying the training needs and provide for the training of all personnel performing activities affecting quality' (BSI, 1987: Part 1). Discussion of small firms has long claimed that employee training in small firms is deficient and needs to be improved if Britain's economic performance is to be enhanced. What is also clear is that the vast majority of small firms use informal methods of employee training (Abbott, 1993; Curran *et al.*, 1996a). 'Informal' can often be interpreted to mean haphazard and unsystematic, but this need not be the case.

Proponents of BS 5750 argue that a result of implementing the standard is the need to have a formal training plan rather than rely on 'ad hoc' approaches (Felstead and Green, 1993). But again, there is no automatic link between adopting BS 5750 and improved training. A training plan can exist but may be implemented only spasmodically or not at all. Holliday (1994) demonstrated the critical distinction between the promise of a quality standard and the reality of its implementation. In one of her small firms, BS 5750 registration occurred without any increased delivery of formal training despite the formal acceptance of such an obligation as part of registration.

Abbott (1993) argues that lower levels of formal training in small firms may not be that important since informal training may be just as effective for small businesses because it is closely tailored to the precise needs of the business. Again, at the least, it is conceivable that forcing small firms to adopt formal training plans with an emphasis on formal, particularly off-the-job training, produces *negative* procedural implications for the firm. This could occur, for instance, where formal off-the-job training adds to running costs by having to replace workers away on training or accepting lower output. If these costs outweigh other benefits from adoption of the standard, the firm suffers dis-benefits.

It is clear that BS 5750 will affect employees and their involvement in the firm and this may be more complex than some suggest or perhaps hope for. Holliday notes that the standard attempts to ensure 'the accountability of individuals and materials to finished product quality' (Holliday, 1994: 5). The quality literature, particularly the TQM literature, goes much further and claims that modern holistic quality strategies 'empower' employees by reducing centralisation and hierarchy in the organisation and pushing decision making down to the appropriate employee level (Barad, 1996). This, it is argued, generates positive commitment to the business and a drive to improve quality. However, others (for example, Kerfoot and Knights, 1995) view the employee empowerment thesis with scepticism. They argue that, in practice, 'empowerment' is often very limited in terms of the devolvement of real decision making and employees are aware of the contradictions between the rhetoric of empowerment and the realities of centralised corporate power in the modern business. Conformity, they suggest, should not be mistaken for commitment in an era of employee insecurity and high unemployment.

Evidence on the impact of the adoption of quality standards on employees is mixed. Research by Blackham (1992) revealed that a majority of firms reported increased employee motivation and participation under BS 5750. Evidence of this kind is often based on managerial assessments of the impact of a quality standard and reaction at the shop floor level may differ among those attempting to integrate formalised quality strategies with their other work role commitments. Holliday (1994) argues, for instance, that if notices are regularly served to employees concerning the 'non-conformance' of their work, then it is likely that 'the system will become dysfunctional as greater supervision will be needed to enforce and police the growing complexity of rules' (Holliday, 1994: 5). Hodgart and Temporal (1991) agree suggesting:

> Imposing a systems approach to quality assurance – and BS 5750 is imposed from above no matter how its supporters rationalise otherwise – has an automatic de-motivating impact. BS 5750 does not provide a context, a purpose, or a meaning all of which reinforce de-motivation. Hence people quickly come to see all of the imposed systems as ends in themselves.
>
> (pp. 15–16)

No doubt the proponents of TQM would argue that evidence of the above kind simply indicates top management failures to implement the quality strategy effectively. This may be the case but as with implementing any other management and human resource strategies, the realities of real organisational life including employees' own agendas, the contradictions between, for example, coping with the exigencies of the market and new technology, on the one hand, and giving employees a secure, challenging and satisfying environment on the other, are always present.

Marketing benefits

Small firm owner-managers may be motivated to implement BS 5750 as a *marketing strategy*. This type of motivation should be seen as analytically separate from the procedural benefits discussed above: they may or may not go together and one can exist without the other. Government, consultants and third party certification bodies are quick to promote the marketing aspects of BS 5750. For example, DTI literature has suggested registration is 'particularly valuable in marketing' (DTI, 1992: 6), and BSI promotional literature gives priority to the assertion that 'BSI certification is a first class marketing tool'.[9] This emphasis again echoes the wider literature on quality strategies. A major theme in contemporary quality exegeses is that the modern business needs to be 'customer driven' (Stokes, 1994). Indeed, the importance of the customer notion is shown by the extending of the supplier–customer metaphor to relations within the business itself. Departments (or individual employees) are 'suppliers' or 'providers' to other 'customers' or 'purchaser' departments (or individual employees) so that the firm may be said to have, of even be constituted as, an 'internal market' (Tuckman, 1995; Barad, 1996).[10]

Small firms, as noted earlier, may view adoption of BS 5750 strategically as a means of presenting a quality image to the market even if internal processes remain largely unaltered. It may be employed as a means of differentiating the firm from competitors, a major problem for many small firms who are otherwise clones of each other with little that is different to offer the market. More radically, it may enable the firm to move up market to access a more profitable higher value added niche. As Holliday (1994) comments:

> the motive for obtaining BS 5750 status is often simply to increase sales. It is a marketing device which allows small firms to tap into vital larger or more 'up-market' customers and more profitable markets. Thus there is no incentive to improve *real* quality within the company, rather this choice is based on a desire to present a *quality image*.
>
> (Holliday, 1994: 5, emphases in the original)

What is worth stressing is that marketing benefits even when they are the main or even sole motivation for adopting BS 5750, are no guarantee of any market advantages. The realisation of potential marketing advantages is dependent on external factors which amplify or diminish the impact of adopting the standard. If a small business operates in a highly competitive sector where growth is inherently difficult such as retailing, adopting BS 5750 may have little or no positive effect on the business. No matter how well planned and implemented the adoption of the standard, the external constraints prevent marketing advantages materialising. For many small businesses in retailing in the 1990s, just surviving is difficult enough. The adoption of BS 5750 will not change the fundamentally adverse external situation faced by these small firms.

External market conditions

A third type of motivation for small firms adopting BS 5750 is where it is a response to *external market conditions*. Much media coverage has stressed the idea that small firms are implementing the standard as a result of competitive, and especially customer, pressures (Tisdall, 1990; Harris, 1991; Batchelor, 1992). For example, Batchelor (1992) suggests that many small firms 'have no choice but to register if they want to retain their customers. Large firms and government organisations increasingly expect their suppliers to meet the standard'.

Bastow (in Rock, 1992) estimates that 10 per cent of large UK companies and 80 per cent of government bodies, insist that suppliers meet the standard or an equivalent.[11] Public sector insistence was intensified when the Ministry of Defence announced in 1991 that in-house assessment of quality would be replaced by external certification using BS 5750 (Tisdall, 1990). There is already clear evidence that this practice is affecting small firms. For example, research by Abbott *et al.* (1996) notes how BS 5750 has become another burden for small firms entering the Compulsory Competitive Tendering (CCT) market. A Small Business Research Trust (1992) survey indicated that 35.4 per cent of small firms reported they were affected by BS 5750 as a supplier. In other words, not being registered could result in being debarred from tendering or being taken off an approved supplier list.

However, it is possible that this influence on BS 5750 registration may have been overstated. Evidence suggests that many large firms are reluctant to use small firms as suppliers anyway (Curran and Blackburn, 1992: 57; Curran and Blackburn, 1994: Chapter 5). Not being registered may bar a small firm from being a supplier to a larger business or public sector customer but being registered may not increase demand for its products or services from such customers if they are reluctant to give orders to small firms anyway.

If registration occurs as a result of customer pressure, it will be highly dependent upon the sector and market position of the firm (Curran and Blackburn, 1992: 47; SBRT, 1992; North *et al.*, 1993). Some small firms will face little or no pressure from customers to adopt a formal quality standard. For example, businesses whose customers are drawn from the general public may find that the latter do not care much whether the firm has BS 5750 or not. Small hotels, for instance, are unlikely to gain much increased custom if they proclaim they have BS 5750.[12] There is also evidence that external pressure on firms to adopt BS 5750 may even be declining. For example, a sample of small firms interviewed twice over a one year period revealed that the proportion of firms expecting BS 5750 to have an effect on their business fell from 43.1 per cent in 1992 to 36.8 per cent in 1993 (Curran *et al.*, 1993: 30).

In summary, the motivations for implementing BS 5750 are complex. Here they have been classified into three distinct groups. This is not to claim, however, that these are the only motivations but merely to review those the existing literature emphasises: it may well be that others are also important. The first two mentioned above, 'procedural benefits' and 'marketing benefits', may be seen by owner-managers as a means to improve the competitive position of their firm. However, the benefits accruing from each should not be seen as mutually exclusive. For example, though firms may implement the standard to achieve procedural benefits, it should not be assumed that they will ignore any ensuing marketing advantages. Conversely, firms implementing the standard to achieve marketing benefits may discover procedural benefits. However, as noted above, some research indicates that small firms who implement BS 5750 to achieve marketing benefits may wish to minimise the effect of the standard on the internal operations of the business, reducing the possibility of procedural improvements (Holliday, 1994).

Finally, small firms may implement BS 5750 as a reaction to external market conditions. Unlike the first two, this motivation can be construed as reactive or even as negative, at least initially. Small firm owner-managers who are forced, for example, by larger customers to implement the standard may consider it an unnecessary burden but feel they have no choice if they are to remain in business. Whatever the main motivation, it can be seen that it will influence owner-managers' attitude towards implementation and this could have longer term affects on the success of the system.

THE PROBLEMS SMALL FIRMS FACE IN IMPLEMENTING AND MAINTAINING BS 5750

There is already an extensive literature on the practical problems small firms encounter in implementing and maintaining a formal commitment to BS 5750 (Ashton and Jackson, 1993; Sadgrove, 1994; Stebbing and Pengelly, 1994). Most of it is based on anecdote or unsystematic research on small firms going through the experience of attempting to adopt and retain BS 5750 (Stephen Hill (1991) makes this point generally in relation to the quality literature). However, some commentators have attempted to take a more critical look at the problems associated with implementing and maintaining the standard (Bannock, 1991; Chittenden *et al.*, 1996). This literature, in other words, offers something of a counter-view to the enthusiastic endorsement of the benefits of formal quality standards for small firms offered by several of the sources discussed earlier.

The first issue small firm owner-managers may consider in deciding whether to implement BS 5750 is its operational relevance. Bannock (1991), for instance, suggests: 'Quality systems may not be relevant in a small firm where quality is the personal responsibility of the owner' (Bannock, 1991:16). He bluntly questions whether formalised approaches towards quality are as appropriate to the needs of small firms as the informal methods of quality management typically developed and applied by small business owners. For example, it is argued that the standard is 'over-complex', 'riddled with jargon' and, as such, simply inappropriate to the archetypal, informally structured, personally managed small firm (Bannock, 1991; Pengelly in Rock, 1992). It is pointed out that the wording in the standard appears to assume implicitly a structured business where there are a number of personnel performing differing distinct and identifiable roles linked to the main managerial functions (see, for example, Bailey, 1992; North *et al.*, 1993). But small firms are rarely organised in this way and it may not be easy to add a distinct 'quality function' to existing managerial responsibilities.

It has also been argued that the bureaucratic nature of BS 5750, formalising the operating procedures and processes of the business, is likely to undermine the often cited key economic advantage of small firms, namely their rapid and flexible responsiveness to the market (Bannock, 1991). These problems have been acknowledged to some extent by the BSI and the DTI in the setting up of a BSI Policy Committee for Small Businesses (Bethell, 1993; SBRT, 1994a: 3). The committee's aim was to ensure that the distinctive needs of the small business sector are recognised in the standard's procedures. The government for its part has responded to these issues and says that it 'will be seeking changes to meet the demands of small firms' (DTI, 1996b: 52) when BS 5750 is next revised.

Since BS 5750 was developed initially with large manufacturing businesses in mind, it is argued that the standard's relevance to small firms is questionable because small firms are not simply large firms scaled down and because most, almost 9 out of 10, are not in manufacturing.

However, as indicated earlier, service sector firms are becoming more aware of the standard, perhaps as part of their increasing identification with quality issues – particularly customer satisfaction – generally. The link here could be with the marketing aspects of registration, that is, firms in service industries may be considering BS 5750 as a means of differentiating themselves from the competition through their marketing to customers. It is sometimes difficult for businesses in services to differentiate themselves and their products from what competitors offer because it can often be easy to replicate each other's images and services. Some kind of quality mark or standard might offer an advantage over competitors, even if only temporary, provided customers could be persuaded that the standard indicates a clear superiority in what is being offered.

But it can also be argued that the standard is equally, if not more, applicable in an operational sense to service sector businesses than manufacturing businesses. There is little distinction between process and product in many services and BS 5750 will be relevant because it is essentially concerned with maintaining high process standards (North *et al.*, 1993). Obvious areas of overlap include service industry processes such as telephone contacts with customers where such contacts are key to the level of sales and an inherent part of the service offered. Such processes may be defined within standard frameworks which can then be adapted to the specific activities and market needs of the firm. Small firms in services, therefore, could possibly adapt such frameworks to their activities to improve their performance and competitive position.

After considering the potential operational relevance of BS 5750 to their businesses, small business owner-managers have to consider problems specific to implementing and maintaining BS 5750. Some have questioned whether many small firm owner-managers have the time and/or financial resources to implement the standard effectively (Bannock, 1991; Batchelor, 1992). Making estimates about the costs of implementing and maintaining BS 5750 are difficult since they vary according to a wide variety of factors (North *et al.*, 1993). For example, owner-managers have to decide what method of implementation they intend to use. The initial guidance available may not be very helpful on issues such as this. The official literature on the subject, for instance, has been described as 'incomprehensible' (Bannock, 1991: 16) and many owner-managers will not have the time, it is claimed, to decipher, let alone implement, BS 5750 on top of all their other responsibilities (Jack, 1991).

In this situation, owner-managers have two options. Many trade associations, industrial training organisations (ITOs), chambers of commerce, training and enterprise councils (TECs) offer inexpensive part-time courses for owner-managers implementing the standard (Bethell, 1994). The more recently established Business Links will undoubtedly offer similar help. Harbourne (1993) argues that industrially based methods of delivery can be very effective since organisations like ITOs are often able to offer sector-specific interpretations of the standard. These offer a more or less ready-made framework which has already been tuned to the needs of firms in a specific sector rather than the often confusing generic approach offered by BS 5750 in its original form. This sector-based approach, the literature argues, has advantages because it encourages a 'hands on' approach to implementation by owner-managers so that they are closely involved in developing and writing their own quality manual. As a result, this gives greater scope for developing the system round the precise requirements of the business as well as making it more likely that the owner-manager will be the champion of the standard.

However, a 'hands on' approach may not be possible given the constraints on owner-managers' time or their ability to absorb the detail of the standard. In these circumstances, small business owners may decide to employ a consultant. Employing a consultant can be expensive. Estimates in the late 1990s vary from £500 to £1,000 a day. Though earlier government help, through the Enterprise Initiative, raised the profile of BS 5750 and undoubtedly encouraged more registrations (see Jay Communications, 1991) it was criticised for subsidising 'over-expensive consultants' who were not always totally competent (Rock, 1992; Bailey, 1992; SBRT, 1992). Criticisms of consultants and their fees are a commonplace among small business owners (Macmillan *et al.*, 1990) and adverse comment on their assistance in helping small firms register for BS 5750 is to be expected. There is an unfortunate paradox here. Owner-managers in small firms (especially smaller small firms) are less likely to be able to afford the time to implement the standard yet are also less likely to be able to afford a consultant's help. A compromise, however, is for owner-managers to write the rough outline of their 'manual' and then employ a consultant to 'tidy it up' for third party certification.

The next stage is gaining registration which involves further costs separate from any fees for advice in implementing BS 5750. Some, but not all, third party bodies set costs according to firm size. Many now offer special rates for small firms. However, it is likely that most small firms will pay around £1,500 (though it could obviously be more for larger small firms) to become registered and around £500–£600 each time they are reassessed to retain their registration. Some people may feel that even after adding all the likely fees together, the total is not excessive. It may well add up to less than £5,000 in total (not counting the periodic fees for maintaining registration). But given the likely capital resources and low turnover levels of a large proportion of small firms, adopting BS 5750 is an investment which owners may need to consider very carefully. Not only will an estimate have to be made on whether the likely bottom line return makes the investment worthwhile but there are often alternative investments which might well have a greater pay-off for the firm.

It is clear that implementing and maintaining the standard will be easier for larger small firms. For the great majority of micro firms, those with say, one but under five employees (of which there are over 800,000 according to the DTI (1996a)), almost two thirds of all businesses with at least one employee) deciding whether to invest in BS 5750 is a serious matter. The likely direct return in the form of greater efficiency or gaining more customers, must be convincing before these owners are likely to embark on the formal quality standard route.

CONCLUSIONS

The importance of the small firm in the UK economy is now well established as measured by its contributions to business turnover and employment. Around a third of business turnover and almost 40 per cent of employment is already in firms with at least 1 but under 50 employees. Moreover, this growing importance is likely to increase further as the economy restructures itself to meet the demands of the next century. Quality is now widely regarded as key to the performance of businesses of all sizes. The UK, it is argued, has paid too little attention in the past two or three decades to producing high quality goods and services and has slipped down the world economic league table as a result.

Managing to achieve high quality is not easy and small firm owner-managers are often seen as poorly skilled in meeting the main management functions required for a successful business. In recent years, thinking about quality issues has spawned a host of quality management strategies. Perhaps most important in the UK has been strong encouragement to adopt BS 5750. However, the evidence indicates small firms have been less enthusiastic about adopting formal quality standards than their larger counterparts.

As the chapter has shown, adopting BS 5750 is a complex process for small firms. Discussion on the mechanics of adoption and the benefits and disadvantages which can result, shows just how complex the process can be. For example, assessing the opportunity costs of adoption is very difficult for small business owners who rarely have the skills or the time, to make a considered appraisal. Most small firms are in services and the problems of devising a formal standard for many kinds of services can be formidable. The kinds of benefits which can result whether procedural (improving the operating processes within the business) or marketing (helping the firm to win more or more profitable customers) are often both difficult to estimate and difficult to translate into reality.

As the chapter has also shown, a great deal of the literature on quality issues is fuzzily prescriptive rather than based on clearly thought out concepts backed by rigorous testing. Often the potential positive benefits are trumpeted while discussion of the possible disadvantages of adopting a formal quality standard is much more muted. Since the main literature on quality issues is almost exclusively concerned with larger enterprises, all these potential benefits and disadvantages are even more problematic for small firms.

What is needed clearly is a non-prescriptive, research-based approach to quality management strategies in small firms. Formal quality standards are only one strategy for improving and sustaining quality in small firms and a research-based approach needs to have an open mind on how the effectiveness of alternatives compares with BS 5750 or similar standards. In the following chapters such an approach is adopted. The aims are first to be clear about what is meant by 'quality', second to use the data from a carefully designed research project to assess how quality is managed in small firms engaged in different kinds of economic activities and, finally, to assess the comparative advantages of different approaches to quality management in small firms, including formal quality management strategies such as BS 5750.

2　Quality: definitions and conceptualisations

INTRODUCTION

The near obsession with 'quality' as the key to improved business performance among contemporary management and political commentators was highlighted in the previous chapter. Evidence indicates that a high proportion of large organisations in the private and public sectors have now adopted this emphasis on quality in some form or another (Bastow in Rock, 1992; Kirkpatrick and Martinez Lucio, 1995). Few mission statements or their equivalents from larger enterprises whether they are banks, retailers, hospitals or the Inland Revenue, fail to mention quality, directly or indirectly, mainly in the form of a declared commitment to high standards of consumer satisfaction.

Small business owners, on the other hand, appear more ambivalent. Explicit adoption of formal quality standards such as BS 5750 is, as the previous chapter showed, much lower among smaller than larger enterprises. Few small businesses have mission statements or offer 'customer charters' leading to the impression that they are less quality conscious than larger enterprises. Smaller firms, it is sometimes suggested, may therefore be falling behind in giving quality the emphasis it deserves if they are to improve their overall performance. Customer demands for high and consistent quality standards are rising, it is argued, but small firms could be in danger of missing out on this important key to business success. At best, as the last chapter indicated, interest in quality issues is low but increasing among small firms (Pera, 1992; SBRT, 1992; Curran *et al.*, 1993; SBRT, 1994a, 1994b).

In the drive to create what almost amounts to a formal 'quality function' ranking alongside the more traditional functions of production planning, finance, marketing, personnel and strategy formulation, what is often neglected is a clear conceptualisation of what is being discussed when the term 'quality' is used (Wilkinson and Willmott, 1995: 7). This is not to say that management texts and gurus do not offer definitions of quality (see the discussion below) but their definitions are often vague or even half hearted. It is almost as if they do not believe they have to work very hard at saying what is meant by 'quality'. Notably, they lack the rigour and precision which is felt needed for the discussion of other equally key and common terms used in management such as 'operations management', 'inflation accounting' or 'cost–benefit analysis'.

One reason for this vagueness is that 'quality' is one of those every-day terms which sociologists refer to as part of the 'taken for granted' realm of culture which underpins routine interpersonal social exchange in modern societies. Such notions are employed so commonly in every-day discourse that users rarely feel the need to say precisely what is meant since it is taken for granted that everybody knows – and agrees – what they mean. Yet if there is to be a more explicit 'quality function' in the modern enterprise, then there is a need to be more precise and to explore the notion of 'quality' in more detail.

The aim of this chapter is to investigate a range of ideas surrounding the notion of 'quality' and the ambiguities associated with how 'qual-ity' is conceptualised. Only then will it be really possible to discuss how 'quality', in whatever formulation, is adopted, is achieved. The concern is to place notions of 'quality' in the context of their use and applica-tion to the activities of the small scale enterprise but the discussion provides a contribution to the conceptualisation and discussion of quality in economic activities more generally.

EXPLORING NOTIONS OF QUALITY

Conventionally, 'quality' is linked with high standards of production, delivery and presentation (Coote and Pfeffer, 1991). It is often associ-ated with the notion of the consummate good or service where costs of production are seen as irrelevant and 'no expense has been spared'. Offering the best possible is the only criterion applicable. Obvious examples include products such as Rolls-Royce cars, designer clothes and the food and wine offered by Michelin starred restaurants. Of course, cost *is* highly relevant since such goods and services have costs of production (reflected usually in their high prices) but where 'quality' is used in this absolute sense, cost and price are often taken out of the equation to emphasise some neo-essentialist idea of 'pure' quality.[1]

'Quality' in the above universalist sense in the discussion of goods and services is close to economic illiteracy. In a market economy cost and price will *always* be part of the production of any good or service and, inevitably, part of any quality considerations. Yet, however obvious the economic context of quality is, absolute notions of 'quality' all too easily eclipse other elements in conceptualisations and applications of the term. Sometimes indeed, the term 'quality' may be used in a universalist way deliberately to direct attention away from economic considerations.

An obvious contemporary example of the above, at least in the opinion of some, is the introduction of 'quality reforms' in the public sector. In education, health and welfare, changes in the way services are delivered are often presented as 'quality reforms' aimed at improving the service received by those benefiting. Critics of these reforms argue that the use of 'quality' in these circumstances is often a way of disguising reductions in public funding (Robinson and Le Grand, 1993). In other words, absolute notions of quality are embedded in the policy presentation and cost elements of the changes are downplayed, with the object of suggesting quality improvements with no resource implications. Contentious measures are also sometimes introduced as 'quality reforms' again using the notion of quality in an absolute sense so that any protests can be labelled 'absurd' objections to introducing services of higher quality.

Whatever the intellectual weaknesses of universalistic notions of 'quality' in any context (which in contemporary society covers virtually all activities, economic and non-economic, in practice) the approach is remarkably common. For instance, the main institution for promoting quality in the UK, the British Standards Institute (BSI) produced a neo-universalist conceptualisation of 'quality' when it suggested the following definition in relation to BS 5750: 'the totality of features and characteristics of a product or service that bears on its ability to satisfy stated or implied needs' (BSI, 1987 – 4778: 3). Leaving aside the temptation to see this as an empty or over-general definition, it was clearly developed with a specific objective in mind, that is, defining 'quality' in terms of customer requirements. In this sense, it picks up on the other key feature of much of contemporary management writing on quality, the alleged importance of the customer.

The original purpose of BS 5750, namely to provide an independently assessed framework which, when applied by businesses to their own procedures, assures customer requirements are consistently delivered, is clearly reflected in the definition. As Chapter 1 made clear, BS 5750 does not and cannot *ensure* that customer requirements are understood or delivered in all circumstances. One reason for this, as the chapter argued, was that much depended on whether or not these 'stated or implied needs' could be explicitly defined and/or recognised by customers. Only where customer requirements can be explicitly stated will definitions of this kind be useful in thinking about 'quality' as a first step to the practical task of applying it in economic activities.

It might be argued that the above requirements, implying an informed customer or consumer, are not really much of a barrier to theorising quality strategies where the implied needs can be stated, that is, where a clear statement of what the customer or consumer would recognise if they were able to articulate their needs, can be made. But where 'quality' and 'quality standards' are said to exist despite customers being unable to state their requirements, there is always the question of 'whose quality?', that is, whose interests are being best served?

Where customers or consumers are uninformed, a supplier 'knows-best-approach' is easily adopted which may not always benefit end users. For instance, in motor vehicle repairing, parts with a shorter life may be substituted for longer life parts because this generates higher levels of repeat business. Consumers, not knowledgeable about the life expectancy of different brands or types of replacement parts, will not receive the 'best' service in one sense even though the parts supplied may satisfy stated or implied needs in other senses including compliance with BS 5750 or safety standards and hence a stated quality standard.[2]

Even when customers are informed about the goods or services in question, this does not mean that the quality issue is easily settled. In many instances, producers and customers may be technically as well informed as each other but nevertheless their relations are still characterised by what economists term conditions of asymmetrical information. This means that though the parties are well informed technically, one or other lacks other information relevant to the current exchange. For instance, customers may not be up to date on what other suppliers could provide or on the capabilities of the producer to produce at a given price/volume. They may therefore accept goods and services of a particular quality at some price when under conditions of better information, they would behave differently.

The quality management literature examined briefly in the last chapter and most often seen as culminating in what is usually labelled TQM, also offers conceptualisations of quality as precursors to recommending specific quality management strategies. Often, however, they are no more satisfactory than the kind of universalist approach discussed above. One well known example is: 'the composite product and service characteristics of marketing, engineering, manufacture and maintenance, through which the product and services in use will meet the expectation of the customer' (Feigenbaum, 1972: 7). It would be tedious to quote the whole range of definitions offered by TQM authorities but some of the key phrases which occur include 'fitness for use' (Juran, 1991), 'conformance to requirements' (Crosby, 1979), that quality means 'to satisfy the needs of customer past and present' (Deming, 1986), and 'delighting the customer by continuously meeting and improving upon agreed requirements' (Macdonald, 1993: 3). Again, there is an emphasis on the customer, now however more explicitly seen (compared with the BSI definition above) as *the* criterion of quality. But much the same kind of objections can be raised as in the discussion of the kinds of definitions emanating from BSI sources or the like.

A further point to be made about customer-based definitions of quality is that they offer a view of economic activities in market-based economies which is potentially at odds with the thinking, strategies and goals of managerial behaviour in practice. For example, there have long been criticisms that marketing often involves dubious strategies to sell people products and services that they do not need or which might actually harm them (Murphy and Laczniak, 1981). The sale of cigarettes is probably the most frequently offered example in such arguments but there are other examples which could be drawn upon such as baby foods marketed to suggest they are superior to the mothers' own milk in developing countries and foods with a high fat or sugar content. These examples offer an implicit criticism of notions of quality which imply or argue, that customer satisfaction is the sole or prime criterion on which the performance of the business should be assessed. The real world of business does not function according to this criterion and is unlikely to ever do so in market-based economies as presently organised.

Nor do the above arguments exhaust the doubts about the emphasis on the importance of the customer in discussions of quality strategies. What of the supremacy of shareholders whose interests UK managers are legally required to give priority to in the operation of the business? It is easy to argue that by satisfying customers' needs, shareholders' expectations are thereby most effectively satisfied, but it is equally easy to offer examples where shareholders' and customers' interests will not coincide. Nor, as environmentalists point out, are customers and shareholders the only people with interests in the way the business performs. There is also the community or public at large. What quality considerations are relevant to them and how are they related to those applicable to the interests of the shareholders and customers of the business?

To the criticisms of the vagueness of conceptualisations of 'quality' in the management literature therefore can be added lack of realism. Universalist conceptualisations of quality are over-normative in their content and often bereft of real practical help to those running businesses (except where they add to a bargaining rhetoric). What is needed is, first, a more pragmatic notion of 'quality' and, second, a recognition that quality strategies are part of the wider management strategies required to operate in a market-based economy. Neither should normative prescription be substituted for the analysis or examination of the ways in which quality strategies are actually implemented under real life conditions.

AN ALTERNATIVE APPROACH TO QUALITY

An alternative approach would reject universalist approaches to conceptualising quality and argue that the notion of 'quality' in any context (economic or otherwise) is relative and socially constructed through a process of implicit or explicit negotiation. That is, the definition of 'quality' in relation to the production of goods or services will be a joint construction of producers (owner-managers and employees who constitute the small firm, for example) and others, especially customers, external to the enterprise.

Any quality issue related to the production of goods and services may impinge on a wide range of people. Besides owner-managers, employees and customers, other external actors may seek actively to influence definitions and practices linked to the quality of goods and services offered. Obvious external sources of influence are the state and the general public (or groups within these larger entities). The state may influence the product or service, for example, by statutory means for health and safety purposes. The general public (or groups within it) may seek to influence the quality of goods and services, for example, for consumer protection, environmental or safety reasons.

While the social construction and negotiation of quality notions and practices necessarily involves cooperation for its successful accomplishment, this does not rule out conflicts of interest between those involved. For example, Bowbrick (1992) suggests that producers may be guided by criteria such as cheap materials, ease of assembly and low rework costs, giving these equal or greater importance than customer satisfaction. Thus while the business attempts an image of 'quality' in the market, customers can still lose out.

Clients or customers have expectations and desires concerning the performance and appearance of the product or the content of a service activity which they believe they should, or could, obtain under given circumstances. Probably the most important of these is price, though time (for instance delivery times), performance and consistency, product life and safety may also be important. In addition, some customers may have special expectations related to their personal needs or how the product or service links with some other product or service in which they have an interest.

The negotiation of quality in the above sense may be straightforward. Suppliers and customers may be in regular contact with each other, both knowledgeable, have no great imbalance of power or bargaining between them and be keen to achieve a settled, stable deal. In the literature on subcontracting, for example, there is often an implicit notion that something approximating to the above is the norm and that such relations are on the increase as more outsourcing occurs (Curran and Blackburn, 1994). However, it is easy to argue that, in practice, the negotiation of quality is much more variable and unstable than is sometimes thought. The widespread existence of customer complaint departments, consumer protection legislation and inter-firm disputes, are evidence that conflicts can occur.

In large areas of production and consumption, negotiation is very much an implicit process. Goods and services are presented to consumers who are nominally free to choose to purchase or to choose an alternative offered by another supplier. 'Negotiation', in other words, may consist mainly of a simple refusal to purchase the specific good or service as currently offered. However, this often causes suppliers to alter the quality package offered by making changes in the product or service, its price or other conditions attached to the sale and the marketing strategies employed. In short, an implicit process of negotiation occurs.

On the whole, it is likely that producers and customers will often have differing or poorly formulated expectations or desires about product performance or service content in relation to other exigencies such as price. Customers in particular may lack accurate, up to date knowledge of the product or service and find it difficult to make well informed decisions. For instance, in the BSE crisis a reason offered for the use of cheap animal feed by farmers was that consumers 'insisted' on cheap food and were reluctant to pay higher prices for safer, better quality food products. But since the general public were largely unaware of the kinds of animal feed being used or of the risks involved, it is hard to argue that they 'chose' the cheap, lower quality food over more expensive, better quality and less risky food products.

The general trend in the development of modern economies, it could be argued, is for more and more goods and services to be offered. This produces problems in negotiating quality between producers and consumers (whether these are other businesses or private consumers). One reason is the increased technological complexity of many new goods and services. Informed assessment is now more difficult in the sense that individuals are likely to be reasonably knowledgeable about a shrinking range of goods and services. Even sophisticated commercial customers, with the resources to carry out detailed assessments of potential purchases, may find it too expensive to undertake this for the whole range of purchases they make.

An increasing proportion of the goods and services purchased by commercial and especially private consumers in an advanced economy, are intangibles. Leisure and communications products and services, for example, are becoming more sophisticated and choice is greater than ever before. But as disposable incomes increase, people devote more of their purchasing to these kinds of products and services. It is often very difficult to negotiate quality for many of these newer products and services. Good examples of the above are films, TV programmes, popular music, meals, books and holidays, where the customer has little control over the original quality of the product or service as offered and can only make an informed judgement *after* the product or service has been consumed. Consumers, in other words, may not know what they like until they experience the good or service while producers may agonise over what they offer with no secure way of predicting what will sell.

The recent history of the US film industry offers an excellent instance of the above. The industry recognises that risks and quality judgements linked to intangibles can be helped by past experience. One result is a growing fondness for making versions II, III and IV of a film which has done well at the box office. It reduces the risks of failure as consumers choose a sequel they hope will be as pleasurable as the original. Word of mouth is also important in helping reduce consumer disappointment. But it remains something of a hit and miss 'negotiation' process for both producers and consumers as more and more goods and services come on to the market.

Bodies such as government, the EU, trading standards departments and consumer organisations may also intervene in the negotiation process. They may help inform both producers and consumers by specifying product or service standards on behalf of less well informed consumers. They may even ban some goods or services from being offered at all. They may also intervene in the negotiating process in other ways. For example, they can 'slow down' the negotiation process by giving consumers a breathing period before they are contractually bound by their purchasing decision or offer advice and information to consumers on how to negotiate better deals.

QUALITY IS DYNAMIC, CHANGING AND UNSTABLE

Perhaps the most important point to stress in the approach to the conceptualisation of 'quality' proposed here is that not only is quality not absolute, it is also not stable. That is, the social construction of quality and the negotiating processes which promote and sustain this construction are continuous. The quality relations in which businesses and consumers engage are subject to all kinds of influences which lead to changing definitions of quality in relation to the product or service. This dynamic aspect of quality relations is often ignored because of the widely accepted cultural emphasis on absolute standards of quality and because, in practice, there is often an interest on the part of both producers and consumers in having some semblance of stability. Yet even those 'quality standards' which are very precisely formulated in a written, even legal, form, are never really fixed in any permanent sense. At the simplest, the expectations and desires of customers as well as producers' production strategies are subject to new technology, changing tastes, strategies and budgets over time and an awareness of how others in the market are behaving (Bowbrick, 1992).

Also, in a market economy price has a special role in influencing quality standards and negotiations. The equation between the product or the content of a service and its price, is inherently unstable. For example, a particular firm or firms in a sector may attempt to change the performance/content of a product or service in relation to price so as to offer customers a better deal. Such changes, however, cannot move too far away from market-dictated exchange bargains otherwise the attempt to 'improve quality' will fail. If the quality offered is markedly higher than that provided by others at a given price, the business may well fail to make an adequate return. Some changes which improve quality may, however, be 'costless' if they result from more effective use of people and resources – a message reiterated frequently by advocates of the adoption of BS 5750 and TQM (see Fox, 1991; Deming, 1986; DTI, 1992).

The basic mechanism of the market economy, competition, causes all kinds of instabilities in price and content. The major recessions of the early 1980s and 1990s played havoc with price–content relations (and therefore quality relations) between producers and customers. The high rate of technological change which is seen as so characteristic of contemporary economies similarly produces dynamic change and instabilities in quality relations. New firms enter the market, new products and services appear to compete with older products and services. The knowledge of how other producers and customers are behaving changes, adding its stimulus to the dynamic of change and instability. Acceptable levels of quality in relation to a particular good or service rise or even fall over time. Influences of this kind may therefore lead to new notions of 'quality' and 'quality standards' but they cannot disguise the facts of change and instability in quality relations.

The above outline of an alternative conceptualisation of 'quality', a socially constructed approach based on the notion of negotiation between all those involved, counters approaches which stress absolute or fixed standards of quality. It also seeks to fill the hiatus resulting from the refusal of previous theorising to offer a clear conceptualisation of the notion of quality. Further refinements are possible of course but it is argued that the above is sufficient for the purposes of a study of quality management in small firms. A socially constructed or negotiated approach offers a way to generate more specific formulations of 'quality' than any attempt to suggest some mystical notion of absolute 'quality' which firms, their customers and employees, should be seeking. In applying the above approach to quality strategies in small firms, it needs to be made more concrete to be useful. The following section offers a way of discussing the approaches small business owners use in practice. However, the notion of quality as a social construction arising out of a wide range of more or less complex processes of negotiation, underlies all the approaches discussed.

HOW DO SMALL FIRMS DELIVER GOODS AND SERVICES TO AGREED QUALITY STANDARDS?

At the practical level of everyday relations between small firms and their customers, owner-managers may see themselves as more or less bound by the market to deliver goods and services to some agreed 'quality standards'. In most instances, the quality standard will be ad hoc in that it exists in the owner-manager's mind rather than as a formalised quality standard. In other cases there may be a formal element, for instance, a brief written specification given to customers as the basis for a later invoice. They will see themselves as having to make all kinds of choices on the methods by which their notion of quality may be achieved. It is argued that for those who have adopted BS 5750, these choices can be made much more systematically. But as Chapter 1 indicated, the widespread adoption of the standard is very far from the case. So how do small firms solve the quality problem in practice?

A common approach to answering the above question is to distinguish between 'informal' and 'formal' quality management strategies.

Small firms, like larger enterprises, often operate both methods of quality control. However, these much used terms can engender considerable ambiguity (Brown, 1992: 52). What constitutes 'informal' and 'formal' methods will not be determined by a firm's *actual* quality practices. They are best understood as the strategies which owner-managers have developed for the purpose of achieving quality as they define the notion. For the purposes of the present discussion, the above informal-formal distinction may be more carefully and clearly elaborated into the following:

1 *Informal methods of quality control* are *ad hoc* or semi-bureaucratised methods developed, controlled and assessed exclusively by the firm's owner-manager or person designated by the owner-manager as responsible for key quality decisions. These methods may be further subdivided in to:

(a) *simple informal methods*, that is, non-bureaucratised, rule of thumb approaches to managing quality, based on day-to-day decisions rather than any longer term, systematic approach;

(b) *complex informal methods*, that is, structured, bureaucratic or semi-bureaucratic approaches which may be paper-based or systematised in some way but which are entirely controlled by the owner-managers. Such approaches may resemble external formal standards but no external body is involved in defining or monitoring the quality strategies.

2 *Formal methods of quality control* are those methods which are pre-determined and usually bureaucratised by being written down and having defined procedures attached to their routine application to the activities of the business. They are assessed by a body external to the enterprise. The external assessment may be (1) *second party assessment* by a customer/supplier or (2) *third party assessment*, as is often the case with BS 5750.

SIMPLE INFORMAL STRATEGIES

Simple informal quality management strategies are common in small firms. Indeed it is difficult to imagine any business surviving for very long which does not have at least some informal quality management strategies. Even those with more formal strategies will usually augment them with informal methods. In practice, owner-managers who rely on simple informal strategies are likely to develop a number of *proactive* and *reactive* measures.

Proactive strategies are those which affect the quality of the product or service, before and during its production, but before, or at the point, it reaches the consumer. They may take a wide variety of forms. The most obvious form is the direct supervision of staff in the production of the good or service. But other common strategies may include monitoring the quality of supplies used in producing the good or service and a rigorous, often 100 per cent, inspection of all goods produced before they are dispatched to the customer (Dale *et al.*, 1990). In service businesses, the owner-manager may try to directly oversee each individual service delivery if at all possible.

Another key proactive strategy may be ensuring adequate staffing by recruiting skilled staff and additional training to maintain or upgrade their skills as required. Research indicates that small firms prefer to use informal methods of recruitment and training (Scott *et al.*, 1989; Curran *et al.*, 1993 and 1996a). For example, many owner-managers recruit employees by word-of-mouth. They seek new or replacement employees through existing employees or other people known to them and who they trust. Small business owners often state they select people on their personal characteristics as much as on their objectively demonstrated skills: recruiting the 'right' people is regarded as crucial. One aspect of being the 'right' person is their potential for maintaining and contributing to the quality procedures of the firm. Most small business training tends to be informal and on the job (Curran *et al.*, 1996a) with owner-managers themselves acting as the trainers, responsible for training and motivating employees to ensure the appropriate delivery of the final product or service to the quality standard desired. The 'right' person for the job therefore has to be someone assessed as receptive to being supervised and trained in these ways.

The attention given to employees represents the fundamental importance of people in a small firm. Much of the writing on the small enterprise concentrates on the owner-manager or 'entrepreneur', seeing him or her as producer and sole mover in the fate of the business. Employees are frequently neglected or seen as inputs into the business on a par with purchases of supplies and materials. Small firms are often, in effect, small teams led by the owner-manager: the enterprise only survives and succeeds if the team works effectively. Interestingly, research shows that small business owners themselves are acutely aware of the importance of others who work in the business (Scase and Goffee, 1989: 58–72; Scott *et al.*, 1989; Curran *et al.*, 1993). Repeatedly in interviews they stress that picking the 'right' people and managing them is one of the most critical (and difficult) aspects of running their businesses and ensuring goods and services conform to the owner-managers' quality standards. Quality strategies, in other words, whatever their specific character, are also people-centred.

Reactive strategies are those used to assess the quality of the good or service *after* production and delivery to the customer, or customers have experienced the service. Follow-up quality strategies take a variety of forms. Small business owners frequently argue that their relations with customers are often ongoing, that is, the business relies heavily on a core customer base providing repeat orders (Curran, 1987; Curran *et al.*, 1991). This often leads to personalised relations between owner-managers and customers. Owner-managers deliberately seek to put their business-to-business relations on a personalised basis to tie the customer to the firm. In services, the creation of quasi-personal relations between the small business and consumers is even more well established (Shaw, 1995). For instance, the popularity and success, even survival, of a pub or small shop, often depends greatly on the personal skills of the tenant or owner.

One of the fashionable recent 'discoveries' in contemporary large enterprise marketing is 'relationship marketing' (Gronroos, 1994; Payne, 1996). This stresses that relations between supplier and customer do not end when a particular sale is made but continues with this after-life being critical to ensuring the customer returns to the supplier for future goods and services. Small business owners have long practised relationship marketing as a way of retaining customers even if they were unaware of the label attached to it by marketing practitioners and academics.

In consumer services, other kinds of reactive quality strategies can be used. One example, is the 'dummy customer' who reports on the service provided. Small business owner-managers can use this quality strategy fairly easily and cheaply. Again, this is a strategy larger enterprises also use. Supermarkets, for instance, use dummy customers to check on how staff present themselves to customers and how helpful they are in dealing with the public. They are also used by franchisors to check on the operation of their franchisees, who are often small businesses. Another reactive strategy involves finding out what competitors are providing. Small business owners telephone competitors posing as a customer to find out how the other business treats customers, what it offers and at what price and delivery times. Service business owners can visit competing businesses as customers, gauging how the other business and its staff serves them. This is a low cost strategy for most small businesses and enables them to stay abreast of changes in what is being offered by similar firms in the market.

Another strategy is customer surveys. These are most useful to small businesses in services, particularly those serving private consumers. In principle, simple telephone, postal or street surveys of customers are easily carried out and might be suited to the needs of small businesses seeking information on how their services are perceived by customers, actual and potential. But there is little evidence that small firms use this reactive strategy very extensively. Perhaps owner-managers see it as inappropriate since they often have very close informal relations with their customers (Shaw, 1995). Or they may feel surveys are technically too difficult and too time-consuming in relation to the information they are likely to produce.

Many of the above examples of simple informal quality management strategies are probably widely used in one form or another by small firms. Previous research has not highlighted their importance, probably for two reasons. First, as Chapter 1 argued, much of the emphasis on the discussion of quality management has been on formal standards such as BS 5750 with much less attention given to non-formal strategies. Second, research on small firms seeking information on management and marketing strategies has usually been of the survey variety asking questions about the use of textbook strategies. This means that the distinctive character of small business owner management strategies in which managerial functions are met in an undifferentiated way, is not properly addressed. For instance, quality management will often not be a separate function but integrated into the other managerial activities of the owner. Indeed, the owner-manager may not be able to easily separate quality strategies from other activities required to manage the business: they may be so much part and parcel of everyday management that they are not explicitly recognised for what they are.

COMPLEX INFORMAL STRATEGIES

It has so far been assumed that, in smaller small firms at least, much of the responsibility for controlling quality falls on the owner-manager. It is unlikely that there will be much scope for delegation of responsibility in firms with, for example, five or fewer employees. However, in larger small firms, or as small firms grow, the ability of the owner-manager to effectively control quality directly will decrease (Churchill and Lewis, 1983). For example, where owner-managers are acting as both production supervisors and quality inspectors, they may opt for only one of these roles because of possible conflict between them or constraints on their time (Gouldner, 1954). Owner-managers may therefore be forced to delegate responsibility to trusted employees, for example. However, this might not be enough. Owner-managers are often reluctant to devolve responsibility in this way (Scase and Goffee, 1989) and may still be concerned that quality will suffer as their business grows. The obvious next step is for the owner-manager to introduce some form of paper-based system to help control those aspects of quality they are not able to supervise personally. This may even include the development of a manual detailing the firm's operating procedures. If so, the firm is operating what can be termed *complex informal strategies* of quality management.

As the definition presented above made clear, complex informal strategies are structured bureaucratised or semi-bureaucratised procedures supervised and controlled by the owner-manager or whoever he or she designates, but with no direct external control or monitoring by second or third party agencies. Again, they may take a wide variety of forms. Simple examples would include the use of a 'job card' which follows the product or service through all stages from the original order to final customer payment. At each stage the person responsible for its completion adds their initials or name to the card before it moves on. Quality failures at any stage can then be traced relatively easily.

More complicated examples of complex informal strategies are complete quality manuals with the different stages from receiving the order, to production, to delivery and follow-up, all documented in detail. Owner-managers may devise such manuals from scratch but more commonly probably use a model of some kind. For example, as the research later in the book shows, some small firms embark on preparing to register for BS 5750 but decide for some reason not to complete the process. The preparation may have gone far enough to include the writing of a manual. This is sometimes retained and used in the business despite lacking external certification.

Another example of the above occurs in franchised small enterprises. Franchisors often prepare very detailed operating manuals for their franchised outlets which offer a blueprint for a very wide range of aspects of running the outlet, including quality issues (Stanworth *et al.* 1984; Felstead, 1991). This is part of the package the franchisee purchases with the franchise and is designed to help the business operate efficiently as soon as possible. In many instances, the franchisee is required to adopt the procedures in the manual as part of the contractual relationship with the franchisor. In this case, the quality strategies may be termed 'second party certified' if the franchisor assesses and monitors how well the manual is implemented and, hence, an example of formal methods of quality management (discussed below). But where the quality recommendations are applied voluntarily, they are examples of complex informal strategies.

Again, as with simple informal strategies, complex informal strategies need not be confined to what goes on in the firm. Owner-managers may well use semi-bureaucratised strategies to systematically follow up customers. A simple example, is an added section to delivery notes, invoices and bills encouraging customers to comment on the quality of the product or service they have purchased. Often the invitation to customers is presented in a form which ensures the reply will be returned directly to the owner-manager.

Earlier, customer surveys were examined as a simple informal quality strategy but they can also be examples of complex informal strategies. For instance, an outside marketing research agency can undertake the work. The systematic use of customer surveys to gauge the quality of service received by customers is, however, relatively expensive. Larger enterprises often use 'omnibus' surveys, that is, have questions included in surveys collecting data for several users. Small businesses could share the costs of consumer surveys but there is little evidence that this occurs much in Britain. This could be a service training and enterprise councils (TECs), chambers of commerce or Business Links could provide for small businesses in their areas.

The extent of the use of complex informal strategies of quality control by small firms is not known, mainly because so little research has focused on such strategies. Even where research reveals their use, the analysis can easily misunderstand what is happening. For instance, where firms have prepared a manual as part of an aborted preparation for BS 5750 registration, this is sometimes seen as a 'failure' in quality strategy implementation. Little attention is given to the benefits, in terms of quality management, that may have resulted from the changes in the way the business operates.

SECOND PARTY CONTROLLED STRATEGIES

Second party controlled strategies are routinely used bureaucratised procedures, externally dictated and assessed by firms' customers or suppliers. In other words, some external second party lays down specific requirements that have direct implications for quality control in the business. For example, customers may demand some minimum level of product or service quality by insisting that the firm adopts their suggested quality control methods. This approach has long been common in the defence sector as Chapter 1 noted and, indeed, was the model for the development of BS 5750 itself. The example of franchisors contractually insisting on conformity to an operating manual which includes quality provisions, is another example also mentioned above. Other examples can be drawn from small clothing manufacturers and their relations with the large high street retailers (Rainnie, 1989: 95–99).

One of the main management trends of the 1980s was the rationalisation of supplier lists by large organisations (Curran and Blackburn, 1994). Studies have shown that large organisations have been rationalising their supplier bases and insisting that suppliers are 'quality assured', depending on the product or service supplied. In many instances, BS 5750 is used as a screening device to ensure minimum quality levels. To secure a place on the preferred supplier list firms must have registered. This is a clear example of a mixed second/third party strategy of quality control. But this is not always the case. Curran and Blackburn, for example, quote one of their respondents in a study of large firm–small firm links as preferring their own approach: 'we don't use a DTI approved list, we use our own compiled by [our] quality assurance department' (Curran and Blackburn, 1992: 47). Internal quality assurance departments in larger organisations in both the private and public sectors are now routine. The label 'internal' is a slight misnomer here where the department also vets the quality of outside independent suppliers such as small firms.

Second party controlled quality strategies are especially suitable where particular kinds of economic activities or specific sectors have very singular characteristics. They enable standardised, widely accepted quality strategies to be devised which fit closely with the needs of both suppliers and customers. They can also reduce the overall costs of quality maintenance and avoid wasteful duplication of quality strategies. On the other hand, there is a danger that larger or more powerful businesses may use such strategies as a way of exerting power over smaller suppliers or to exclude some firms so reducing opportunities and competition in the sector.

THIRD PARTY CONTROLLED METHODS

Third party controlled methods are fully bureaucratised procedures externally dictated and assessed by a third party agency, such as BS 5750. These are intended in principle to be applicable to any kind of economic activity or equivalent in the public sector. This broad reach has, however, been seen as a weakness as much as a strength. Critics have made the obvious point that by attempting such wide coverage, these standards often end up being too general to be really helpful in generating well focused quality strategies (North *et al.*, 1995). As discussed earlier, firms adopting BS 5750 often feel a need to find a version already tailored to the needs of their specific kind of business rather than starting from scratch with a generic standard.

As shown in Chapter 1, BS 5750 provides a set of requirements for the development of a quality management system (Fox, 1991: 5). Its aim is to provide firms with a framework by which they can improve their operating procedures which, in turn, is intended to have implications for raising quality levels. Other benefits may include increased provision of employee training or reductions in operating costs through increased efficiency (Fox, 1991: 2). In theory, this is achieved through the auditing and augmentation of existing procedures in line with those suggested by BS 5750. The system is then documented and assessed independently by a third party certification body to see whether the newly developed procedures and practices meet the standards set. Subsequently there is periodic monitoring to ensure that firms maintain the system to which they have committed themselves at the original registration.

Other third party schemes are sector-based. One example is the *Retail Motor Industry Quality Control Scheme*. This a third party controlled, operated and assessed quality control scheme by the Retail Motor Industry Trade Association similar to BS 5750 but specific to the requirements of the garage and vehicle repair sector.[3] Schemes of this kind try to be sufficiently broad to cover a whole area of economic activity yet specific enough to provide detailed, tailor-made and meaningful quality strategies for the firms and customers involved.

TOTAL QUALITY MANAGEMENT AS A QUALITY STRATEGY

Total quality management (TQM), discussed in Chapter 1 is, in effect, the attempt to take quality strategies to their highest level (Dale *et al.*, 1990). It will be remembered from the earlier discussion that, in essence, TQM is a holistic approach which seeks to convert the entire culture and structure of the enterprise into a total commitment to quality (Barad, 1996). In application, TQM inevitably falls short of attaining this ideal (Taylor, 1992; Jackson, 1993; Webb, 1995). As Chapter 1 argued, the real world is too complex and too unpredictable, to allow a full blown TQM organisation to be realised.

Recommendations on the practical implementation of TQM in Britain are usually linked closely to BS 5750 which is seen as the first step towards attaining TQM (see, for example, Oakland in Nuttal, 1991; Drummond, 1992). The alleged virtues of TQM are very similar to those claimed for BS 5750. There are a number of quality/management gurus, consultants, government, large firms, and some academics who appear to support the TQM philosophy regardless of the criticisms levelled against it elsewhere.[4] But there are also others – mainly other academics – who are making genuine attempts to research and discuss the implications associated with implementing TQM (see, for example, Hill, 1991; Wilkinson *et al.*, 1992; Wilkinson and Willmott, 1995).

The criticisms of TQM, rehearsed in Chapter 1, are therefore not surprisingly similar to those levelled at BS 5750. The milder criticisms suggest that its claims on raising quality levels are as yet unproven but, again as pointed out in the opening chapter, a number of commentators dismiss the TQM philosophy outright:

> If good TQM should have a philosophy, principles and methods, and these should embrace the technical and human aspects of the organisation, then we can say that TQM is good at telling you how to design the process so that you have zero defects . . . It is not good at telling you about the sort of organisational design which will enable you to produce a quality product. How do you design an organisation so that people can give their best and can get quality for you? In terms of culture, quality gurus talk a lot about the philosophy of culture, but there are few principles and few well tested methods for bringing them about . . . And, in terms of politics, then no-one talks about the politics of quality.
>
> (Jackson, 1993: 19)

More important for the focus of this book is the criticism that TQM is irrelevant to the discussion of quality strategies in small firms. Davies (1990) suggests that most small firm owner-managers consider TQM irrelevant, believing that by virtue of their size, they already practice TQM. They believe they hit all the cultural and organisational targets advocates of TQM stress as integral to the quality concerned enterprise. They produce high quality goods and services; employees all understand and adhere to the firm's quality 'mission'; everybody's tasks are clearly defined; communications within the company and with customers are excellent; and that the small firm culture makes the embodiment of TQM principles in the organisation and motivation of workers relatively easy. This may be wishful thinking on the part of small business owners but as will be seen in the following chapters, an explicit commitment to TQM in a formal sense is rare in small firms.

CONCLUSIONS

The fixation on quality as the key to business performance and national economic success is now proclaimed in the management and marketing literatures and government policy. Large enterprises in the private and public sectors have accepted the quality emphasis to a greater or lesser extent. Small businesses, on the other hand, have been seen to be dawdlers in accepting the 'quality message', at least as measured by their lack of enthusiasm for formal quality standards such as BS 5750. On the other hand, small businesses survive in the UK economy and their numbers have been increasing sharply since the mid-1970s. Even if they are not committed to formal quality standards, they must be dealing with quality issues in some way. Yet it is also clear from national statistics that large numbers of small firms cease to trade within a short time of being launched. Businesses cease to trade for all kinds of reasons, of course, but weaknesses in quality management could be one of the key reasons. How small firms deal with quality issues therefore deserves closer inspection and analysis than has hitherto been the case.

What has clouded much of the discussion of quality issues in economic and non-economic contexts, has been a failure to offer a clear conceptualisation of what is meant by the notion. We have suggested that one reason for this is that 'quality' is one of those terms which sociologists term 'taken for granted', that is, they are used so commonly that people feel no need to state clearly what they mean by the term when they use it: 'everybody knows' what it means and this is taken to mean also that everybody agrees on what it means.

In the quality literature and in a lot of popular thinking, absolutist notions of 'quality' are often implied. 'Quality' is seen as a synonym for 'the best', often regardless of other considerations such as price. Of course, in the real world 'quality' is much more problematic. Management writing on quality stresses the customer as the key test of quality achievement. Quality is seen as customer driven and businesses should be dedicated to meeting customer expectations. This view was criticised as facile since it neglects other powerful influences on business behaviour, particularly those of management itself and those which require the interests of shareholders to be given maximum priority. Customers often come second in the real world, and quality strategies, however well thought out or implemented, cannot dissolve differences of interest between the main groups involved in any business. Moreover, others also have interests which they will seek to exercise. The negotiations between these groups may be explicit and formalised but also often tacit and subtle.

An alterative approach was presented which saw quality as socially constructed and negotiated. In other words, quality is specific to any particular context. It will be the outcome of a complex set of influences ranging from the interests, knowledge and bargaining power of particular groups (managers, customers, shareholders, employees, the state, pressure groups etc.) to market effects resulting from competition (and especially its impact on price) and the availability of other relevant products or services. Quality is never absolute but relative and context-bound.

What also follows from the above is that quality standards will also be dynamic, unstable and changing. The interests and influences which underpin the social and economic construction of quality, change and realign themselves with the result that agreed notions of 'quality' in a particular context will be subject to change even though those involved may attempt to stabilise them in the interest of smoother and more predictable relations. Quality relations and the strategies which underlie them, therefore, are often complex and difficult to embody in simple management admonitions to 'drive for maximum customer benefit' or aim for 'zero defects' or the like.

From the general to the particular, the chapter shifted from basic conceptual issues to presenting an initial typology of how firms, specifically small firms, manage quality. The typology posited a main distinction between informal and formal strategies of quality management. Informal strategies were further divided into simple informal methods and complex informal methods. Formal methods included the most widely discussed formal quality standard, BS 5750. Each type was examined in detail, with examples, to show how they were related to the way small firms manage quality. Finally, TQM was discussed as a separate case, albeit related to the above types. It was suggested that even in its formal business literature form, TQM appears to play relatively little part in the quality management strategies of small firms.

It should be stressed that the typology is a first step in examining quality management strategies in small firms. In the study and findings reported in later chapters, it will be shown that much needs to be added to the above approach to understand small firm approaches to quality. Moreover, typologies are not explanations: to explain how and why small firm owner-managers manage quality issues in particular ways requires a great deal of additional analysis. Equally, how small business owner quality strategies compare with those used in larger enterprises also requires its own analysis.

3 Researching quality in small firms: the methodological issues

INTRODUCTION

Researching small firms is notoriously difficult. Even saying what is meant by a 'small firm' is far from easy because there is no official or universally accepted definition. Both government and academics have used varying definitions, depending on the purpose for which they are being employed. For example, different government departments and pieces of legislation use different definitions (Smith, 1985). Researchers use various quantitative definitions (usually based on the number of employees),[1] qualitative definitions or some combination of both (Curran and Burrows, 1988; Curran and Blackburn, 1994: 53–59). Similarly, the European Union has used various definitions, in attempting to arrive at one which can be applied across the whole community (European Commission, 1996; DTI, 1996a: 8).

In this study a small firm was defined as a legally independent business employing at least 1 employee (or full-time equivalent) but less than 50 people.[2] This definition has been chosen for the following reasons. First, it can be argued that in size terms (measured by number of employees) it accords broadly with what most people would accept as a 'small business'. It is also close to the definition now used by the European Union[3] and accepted as a useful definition by the Department of Trade and Industry's Small Firms Statistics Unit. On the other hand, this upper size limit is lower than other research on small business quality issues (see, for example, SBRT, 1992). However, it is argued that the lower upper size limit is more realistic for a study of quality management strategies in *small* firms. As Chapter 1 reported, the most recent DTI estimate of the UK business population suggests that this 1–50 employees definition covers 97 per cent of *all* businesses in the UK with at least 1 employee.

In relation to research on quality management strategies, the criterion of legal independence is also important. Where a business unit is not independent because it is a branch of some larger enterprise or a business which is controlled by another business, this is likely to affect how quality issues are handled. For example, as previous research has established, the use of formal quality standards is positively related to size of enterprise (SBRT, 1992; Chittenden *et al.*, 1996: 129–131) Where a small unit is part of a larger enterprise rather than independent, therefore, it is more likely to be associated with some kind of formal standard such as BS 5750, perhaps as part of a group strategy. In this research although the original focus was on small firm experiences of BS 5750, this was widened to investigate the more basic issue of small business quality management strategies generally. To include small establishments of larger businesses would lead to an over-representation of businesses committed to formal quality standards and would make the findings much less valuable as a picture of how small firms typically manage quality.

A second problem in small business research is the lack of suitable sampling frames, that is, accurate and up to date lists of small firms defined in whatever way is deemed suitable by government or researchers for the purposes of the research. Sampling frames of this kind are required if the research is to have any claims to be statistically representative. To many people's surprise, despite all the different kinds of information collected on the UK economy for economic policy, legal and taxation purposes, there is no comprehensive register of businesses in the UK (Storey, 1994). Anybody can legitimately run a business in the UK and while the individual person may register as self-employed, there is no legal requirement that the business itself be registered as a company. Nor is a business the equivalent of a self-employed person since two or more people may own and run the same business.

Neither are all businesses on the VAT register since businesses need not register for VAT if their turnover is below the registration threshold. This is currently £48,000 (November 1996 Budget), a turnover level which a high proportion of businesses, perhaps between 40 and 50 per cent, do not exceed (Jennings, 1991).[4] In other words, whatever official listing is consulted (assuming that the public are allowed to consult the list in question) a substantial number of existing businesses will not be included.[5]

Thirdly, even if a close approximation of a list of businesses exists for a particular locality or sector, they are almost always out of date within a short time of being published:

The Small Business population changes constantly. New businesses are started, others close, while some change ownership . . . In recent years, information collected about business bank accounts indicates that, in England and Wales, around 400,000 new businesses start each year and that similar numbers closed down.

(*Small Firms in Britain Report*, 1996 – DTI, 1996b: 84)

In short, even though the number of small businesses is estimated to be large (around 1.2m employ at least 1 but under 50 people) the high numbers of start-ups added to the similar number ceasing to trade, means that the level of 'churning' is so high that it is not so much a population as a 'flow of businesses'. Lists which seek to capture the numbers and kinds of businesses at any one moment in time will date very quickly unless considerable resources are devoted to updating them. The latter rarely happens in practice.

Finally, there is the issue of heterogeneity. Small businesses exist in virtually every sector of the economy.[6] This presents a problem for any adequate statistical analysis since this requires that the population (or appropriately selected sample) subject to statistical manipulation should have sufficient relevant common features for the claim to be made that the units are similar in key respects. But where a simple size measure such as number of employees is used to define 'small', there may be considerable doubts about whether the homogeneity in relation to key features relevant to the subject of the research is sufficient for meaningful statistical analysis. For example, despite the fact that they all employ under 50 people, it may be questioned whether a small print business has a lot in common with, say, a small hotel or a small employment agency or a computer software firm for many of the issues (including quality issues) which are typically the subject of small business research.

Of course, the above problems are not that easy to solve. It is very difficult, for instance, for researchers with no access to official lists and limited resources to magically resolve the problem of accessing (or constructing) sampling frames that are fully statistically representative. In practice, most small business researchers have to do the best they can under the circumstances. They have to exercise as much care as possible within the resources at their disposal in constructing samples and be aware of the limitations their findings have in relation to any larger population of small businesses. Considerations of these kinds, whether acknowledged or not, always underlie the research designs adopted in all small business research.

THE RESEARCH DESIGN

The approach adopted for the present study was a popular two stage quantitative–qualitative research design used in much contemporary small business research. This is a common compromise approach which seeks to be able to claim some statistical power for the generalisations drawn from the findings combined with an understanding of the motivations, logics and strategies of the human actors involved, in this instance small business owner-managers, but also to a lesser extent their employees and customers. Other research on quality management strategies in small firms such as that conducted for the Small Business Research Trust (1992 and 1994; Chittenden *et al.*, 1996) has faced similar problems but adopted less sensitive research strategies using simple postal questionnaires. This has the advantage of permitting larger samples for a given level of resources but at the expense of high response rates and depth. Insights into the motivations and situations which influence and constrain owner-managers' quality management strategies, as well as information on the content of the latter, are difficult or impossible to obtain using such approaches.

The first, mainly quantitative, element of the research design in this study involved 150 telephone interviews with small business owner-managers. The problem of accessing suitable sampling frames was solved by using updated sampling frames constructed for other recent research projects conducted by the Small Business Research Centre (Curran *et al.*, 1991: Curran and Blackburn, 1992). One reason for this was that these sampling frames had been constructed to high standards, in one case to an exceptional level in a very resource expensive fashion and then regularly updated.[7] Not only would it not have been possible to replicate this sampling frame construction because of resource limitations but using the original sampling frame offered other advantages. For example, the data on the firms collected in earlier projects provided excellent background information on the firms' histories and other characteristics. The other main sampling frame used was constructed for a project conducted immediately before the research reported in this book.[8] The use of sampling frames of this kind in this way is therefore not only resource effective but of direct benefit to the research itself.

Respondents were invited initially to participate in the project by letter and a few days later were contacted by telephone. Many had already indicated their willingness to cooperate in further research in earlier interviews for other projects. This helped solve another potential problem bedevilling small business research, that of low response. Busy small business owners are sometimes reluctant to give time to researchers – especially for telephone interviews – and response rates in small business research are frequently well below 30 per cent (Storey, 1994: xvi-xvii). (In the study of BS 5750 and small businesses by Chittenden *et al.* (1996), for example, the response rate was below 20 per cent.) Those who have already participated in research, particularly as in this case face-to-face interviews and who know something of the value of previous research,[9] are likely to be much more receptive to requests to take part in future research and telephone interviews. The outcome here was a very high 90.4 per cent response rate.

A telephone survey strategy was chosen because a considerable amount of data can be collected even in a relatively short interview providing the schedule is carefully constructed and well focused. The centre has gained considerable experience in conducting telephone surveys with small business owners using a CATI (computer-aided telephone interviews) approach. Here a skilled, experienced interviewer (in this case one of the authors) asked respondents questions prompted by a specially constructed screen-based interview schedule and coded the answers immediately on to a suitable database (SPSS PC+ in this case). Answers were mainly of the 'yes' or 'no' kind or some discrete quantity but qualitative answers were also summarised where the type of question required a fuller response.

The telephone questionnaire was developed to cover a range of issues concerning quality while minimising the time commitment of the respondent.[10] Many small firms have only one telephone line and owner-managers may worry that while they are answering the questions, a customer cannot get through. By careful design and testing, it is possible to ask well targeted questions and still keep the interview short. The specially designed CATI–SPSS PC+ strategy for data entry and coding also helped save time. The interviews varied from an average of 5 minutes for those firms who had not implemented formal methods of quality control, to an average of 15 minutes for those who had. Some interviews lasted much longer because the respondent was both articulate and interested in quality management issues.

Table 1 shows the size distribution of the small firms sampled in the first, telephone interview stage of the research design. Almost 90 per cent of the businesses employed less than 20 people. Although the upper size limit was 50 employees, the strong representation of smaller firms was desirable since this reflects the skewness of the size distribution of businesses in the UK. For example the DTI Small Firms Statistics Unit estimates suggest that over 80 per cent of businesses employing at least 1 but under 50 people actually employ under 10 people (DTI, 1996a: 9).

Table 1 Size distribution of surveyed firms

Employees	Frequency	%
1–4	46	30.7
5–9	53	35.3
10–19	31	20.7
20+	20	13.3
	150	100.0

Notes: Mean = 10.313; median = 7.00

This implies that the distribution shown in Table 1 actually *under-*estimates smaller businesses (1–4 employees) but over-represents those employing 5–9 people but nevertheless it can be claimed that smaller businesses are well represented in the sample. Moreover, the distribution in the table avoided a more serious problem. Recruiting a sample reflecting the DTI size estimate profile more accurately would, given previous estimates of BS 5750 registrations (see SBRT, 1992), run the risk of producing very few, if any, registered firms in a sample of this size.

Another important point is that BS 5750 has a differential impact on different sectors: firms is some sectors, particularly in manufacturing, are more likely to be registered than firms in services (SBRT, 1992; Chittenden *et al.*, 1996). On the other hand, the small firm population contains many more service than manufacturing businesses. This second point was considered to be especially important since there is a tendency in research and policy discussions to give more attention to small firms in manufacturing than their statistical importance in the economy warrants. Firms were therefore selected to ensure a balance between services and manufacturing to reflect broadly the representation of the two categories among small firms overall (Table 2). It was reported earlier that the DTI Small Firms Statistics Unit (DTI, 1996a: Table 1) indicates that about 75 per cent of small firms are in services and the remainder are in construction and manufacturing. To reflect this, a broad 75/25 split between services and manufacturing was aimed for in the sample. As Table 2 shows, this division was met closely in the main sector distribution.[11]

Emphasis was also placed on services because official and other literature on quality management strategies and standards, appears over-concerned with manufacturing, though the bias appears to be diminishing (North *et al.*, 1993). Frequently this has resulted in too little attention being given to small businesses in services. This is

Table 2 Sector distribution of surveyed firms

	Frequency	%
Manufacturing		
Electronics	18	12.0
Printing	16	10.7
Services		
Advertising	17	11.3
Computers	26	17.3
Employment agencies	15	10.0
Garages	34	22.7
Plant hire	24	16.0
Total	150	100.0

particularly well shown in several previous studies of small firms and BS 5750 (see, for example, SBRT, 1992). Within the main manufacturing-services division a limited range of sectors were selected. Given the overall size of the telephone interview sample, it would have been impossible to have anything like a full representation of every kind of economic activity in manufacturing or services let alone a representation reflecting the relative importance of each kind as measured by their contributions to employment and/or turnover.

The alternative, used in the research design, was to select sectors which, it could be argued, are key in understanding the current UK economy and issues of quality management. In manufacturing, for instance, printing is a long established industry providing products and services mainly to other businesses. Electronics, in contrast, is representative of a relatively new sector in manufacturing linked to high technology and to the kinds of activities likely to be represented strongly in the post-2000 economy (FEI, 1995). In services the sectors were again chosen to ensure that traditional and more recently emerging activities serving the needs of other businesses and private consumers were represented.

Two other influences were also taken into account, legal form and locality. For some issues in small business research, legal form and locality are considered to be important and hence need to be given methodological consideration. In the present research neither of these influences was seen as requiring any special provision in the research design. On the legal issue, after the exclusion of public limited corporations, their branch plants and subsidiaries, legal form is likely to provide a statistical rather than causal relationship since legal form tends to be related to firm size as does attitudes to BS 5750 registration. In other words, larger firms are much more likely to be incorporated than smaller businesses which are much more likely to be sole proprietorships or partnerships. But since BS 5750 registration is also positively correlated with size, legal form is unlikely to affect the findings from the research at a level which could be detected in a sample of the size chosen.

On locality, previous research appeared to show a regional effect. The Small Business Research Trust study (SBRT, 1992: 11), for example, suggested that firms in the north were more likely to have registered than firms in other regions and that firms in the midlands were more likely to be intending to register. However, closer inspection of the SBRT sample shows that manufacturing firms and larger firms were more strongly represented in the north and midlands than among firms responding in the south (SBRT, 1992: 21). Since both manufacturing and larger firms are more likely to register for BS 5750, it was concluded that the reported differences in locality were actually related to sector and size rather than locality. Intuitively, there is no good reason to expect small business owner-managers' quality management strategies to be related in any marked way to locality apart from any effects related to sector and size influences in the different regions. It was therefore decided that the research design did not need to incorporate specific spatial considerations, even though the firms participating would come from a variety of localities.[12]

STAGE 2 OF THE RESEARCH DESIGN

Stage 2 of the study comprised the main qualitative element of the research design. This was aimed at providing in-depth information on the motivations, logics and strategies upon which quality management decisions are made by owner-managers. Some of this data was provided by the respondents in the telephone interviews. Owner-managers often explained the reasoning which guided their answers to the questions in the telephone interviews but it was felt that a face-to-face, case study research strategy would provide much more information. This use of combined strategies to gain information, by ensuring that a reasonably sized sample is approached and augmented by a case study approach to provide in-depth qualitative data, is widely used in small business research as noted earlier.

Face-to-face interviews with 10 owner-managers selected from the telephone sample comprised the second, case study element of the research design. Case studies are potentially a very revealing strategy since the researcher not only interviews the main respondent (the owner-manager) but often has a chance to talk to others in the business and to gain a 'feel' of how the business is run (including the attention given to quality issues) as well as the social relationships between those involved. Quality strategies are related intimately to these less tangible elements of a small business and this additional information is therefore potentially very valuable.

To achieve a balance and coverage likely to provide the maximum support for the project, the research design initially proposed a division between five businesses that had a formalised approach to maintaining quality, including implementing and registering for BS 5750, and five that did not. It was also intended that these would also be matched by sector, size and customer profile using telephone sample data. The object was to compare the quality strategies of the two groups of firms and investigate how they affect the performance of the two groups of businesses.

In practice, as other small business researchers have found (see, for example, Barkham *et al.*, 1996) finding exact or even close matches when bringing two or more samples together is sometimes very difficult. This was partly a result of the numbers involved, particularly the relatively low numbers of firms who had registered or were implementing BS 5750. There was also less enthusiasm among respondents who were not using formal quality management strategies to talk about quality issues. For many of these, quality issues were so much part of their everyday activities that they sometimes found it difficult to see what ends the research would serve. For these reasons obtaining close matches to the BS 5750 registered or near-registered firms was more difficult than expected.

However, the actual choices provided interesting and insightful case study data for the project. The final selection of firms could not take place of course until the appropriate part of the telephone survey was completed and this then suggested what kinds of firms might be selected. As soon as the manufacturing sub-sample interviews were completed three firms from the electronics sector and two firms from the printing and publishing sector, were chosen. Though they matched broadly in terms of economic sector, interviewees were chosen more to represent different respondent 'types' as identified in the telephone interviews. For example, two electronic firms were chosen who operated formalised methods of quality control because they exhibited different attitudes to operationalising quality procedures identified to be common in the telephone interviews. The other electronics firm was chosen because the owner-manager had experience of formal methods but still preferred to operate quality strategies using mainly informal methods.

Two firms were chosen from the printing sector but were not a match. Again both were representative of particular respondent types. The first, a general jobbing printer, was of similar size, market position, customer profile and organisational structure to the other 13 general printing firms. The second, is one of the two paper merchants. None of the former operate formalised methods whereas both of the latter had implemented or registered for BS 5750. These selections worked well in practice, as the data reported in the later chapters illustrates.

During and after completing the service industry telephone interviews, the service industry case studies were organised. As with the manufacturing interviews, broad sector matches were made covering computer services, and the plant and equipment hire sector. In each, one firm was chosen which was currently implementing or registered BS 5750, and the other not. The final case study interview was of a garage and vehicle repair business. This was chosen because it was realised during the telephone interviews that it would provide a very interesting case study. The owners of the firm had decided to implement BS 5750 procedures but with no intention of formally registering. More details of this firm, the telephone interviews and case studies are presented in Chapters 5 and 6.

SUMMARY

The research project was aimed at investigating the quality management strategies of a sample of small firms. The research design was carefully constructed to minimise the formidable problems normally associated with research on small businesses. The small firm was defined for the purposes of the research as a legally independent business with at least 1 but under 50 employees. This definition accords well with both common sense views on what constitutes a 'small business' and the kind of definition often used for official or semi-official purposes. It also fits well with the actual size distribution of businesses in the UK economy. For instance, the most recent DTI estimate suggests that 97 per cent of all businesses with at least one employee in Britain have under 50 employees. Legal independence was stressed because quality management strategies are likely to be related to whether or not a small business is part of some large economic enterprise.

Firms participating in the research were selected from two sampling frames compiled by the Kingston University Small Business Research Centre for previous research projects. The main sampling frame had been carefully updated since its original construction and the second sampling frame had been used very recently relative to the project reported here. These sampling frames contained small businesses from both manufacturing and services so that a broad sample could be constructed.

The research design had two stages. The first stage consisted of 150 telephone interviews with owner-managers of small firms. The interview schedule was carefully constructed to focus on the research problem, small business quality management strategies, using a CATI strategy with data coded on a SPSS PC+ data base. The firms had taken part in previous research projects conducted by the Small Business Research Centre and this helped in producing a very high response rate of over 90 per cent, an exceptionally high level by the normal standards of small business research.

The mix of firms between the main sectors in the economy was designed to replicate the distribution of small firms nationally between manufacturing and services. Broadly, a quarter of the firms were drawn from manufacturing and three quarters from services. Because in a sample of this size it is impossible to ensure every kind of economic activity within manufacturing and services are represented, it was decided to select two areas of manufacturing and six areas of services. The economic sectors were selected to represent traditional and more recent types of business activities including businesses serving the needs of other businesses as well those serving mainly private consumers.

The second stage of the research design was a sub-sample of 10 case studies drawing on face-to-face interviews with owners who had participated in the telephone survey. These face-to-face interviews were used to investigate the motivations, logics and strategies behind decisions and practices related to quality management in the firms. The in-depth data from these case studies was aimed at revealing the ways in which quality strategies actually function in small businesses and to support the analysis of the data from the telephone interviews.

In the following chapters, the findings from the investigation based on the above research design are reported. Quality management strategies are not easy to research and no research design is ever perfect but we believe that the selected research design worked well here. The aim of the research to collect and interpret data on quality management strategies, formal and informal, was met enabling a more theoretically assured analysis of just how quality strategies are related to the functioning of the small firm in different sectors of the economy.

4 Small firms and quality: a quantitative approach

INTRODUCTION

As the last chapter outlined, the first stage in the research was a tele-phone survey of 150 small business owners of firms employing at least 1 but under 50 people (or full-time equivalents). The businesses them-selves were in a variety of manufacturing and service activities selected from traditional and newer kinds of economic activities to ensure a good representation of sectors with different kinds of approaches to quality management. In this way the aim was to gain a broad but detailed picture of small business owner quality management strategies in Britain today.

In this chapter the main emphasis is on introducing the quantitative findings from the research before integrating these with the qualitative data in the later chapters. The data covers several key issues. To begin, the chapter considers small firm owner-managers' awareness of quality issues. The easiest way to do this was to begin by focusing on 'quality' as it relates particularly to the introduction of BS 5750 and similar formal quality standards. To put it another way, the questionnaire used awareness of BS 5750 as a means of broaching the whole issue of quality management strategies in small businesses. Of course, as the earlier chapters have made clear, formal quality standards are *not* being equated with 'quality' but BS 5750 and similar formal standards offered a relatively easy way to begin exploring an issue which might otherwise be too abstract to investigate easily in telephone interviews with busy owner-managers.

From earlier research we expected (and as findings later in the chap-ter confirm) that relatively few businesses would be fully registered for a formal quality standard of any kind. On the other hand, awareness of such standards is a separate and important issue: if relatively few owner-managers have adopted formalised approaches to quality management is it because they lack awareness of their existence or is it due to other reasons? As will be seen, the questions did not cover TQM. The reasons for this were two-fold. First, as other research has made clear, TQM in its formal business school, management guru form, is extremely unlikely in small firms (Tomes, 1989; Holliday, 1994). Second, given the restrictions on the time which owner-managers could reasonably be asked to give to the interview, it was felt that the time would be better spent gaining information on BS 5750 or their own, individually developed, quality strategies.

This chapter presents a good deal of quantitative data on small firms' current methods of controlling quality in their businesses. To organise the data in a helpful fashion the typology developed in Chapter 2 is employed. The main elements of the typology are reprised below to help the reader. The data offers information on small firm owners' adoption of the different quality strategies in relation to firm size and sector. For instance, other research (SBRT, 1994a, 1994b; Chittenden *et al.*, 1996) has indicated that smaller small firms are more likely to use informal methods and larger small firms formal methods. Some research (for example, Curran and Blackburn, 1994) has suggested considerable sector variation might be expected on the levels of adoption of formal methods of quality management. What does the present data have to say about these earlier findings?

Small firms owners' methods of quality control

Informal methods

- *Simple informal methods*: *ad hoc*, non-bureaucratised procedures supervised and controlled by the owner-manager or person in the firm responsible for quality.
- *Complex informal methods*: structured, bureaucratised or semi-bureaucratised procedures supervised and controlled by the owner-manager or other person to whom the owner-manager has delegated this responsibility, but with no direct external control or monitoring by second or third party agencies.

Formal methods

- *Second party controlled methods*: routinely used bureaucratised procedures externally dictated and assessed by firms' customers or suppliers.

- *Third party controlled methods*: bureaucratised procedures externally dictated and assessed by a third party agency, such as BS
5750 as well as sector specific schemes such as the Retail Motor
Industry (RMI) Quality Control Scheme.

In presenting the quantitative findings from the telephone survey in
relation to size and sector, particular attention is given to the characteristics of the sectors as contexts which produce influences on the use of
particular kinds of quality management strategies. Each of the sectors
covered has a historical dimension to the development of quality management strategies and the ways in which this affects present attitudes
and practices towards the adoption of formal quality strategies currently is important. Firms in each sector also face different supplier and
customer environments and in presenting the quantitative findings,
suggestions are made as to how owner-managers' quality management
strategies might be linked to these.

SMALL FIRM OWNERS' AWARENESS OF QUALITY STANDARDS

Unsurprisingly, given the enormous media attention, there is little
doubt that small firm owner-managers are increasingly aware of formal
methods of quality control such as BS 5750. For example, a follow-up
survey of small businesses by Curran *et al.* (1993) revealed that just over
70 per cent of small firms sampled were aware of the BS 5750 standard
compared with less than two thirds of the same firms in 1991. More
recent surveys have indicated that awareness is approaching near saturation. For instance, a study by the Small Business Research Trust
(SBRT, 1994b) indicated that 92 per cent of small firms were aware of
the standard.

In the present survey almost 95 per cent of respondents were aware
of BS 5750 (Table 3). This high level is particularly striking because the

Table 3 Small firm owners' awareness of BS 5750, by firm size (%)

	1–4	5–9	10–19	20+	All
Unaware	10.9	5.7	—	—	5.3
Aware	89.1	94.3	100.0	100.0	94.7
N =	46	53	31	20	150

Base: All respondents participating in the telephone survey

sample contained a high proportion (around 75 per cent) of service sector firms. As the last chapter noted, much of the previous research has over-represented manufacturing firms relative to their importance in the UK economy of the 1990s and since BS 5750 and its equivalents originated in manufacturing, there has been a suspicion that its reported importance has been exaggerated. Conversely, it is usually assumed that the standard has had less of an impact on service industries (Bannock, 1991) and we might therefore have expected that a more representative sample such as that in the present research, might show this bias in the form of lower overall awareness. But whatever might have been the case in the past, the results show the effect is not apparent in the mid-1990s.

On the other hand, the often alleged size effect with owners of smaller small firms (those employing 1–4 people) showing lower levels of awareness of BS 5750 is shown to be still present, albeit if only slightly, in Table 3. Awareness saturation is clearly reducing any size effect which may have existed in the past. Even among the very smallest firms, awareness levels were almost 90 per cent. Among the larger firms awareness was total. Answers also revealed that owners were often also aware of BS 5750 equivalents specific to their area of economic activities (for example, the RMI equivalent in the vehicle repair sector discussed again below).

SOURCES OF INITIAL INFORMATION ON BS 5750

The main sources of owner-managers' awareness of BS 5750 were also apparent from the answers to the telephone survey questions. Since quality and BS 5750 have emerged as issues in relation to small firms, they have received wide coverage in newspapers, trade press and journals and in other sources. Because of these multiple origins respondents could reasonably claim to have become aware of BS 5750 from a number of sources and they were therefore allowed to give more than one rather than being asked to remember the actual first source of information. (In all likelihood, many of the respondents would not be able to recall accurately this information anyway, especially if their first awareness occurred some time ago.)

Respondents cited the mass media (national newspapers and television mainly) most commonly as the main source of information on the standard (Table 4). The importance of the mass media as a transmitter of information to small business owners has been reported by other research (see, for example, Macmillan *et al.*, 1990). Despite the very considerable resources devoted to information provision for small firms

Table 4 Sources of awareness of BS 5750 (%)

Mass media	59.3
Customers	42.7
Trade association	36.7
Training and enterprise council	25.3
Chamber of commerce	18.7
Other	34.7

Base: The replies of the 142 respondents who claimed to be aware of BS 5750. Replies do not sum to 100 because more than one source could have been mentioned

by government departments such as the DTI, it is the mainstream media (augmented as shown below by the trade media) which appear very much more effective as information providers in relation to quality standards. However, media treatments of BS 5750 have often not portrayed formal quality standards positively (see, for example, Woodcock, 1992; Batchelor, 1993) and therefore may not have helped actual take-up greatly.

The second most commonly mentioned source of awareness of BS 5750 were customers. This source has been emphasised by some commentators (see, for example, Tisdall, 1990; Harris, 1991; Batchelor, 1992) who have argued that small firms are being forced by customers to adopt BS 5750 on the threat of being dropped as suppliers if they do not register. However, although just over 40 per cent of the owner-managers report that customers were one of their sources of information on BS 5750, this need not be taken as supporting any interpretation that customers have been important in forcing them to adopt the standard. Indeed, as will be shown below, customer pressures towards adoption appear unlikely as an explanation for more than a relatively small proportion of small firms registering for the standard. Moreover, Bryson *et al.* (1993) and Shaw (1995) show how informal contacts with customers and suppliers are an important source of information for small business owners. The above figures, therefore, may reflect the actualisation of these important information networks.

Trade associations have become involved heavily in increasing the awareness of members in relation to quality issues. Quality standards and strategies are often referred to in trade magazines, journals and newsletters. Many trade associations have taken a lead in developing formal quality standards for their members. This has manifested itself through sector-specific interpretations of BS 5750 (see, for example, the Construction Industry Research and Information publication, *Quality*

Management in Construction – Interpretations of BS 5750 (Oliver, 1990)), as well as through running quality management courses for owner-managers (Bethell, 1994). Some trade associations have their own schemes which are operational equivalents of BS 5750 such as the Retail Motor Industry Federation Quality Control Programme for vehicle servicing and repair. Overall, a little over a third of the respondents reported that they became aware of BS 5750 through a trade association. This might actually be seen as relatively high since recorded rates of trade association membership amongst small firms are typically under 30 per cent (see, for example, Curran *et al.*, 1991) though highly sector variable (North *et al.*, 1996). The level of awareness produced by this source in the present research may, of course, be related to the specific mix of sectors from which the firms were recruited.

The other archetypal small business membership body in the UK is often seen as the chamber of commerce. It is sometimes assumed that belonging to the local chamber is common among small firms. But in fact, chamber of commerce membership among small firms is highly variable and very dependent on sector (Curran and Blackburn, 1994). For instance, the latter report that small businesses, such as employment agencies or other providers of business services such as accountants, are likely to belong to their local chamber of commerce since the latter is an important source of potential customers. Conversely, owners of businesses such as small vehicle repairers, restaurants and hotels and other leisure businesses are much less likely to join. Their customers are mainly private consumers rather than other businesses and owner-managers in some of these areas work long, unsocial hours and cannot spare the time. The low level of overall membership of chambers of commerce offers a reason why they were a relatively minor source of information on BS 5750 and quality standards (18.7 per cent of respondents).[1]

Curran and Blackburn (1994) have also argued that the idea that small firms are typically at the heart of their local economies serving the needs of other local businesses and private consumers, is based on a nostalgic view of Britain's economy whose accuracy is very easy to overstate. They maintain that while such close small business–local economy links might have been the case in the past, it is much less so today. The small businesses most likely to be serving local markets are among those which have either declined (small retailers, for example) or at best only held their own in recent decades. The small business sectors that have shown the highest rates of expansion tend to be in the newer expanding sectors of the economy linked to knowledge manipulation,

IT and business and financial services (Keeble *et al.*, 1992). These businesses are less likely to be tied to local markets or to be able to find the major market for their services in a small local area. Further, there is the alleged decline of community in the more general social and political senses which has also been seen as undermining local business and economic relations (Rutherfoord, 1996).

Yet much of the support for small businesses is predicated on the notion of the local economy. Like the historically older chambers of commerce which arguably emerged when local economies and their small businesses were the significant building blocks of the national economy, more recently established small business support bodies such as enterprise agencies, TECs and Business Links, all rest greatly on the assumption that they serve the needs of local economies and local businesses. The above arguments on the decline of business connections with their local areas and communities suggests that this may be increasingly mistaken. It is not surprising therefore that one of the lowest sources of awareness of formal quality standards such as BS 5750 were TECs (25.3 per cent of respondents) though they were ahead of the chambers of commerce.[2]

Finally, government itself has also taken a direct active interest in the promotion of BS 5750, especially through the Department of Trade and Industry's Enterprise Initiative but also in support through Business Links etc. This appears to have been relatively successful when compared with the other sources discussed above. Awareness of the DTI scheme (48.7 per cent) might be seen as high at first sight but measured against the high overall awareness of BS 5750 in the sample (almost 95 per cent) it might be suggested that the DTI had not been as successful as it might have hoped.

Overall, therefore, the small firm respondents in the research were aware of BS 5750 to the point of near saturation. The information blitz surrounding quality issues and specifically formal quality standards such as BS 5750 has clearly been highly successful. Multiple sources of information have played a role in this blitz but what is perhaps slightly surprising is that the most important source has been the ordinary mass media rather than specialist business sources such as trade associations, chambers of commerce and TECs. The latter sources all played a part but some such as chambers of commerce, were mentioned by a surprisingly small proportion of respondents. However, when the various business-related sources were put in their contexts, particularly their likely importance to small business owners, the often relatively low levels appear understandable.

SMALL FIRMS' METHODS OF CONTROLLING QUALITY

The above has established that small business owners in the study were aware of BS 5750 (and often of other similar formal quality standards relevant to their sectors). It might be expected therefore that a significant proportion, perhaps even a majority of the small firms, would have adopted BS 5750 which had been so widely touted as a mark of a go ahead, successful business in the 1990s. However, as the opening chapter made clear, previous research has suggested that, in fact, only a minority of small firms have opted for the standard. Even relatively recent research (see, for example, SBRT,1994b: 6–11) reported that only 10 per cent of small firms were registered for BS 5750 and, all told, around 40 per cent of small firms operated formal procedures of some kind.[3] In the SBRT sample, however, most of the firms (58 per cent) operated informal quality control methods.

On the other hand, the present survey might have been expected to show a rise in the adoption of formal quality standards such as BS 5750. Small business owners are often cautious about embracing new methods but may now be responding to the huge propaganda onslaught on business and public sector organisations urging a total commitment to quality demonstrated by opting for BS 5750 or TQM. In fact, at first sight the present research records a lower level than the SBRT research quoted above. Just over 13 per cent operated any formal methods of quality control of any kind (including registration for BS 5750) while 88 per cent used informal methods (Table 5).

The variation in findings from the two sets of data are most likely due to methodological differences. Asking small business owners whether they use formal quality control strategies using mail or telephone

Table 5 Small firm owners' main methods of maintaining quality, by firm size (%)

	1–4	5–9	10–19	20+	All
Simple informal method	89.1	73.6	51.6	35.0	68.7
Complex informal methods	6.5	20.8	22.6	30.0	18.0
Second party standard	2.2	1.9	—	—	1.3
Third party QA application	2.2	3.8	19.4	20.0	8.7
Third party QA registered	—	—	6.5	15.0	3.3
N =	46	53	31	20	150

Base: All respondents in the telephone survey

surveys, is not easy. Answers depend very much on the wording of the questions and on what the respondent regards as a 'formal' approach to quality management. Claiming 'formal' quality procedures may actually mean a very minimal commitment to systematic quality strategies. For example, a business may report having a written quality statement or quality policy to guide the business's operating procedures. But we have encountered cases where closer inspection shows that a written quality policy may be as little as a single paragraph on one side of A4 paper.[4]

The 40 per cent of firms recorded by the SBRT (1994b) research as having a formal quality management approach of some kind should therefore not be seen as suggesting that this proportion of businesses operate with quality strategies equivalent to BS 5750. The SBRT mail questionnaire study relied on respondents themselves making the distinction between formal and informal methods. The SBRT figures may consequently include not only some fairly basic quality control strategies treated as formal methods but a proportion which would approximate to what we have called *complex informal methods*. As will be seen below, once allowance is made for differences of these kinds as well as the different mixes of firms from different sectors, the two studies can be seen to produce broadly similar results for overall levels of bureaucratisation of internal procedures – 40 per cent SBRT and 31.4 per cent from this study. The results for externally monitored formal quality procedures – 10 per cent SBRT and just over 13 per cent in this study – are also similar when this definitional difference is allowed for.

Using the typology presented earlier, the results from the present research may be summarised as shown in Table 5. They have been subdivided into the two major categories adopted – the autonomous, internally controlled quality strategies (*simple informal* and *complex informal methods*) and the externally certified and/or monitored varieties (that is, *second* or *third party controlled*). The latter which contains all those which have completed the full BS 5750 certification process, comprises just under 4 per cent.

What needs to be stressed is that despite the different classificatory approach adopted by this research and the differences in sample make up, the overall results are broadly similar to those of previous research. A majority of small firms operate *ad hoc*, non-bureaucratised informal methods of quality control. However, a significant proportion (almost a third) operate more bureaucratised procedures, though only just under 5 per cent have formalised these procedures through links with an external body though another 8 per cent report they are preparing for registration. The reasons for the different classification used in the present research have been explained earlier: essentially we argue it enables us to provide a more powerful theorisation of quality management strategies in the small business.

QUALITY MANAGEMENT STRATEGIES AND SIZE OF FIRM

As indicated in the literature review in Chapter 1, there is a well reported direct positive relationship between the use of formal quality control methods in small firms and firm size (SBRT, 1994a, 1994b; Chittenden *et al.*, 1996: 130). The earlier SBRT (1992) study showed that larger small firms were over ten times more likely to be registered for BS 5750 than very small firms. While only 0.6 per cent of very small firms (1–4 employees) had registered BS 5750, 6.8 per cent of larger small firms (those with over 10 employees) had done so. More recent research, also conducted for the SBRT (1994b), indicated that 17 per cent of small firms with between 20 and 49 employees had registered for BS 5750.

Data from the present survey provides further evidence on the relationship between size and propensity to register for a formal quality standard. Whereas only 4.4 per cent of the very small firms (1–4 employees) were operating formal methods of quality control, 35 per cent of larger small firms (20+ employees) were doing so (Table 5). Moreover, it appears that not only is there a direct relationship between small firms' adoption of formal methods more generally and firm size, but also the adoption of bureaucratised procedures and firm size. For example, whereas only 6.5 per cent of very small firms (1–4 employees) had semi-bureaucratised *complex informal methods* of quality control, the level was almost 20 per cent among the larger small firms (20+ employees).

This suggests that small firm owner-managers adopt more bureaucratised methods as their firms grow though without necessarily accepting or seeking external monitoring. This may help combat managerial difficulties in controlling quality which, as the data in Chapter 5 shows, appear to be more significant in larger small firms. There may even be a three stage process here: as firm size increases, firms move from *simple informal* to *complex informal* to *formal* externally validated quality control strategies. However, the findings merely suggest this association with size. It is based on data collected at a single point in time and does not therefore demonstrate that individual firms actually move through the three stages in the above order.

As noted previously, the majority of small firms operated what are labelled *simple informal methods* of quality control in our typology as their main quality strategy. Indeed, almost 90 per cent of firms with between 1 and 4 employees use these methods. In larger small firms (20+ employees) *simple informal methods* were still more popular than formalised methods but the difference was much less marked. In other words, establishing the link between size of enterprise and the adoption of formal strategies of quality control is relatively easy. Establishing the statistical link, however, is not an explanation of *why* the link exists.

The size effect shown in Table 5 may actually be understated by concentrating on the distribution of informal and formal quality control strategies at any one moment in time, especially if there is any trend towards higher levels of adoption of formal standards. Data from the present study indicates that there might be such a trend. Of those firms who have not yet implemented BS 5750, larger firms appear more likely to adopt the standard in the future (Table 6). For example, while only 13 per cent of owners of smaller small firms (1–4 employees) were thinking about or intending to implement, BS 5750, almost a quarter of the owners of larger small firms (20+ employees) were doing so. Correspondingly, almost 85 per cent of the firms with 1–4 employees have no intention of implementing, or are unaware of, BS 5750 compared with just over half of those with 20 + employees.

There are several possible explanations for this pronounced size effect including influences unrelated to size which may be at work. Size and other influences may also interact by mutually supporting or cancelling each other out. For example, a common sense explanation would be that owner-managers in the smallest small firms such as those with one or two employees, feel that their ability to oversee all aspects of their businesses is so complete that no formal procedures are required. But in larger and especially growing businesses, it is likely that more bureaucratised formal methods are used simply because owner-managers find direct control of all the firm's operations no longer possible (Churchill

Table 6 Small firm owners' intentions towards implementing and registering for BS 5750, by firm size (%)

	1–4	5–9	10–19	20+	All
No intention/unaware	84.8	67.9	41.9	55.0	66.0
Thinking/intending	13.0	30.2	32.3	15.0	22.0
Implementing/registered	2.2	1.9	25.8	30.0	12.0
N =	46	53	31	20	150

Base: All respondents in the telephone survey

and Lewis, 1983). It is virtually impossible for a person managing more than 20 people (often in practice a much lower number) to directly oversee their activities and be totally confident that their actions conform to a desired quality standard.

While explanations like the above have been common, a simple size-related explanation which concentrates solely on the internal operation of the enterprise cannot be the complete explanation. If this were the case then we might expect a much *stronger* size effect, that is, the actual level of adoption of BS 5750 or equivalent formal approaches among firms with say more than 20 employees, would be very much higher. This is especially the case in the service sector where most small firms operate in situations where production and consumption by the customer often occur simultaneously making quality supervision even more difficult.[5]

It could also be argued that larger small firms are more able to digest the costs of implementing formal procedures (North *et al.*, 1993) and that the main barrier to small firms adopting externally assessed and monitored formal quality standards is therefore cost. This is examined in more detail in later chapters but although cost is a factor, especially for the very smallest firms, it does not appear to be a prime negative influence on the decision to adopt BS 5750. Motivational factors and owner-managers' interpretations of the need and likely pay-back from adopting formal quality strategies appear more important than cost by itself.

An alternative explanation might bring in another possible external influence. One of the most popular external influences and one frequently mentioned in the media, is customer pressures. As was established earlier, customers were the second most important source of information on BS 5750 (Table 4). It is argued by academic and non-academic sources that small firms are being forced, often against their wishes or better judgement, to implement BS 5750 or an equivalent by customers under threat of being dropped as suppliers (Tisdall, 1990; Harris, 1991; Batchelor, 1992; Chittenden *et al.*, 1996: 134). Undoubtedly, this has occurred particularly in some areas of manufacturing but the importance of such pressures in explaining the adoption of formal quality standards generally, is another matter.

In the present study, well under half of the respondents (42.7 per cent) reported that awareness of BS 5750 came from a customer. Being made aware of BS 5750 by customers of course is not the same as pressure to adopt. In fact, less than 20 per cent of respondents stated that customer pressures were responsible for their adoption of BS 5750 (see Chapter 6). Three reasons for this finding may be suggested. First, as the data has made clear, only a small minority of respondents have registered. So if customer pressure is common, it cannot be said to be very effective. Second, large numbers of small businesses are in services and have customers unlikely to raise the issue of formal quality standards. Businesses whose customers are mainly private consumers, for example, are not likely to be besieged by customers insisting that future purchases will depend on the business having BS 5750.

Third, even those small businesses who mainly meet the needs of other businesses often have relatively little to do with large firms, the most likely customers to insist on BS 5750 adoption by suppliers (Curran and Blackburn, 1994). Curran and Blackburn report that large firms are very hesitant about giving orders to small firms for a variety of reasons. For instance, they often have doubts about the capabilities of small firms and their staffs' abilities to cope with orders, or doubts about whether it can be assumed that small firm suppliers will stay in business at all. A small supplier going out of business can cause all kinds of problems for a larger business. On balance, therefore, larger firms will often opt for larger suppliers seeing them as more likely to meet their needs reliably.

At this point it needs only to be noted that the analysis shows that while sector is important in influencing adoption of BS 5750 and needs to augment any explanations linked to size or the internal operations of firms, customer pressure in the above sense can only be one, perhaps minor, influence. Customer pressures are important in *some* sectors but as the analysis below shows, where this is the case it is not likely to be a new influence but one related to the history and long standing characteristics of the sector.[6]

Looking at the above size relations with propensities to use different kinds of quality management strategies, there is clearly a positive relationship between size of enterprise and the use of formal quality strategies. Yet the obvious explanations considered – internal operational issues and management control of quality and cost – do not seem strong enough to explain the relationship by themselves. Other factors such as sector may be important. The next section focuses on sector to examine its effect in more detail and perhaps suggest ways in which it may interact with the size effect influences already considered.

ECONOMIC SECTOR AND QUALITY MANAGEMENT STRATEGIES

It was expected that at the broadest level of the division between manufacturing and services, there would be a marked difference in the levels of adopting BS 5750. Research by the SBRT (1994b) and Chittenden *et al.* (1996) for example, has highlighted this broad sectorial variation. For instance, 16 per cent of manufacturing firms in the SBRT (1994b) sample had registered for BS 5750 against 4 per cent of business service enterprises. The findings from the present study also show this pronounced difference. Among the firms from the two manufacturing sectors (electronics and printing) just over a quarter were using formal methods, including BS 5750. Among the services firms, in contrast, only 5 per cent had adopted formal methods (Table 7). Again, however, a simple distinction of this kind does not tell the whole story as the discussion below shows.

Previous research in suggesting a relationship between sector and the likelihood of a firm adopting formal quality management strategies, has sometimes emphasised sector over size as an influence. One proponent of the thesis that small firms' methods of quality control are likely to vary significantly with economic sector is Holliday (1994). She suggests that this may be linked with the internal operational problems faced by owner–managers: quality strategies are likely to reflect the solutions to these problems. However, where it might be thought that she had in mind service sector small businesses where quality control problems are often related to the simultaneous production–consumption characteristics of many services, she was actually referring to some areas of manufacturing. She was suggesting that particular kinds of manufacturing were especially suited to formal quality control.

The kind of argument Holliday offers is by no means new. One of the classics of organisational analysis (Burns and Stalker, 1966) made the point that manufacturing activities with a high level of predictability both in relation to internal operational aspects and a stable external environment, might well be most efficiently managed utilising highly bureaucratic strategies. Highly formal quality control strategies could well be a key element of such management strategies. On the other hand, other kinds of manufacturing displaying the opposite characteristics – low levels of internal operational predictability especially when combined with customer unpredictability – would be much more difficult to control or monitor with formal quality controls.

Other external influences on the adoption of formal quality standards have also been stressed in the discussion of small firm quality management strategies and sector. A frequently mentioned external factor is customer pressure, discussed earlier and seen as much less important than popular views would suggest. Nevertheless, it has some effect in certain sectors. For example, Curran and Blackburn (1994) who were critical of what they saw as the over-emphasis on customer pressures as a factor in the adoption of formal quality standards, still showed in their earlier work (1992) how large firms' insistence on supplier adoption of formal methods varied between the electronics and printing sectors. The pressures were much stronger in electronics. The two studies did not, however, conflict since the same authors also showed that the conditions which produced this customer effect in electronics were not common in the economy generally.

When the data on the individual sectors in the present study are examined, the findings on the broad manufacturing-services division in relation to adopting formal quality control methods is shown as only part of the story: within the two main categories there is considerable variation. Data from the present research showed that firms in the electronics sector were most likely to use formal methods of quality control. Echoing the findings and argument of Curran and Blackburn (1994) discussed above, nearly 4 out of 10 electronics firms used formal methods (Table 7). General printers, on the other hand (excluding the two paper merchants in the sample) and the small garages were the least likely to adopt formalised methods. Indeed, none of the general printers and only one of the garages had adopted formal standards.

Electronics

The reasons why electronics firms were the most likely to adopt formal standards appear likely to be related to the factors that Holliday (1994, 1995) touched upon as important. Put simply, she might be taken as suggesting that BS 5750 and the like are more applicable to industries, such as electronics, where the development of the industry over a considerable period has included a specific concern with quality standards and where production typically involves a chain of separate enterprises usually in the form of extensive subcontracting relations. This concern and these conditions, interact with the operational processes used in businesses in this sector. That is, where new or alternative operational processes are evolved, they are often consistent with existing formal quality management approaches, reinforcing the use of such quality approaches. The history of the evolution of defence products illustrates this trend well: the development of operational and product technologies and producer–customer relations is integrated closely with formal quality standards.

In the electronics industry, government bodies, large firms and trade organisations, have been highly instrumental in developing quality standards, such as BS 5750 and its predecessors, for electronic components. Given the historical association with formal methods of

Table 7 Small firm owners' methods of maintaining quality, by economic sector (%)

	Electronics	Printing	Advertising, marketing, design	Computer services	Employment agencies	Garages	Plant and equipment hire	All
Simple informal methods	38.9	87.5	76.5	46.2	80.0	82.4	70.8	68.7
Complex informal methods	22.2	—	17.6	34.6	6.7	14.7	20.8	18.0
Second party methods	11.1	—	—	—	—	—	—	1.3
Third party QA application	16.7	6.3	5.9	15.4	6.7	2.9	8.3	8.7
Third party QA registered	11.1	6.3	—	3.8	6.7	—	—	3.3
N =	18	16	17	26	15	34	24	150

All manufacturing: informal methods 73.5; formal methods 26.5
All services: informal methods 94.8; formal methods 5.2

Base: All respondents in the telephone survey

quality control in the electronics industry and a relatively high level of contractual and subcontractual relations compared with other sectors (Thorburn and Takashima, 1992), there are significant external pressures on small electronics firms in the production chain to adopt formal quality measures, though not necessarily BS 5750. Two firms in the electronics sector in the present sample, for example, operated formal methods controlled by second parties in the production chain, that is, other larger businesses. In one case it was the firm's suppliers, in the other it was the firm's customers. (For further details see Chapter 6.)

What is important to note here, therefore, is not just the existence of pressures on small firms to adopt formal quality strategies but the ways in which these pressures have come about and are sustained. The historical conditions of the development of the sector and its operational practices have moulded, and been moulded by, its technology and the inter-firm production chains. These are crucial to understanding how formal standards have developed and are maintained in the electronics sector.

Ironically, while there is pressure on electronics firms of all sizes to adopt formal quality standards if they want to win business, this may actually reduce the need for small firms to adopt BS 5750. Since over 60 per cent already operate some form of bureaucratic or formalised system, it might be assumed that most would favour adopting the widely recognised BS 5750 or an equivalent. But some evidence suggests that BS 5750 registration in the industry may be losing ground. For example, in a case study presented in Chapter 5, a large electronics business is shown to be changing its purchasing policy from insisting on BS 5750 registration to reverting to older criteria after finding that the quality required was not being achieved by BS 5750 registered suppliers. This illustrates the point made in an earlier chapter that BS 5750 refers to a standardised framework for quality management but does not itself guarantee quality. Where it is widely adopted in a sector, this potential weakness of BS 5750 may be more apparent to customers.

A significant proportion of electronics firms have been seen to be implementing or are already registered for BS 5750 or an equivalent, not so much for its potential to improve operational efficiency but as a *marketing* tool (Holliday, 1994). If gaining access to a larger proportion of the market in a sector, especially the more lucrative parts, requires registration or approval to an accredited quality standard, then owner-managers will acquire this badge of respectability to help reach potential customers. But as more firms become registered or approved in the sector, the marketing value of registration loses its special advantage and simply becomes a basic condition of doing business.

The above reasons may go some way to explain why half of the small electronics firms owner-managers in the survey report they had no intention of registering for BS 5750 (Table 8). However, it is still the case that 22 per cent have some kind of externally validated formal quality strategy and over a quarter of the firms in the sector are thinking of, or intending to, register for BS 5750. One possible reason for this is that some of the firms are relatively new and want to establish their presence more firmly in the sector. But another reason may be that these firms are operating in subareas in the industry where registration is still viewed externally as important ('electronics' covers a wide variety of economic activities and markets) or, at least, the owner-manager believes it would serve the interests of their business.

Computer services

In computer services a similar story to that in electronics emerges, albeit with some interesting differences. It is a technologically highly developed sector (some aspects of which are consequences of its links with the electronics sector). This helps account for 54 per cent of firms operating some form of bureaucratic procedures (Table 7). However, the number of firms operating fully formal quality strategies is much lower (19.2 per cent) than in electronics. A majority (57.7 per cent) did not intend to register, or were unaware of BS 5750 (Table 8) but almost a quarter (23.1 per cent) were thinking of and/or intending to register.

One reason why there is a difference between electronics firms and those in computer services, despite the technological overlap between them, may be that computer services contains a larger non-manufacturing element than electronics. This non-manufacturing component consists of software design, software application and combined hardware–software service packages tailored for users (Keynote, 1993). Because these activities have a strong service emphasis, establishing formal quality standards is much more difficult than in the manufacturing activities typical of mainstream electronics. Customers are much less likely to insist on formal quality standard registration or recognise such registration as having value: they are often more like the typical private consumer who knows and cares little about formal quality standards. Many of the customers of small computer services firms are other small firms in sectors not connected with electronics or computing (Curran and Blackburn, 1994) reducing again the need for, or value from, adopting a formal quality strategy.

Table 8 Small firm owners' intentions towards implementing and registering for BS 5750, by sector (%)

	Electronics	Printing	Advertising, marketing, design	Computer services	Employment agencies	Garages	Plant and equipment hire	All
No intention/unaware	50.0	81.3	76.5	57.7	33.3	79.4	70.8	66.0
Thinking/intending	27.8	6.3	17.6	23.1	53.3	20.6	20.8	22.0
Implementing/registered	22.2	12.5	5.9	19.2	13.3	—	8.3	12.0
N =	18	16	17	26	15	34	24	150

Base: All respondents in the telephone survey

Employment agencies

Employment agencies, a key area of business services which has grown rapidly in the late twentieth century, offers another sectoral pattern in quality strategies which contrasts sharply with those discussed above. The current level of bureaucratization in employment agencies (that is, the use of complex and/or second or third party certificated methods of quality management as defined in the typology adopted for the study) is relatively low. Full second or third party certification is recorded for only 7 per cent with a similar proportion in the process of implementation at the time of interview (Table 7). Yet, the evidence indicates that BS 5750 was very much a live issue in this sector. The data shows that only one third had no intention of implementing the standard, whereas among the remaining firms, over half (53.3 per cent), were either thinking about, or intending to adopt, a formal quality standard.

Developments within the employment agency sector and the conditions influencing the adoption of formal quality standards can certainly be differentiated from those in electronics and computer services. First, the applicability of BS 5750 or other formal quality standards is not so directly obvious as it would be in manufacturing sectors such as electronics. Nor historically have employment agencies had close links with manufacturing which might positively influence the adoption of formal quality standards. Indeed, historically, employment agencies have had *less* contact with manufacturing than services firms. One main reason for this is that in the past the main 'employment agencies' supplying labour in much of manufacturing were trade unions, particularly the craft trade unions who controlled the supply of manual and often much of the lower level white collar labour.

As the UK economy's traditional manufacturing industries have declined, the market for employment agencies has grown. The expansion of services and knowledge-based activities in which trade unions are weak together with shortages of skilled labour (for example, in computing and IT related activities) or high labour turnover (for example, in areas such hotels and catering) has helped create an expanding market for the agencies which has persisted even through periods of high unemployment. Moreover, some newer areas of manufacturing have never been heavily unionised either and have suffered from labour shortages which again has offered opportunities for employment agencies. More generally in manufacturing in recent years, there has been a rise in the use of temporary staff and the self-employed, some of whom are recruited through employment agencies.

Another characteristic of the growth areas in business services since

1980 has been a rapid increase in the numbers of enterprises engaged in these activities (Keeble *et al.*, 1992) and employment agencies have themselves been part of this very rapid growth. Like many areas of business services, entry costs are low and spin-off enterprises are easily generated, so response to the growing market for employment services has been rapid. While there are some national chains in the sector, there are also a large number of very small agencies, serving local or specialist markets. It is possible that, as the employment agency sector has become more competitive,[7] firms have been resorting to BS 5750 as a marketing weapon to distinguish themselves from their competitors, particularly in marketing themselves to large, including public sector, organisations in their localities. This policy may have been so successful that other firms in the industry have had to follow suit or seriously consider doing so, merely to remain competitive. Conversely, some, especially larger, clients of the agencies, may have made BS 5750 a criterion for doing business although there is no strong evidence for this. It appears that the former is more likely, given the attention that now surrounds BS 5750 in the sector's trade press.[8] More widely, similar trends have been observed in the legal and accounting professions and there is evidence that increasing numbers of professional services, like business services more generally, are being affected in this way (Fennel, 1991).

The emergence of market advantage motivations among owners of employment agencies as a stimulus towards BS 5750 adoption appeared to mirror other evidence from the study and other secondary anecdotal evidence. For example, in the printing and publishing sector, the two firms which had adopted BS 5750 were paper merchants (all the others being general printers). Both stated their motivations for implementing the standard was as a marketing strategy and/or as a reaction to competitive pressures. Holliday (1994) as noted earlier, also observed the same phenomenon in electronics in her study.

Printing

The lack of adoption of BS 5750 by the general printers is interesting and significant in the context of this study. Not one firm had adopted BS 5750 and only one was thinking about implementing the standard. One reason for this lack, it might be suggested, is that, historically, general printing has long been a craft industry with strong trade unions controlling the supply and work standards of labour (Rainnie, 1989). Although this is now no longer the case in much of the sector, historical influences may be continuing to exert a strong sway. General printing has also been a sector with strong, internally developed quality strategies (Kuusisto, 1997). Again, in part, this was related to strong unions and their insistence on maintaining craft skills which not only affected shop floor employees but employers also since many of these rose to be owner-managers from the shop floor. Craft skills and quality standards were (and still are) also supported by the public provision of training for all those involved in the industry by technical and further education colleges who train shop floor and higher level technical employees and the art schools who train the graphic designers.

Looked at more closely, general printing presents an interesting variation on the possible forms of interaction between informal and formal quality strategies. Inside the firms, quality management strategies are typically *simple informal* in terms of the typology being used in this study. Usually, this amounts to simple inspection at each stage of production from receipt or creation of the original matter through to the final product delivered to the customer. Yet, externally, highly formalised bureaucratised processes play a key role in underpinning the simple informal quality management strategies. These mainly take the form of well defined skills training standards (in the past traditional apprenticeships, City and Guilds, and their more recent equivalents, and formal qualifications from art colleges)[9] with very strong built-in quality norms which are internalised by those trained (Kuusisto, 1997).

In other words, here is another sector where specific historical conditions and organisational arrangements have produced distinctive kinds of quality management strategies which have reduced the likelihood of adopting non-sector based, externally validated and monitored quality management strategies such as BS 5750. While there may be some market advantages in adopting the standard, the sector's internal quality strategies have been the mainstay of quality management. There are routine elements in the industry's production processes which might be served well by a formal quality control strategy but these are offset by substantial non-routine elements in many customers' orders. Overall, it is clear that so far the industry's subculture has sustained quality norms which offer an effective functional substitute to formal quality standards. The result is a low take-up of the latter.

Advertising, marketing and design businesses

Related in some ways to printing, particularly as a user of print products, are the advertising, marketing and design firms. They are less likely than the printing firms to adopt BS 5750, though they are more likely to use *complex informal methods* of quality control. Of all the types of businesses in the sample, these are the most representative of the knowledged-based economic activities which many believe are key to the UK economy's future success. Britain's economic advantage as a cheap, semi-skilled labour market, it is argued, will be difficult to sustain because eastern bloc transitional economies such as Hungary and the Czech Republic as well as many of the developing economies in the far east, will more than match Britain on these criteria (Meadows, 1996). Nor, it is sometimes suggested, will Britain perform outstandingly enough in the high tech sector to give it any great advantage over its competitors (Oakey, 1991). But Britain does do well in sectors requiring creative ability and knowledge manipulation, such as advertising, marketing and design.

The character of operations in firms in the advertising, marketing and design sector works against the use of standardised quality approaches almost by definition. Each customer in principle wants something different, something which is original and tailored to their product or service.[10] The firms market themselves as being creative and original, promising customers something new and specially designed to meet their needs. Yet because of the complexities of organising non-routine work, owner-managers in the sector may feel that some formalisation of quality control is necessary to avoid disastrous failures in meeting customers' needs. This is particularly the case where the owner-manager is not able to directly oversee every design or campaign produced for customers. But the potential of standardised quality control strategies will be limited by the inherent character of the products and services being produced. Moreover, this relates to the difficulties of defining 'quality' in creative activities. Customers will almost certainly have little confidence in formal quality standards such as BS 5750 as guarantors that products and services will be original and offer creative solutions to their problems. Therefore it is unlikely that firms will face strong pressures from customers to adopt such standards.

Small vehicle repairers

All but one of the garages operated informal methods of quality control (Table 7) and only one in five of the firms were thinking about, or intending to implement, BS 5750. Again, an examination of the sector's history and organisational structures plus relations with customers, helps to explain the pattern found, including the apparent reluctance to adopt formal quality standards such as BS 5750. Like general printing, this is a sector where historically the craft skills of workers and employers were based on traditional apprenticeship training supported by public provision through technical and further education colleges.

However, the quality element in the training was much less developed than in printing. It was not that the training was inferior in imparting quality standards but that the need to utilise these so explicitly in practice was much less. This lack was linked to the character of the sector's customers. They were (and are) much less able to assess whether the service received reaches a particular quality level. In printing the customer finds it much easier to judge quality because so much depends on the appearance of the final product. If colours do not register or printed characters do not align, this is instantly apparent. On the other hand, if a car is not well serviced or repaired, the customer may find it impossible to detect this just by looking at the vehicle when it is returned. Tests of the quality of motor vehicle repairs and services by the Consumers' Association (published from time to time in *Which?* magazine: see, for example, October 1993) have sometimes reported low standards of servicing. Even though they are sometimes critical of the service they receive, there is no apparent clamour among customers for BS 5750 to be adopted by garages, so the marketing advantage to businesses appears minimal. The sector does have its own formal quality standards such as the trade association run RMI standard discussed earlier, but again whether this influences consumers greatly in distinguishing between one repairer and another might be doubted.

Plant and equipment hire

The plant and equipment hire sector offers yet another pattern of adoption and attitudes to BS 5750 and formal quality standards. While in all the sectors, the majority of owner-managers use informal methods of quality control, owner-managers of plant and equipment firms are more likely to use *complex informal methods* of control than most. On the other hand, they appear no more keen than other owner-managers on adopting BS 5750. The need to use complex informal quality control strategies might be explained by the character of the business in which they engage. Equipment, whether on hire or, as in some instances, operated by the firm's own employees, is frequently not used routinely. Every task in every week or every month is different.

Customers use plant for differing periods and keeping track of which plant and equipment is where and for how long, is a key requirement. At the same time, a lot of the equipment is subject to health and safety regulations and needs to perform reliably. Extensive maintenance and often frequent replacement are needed to ensure these regulations are met. Where the firm operates the equipment itself, it is also directly responsible for operator health and safety. The lack of routine in the use of equipment and the seriousness of the health and safety issues support the adoption of formal controls. However, firms in the sector favour their own approaches to quality control rather than adopting an external strategy such as BS 5750. Many firms in this sector are members of trade associations who offer help in meeting health and safety standards (North *et al.*, 1996). But each firm tends to have its own mix of plant and equipment and may specialise in particular kinds or in serving particular sub-markets so quality control needs and strategies may vary considerably.

At the same time there appears little pressure from the hirers of plant and equipment to adopt BS 5750. Customers are mainly in construction or construction-related activities where again the most important quality considerations are linked to health and safety and reliability. In effect, in this sector legal requirements in the form of health and safety regulations function as quality control strategies and reduce the chances of firms opting for other or additional formal strategies. Nor is it likely that this situation will change in the future unless new legislation, for example, from the European Union, pushes firms to adopt a general formal standard incorporating existing and a new health and safety rules.

CONCLUSIONS

In this chapter, the levels and types of quality management strategies reported by the 150 small firms in the telephone survey have been examined. The results provide basic quantitative data and suggest several themes in relation to small firms' methods of quality control and the adoption of BS 5750. The quality strategies were classified in terms of the typology developed in Chapter 2, ranging from simple informal methods to formal externally certificated quality management strategies. Much as expected from previous research, relatively few (around 4 per cent) of the firms had adopted formal, externally certificated strategies including BS 5750. Over two thirds of the firms relied upon highly informal, *ad hoc* methods of quality control.

The propensity to adopt BS 5750 was found to be positively related to size of firm and, rather less well established by previous research, to sector. A quarter of the firms which had not adopted BS 5750 were either thinking about, or were intending to implement, BS 5750. However, it is important not to interpret the latter as indicating definite future registrations or necessarily showing an accelerating trend towards registration. Many owner-managers explore the potential of formal standards such as BS 5750 and then later reject the option or simply do not proceed to full registration for one reason or another.

The use of the typology of quality management strategies enabled the analysis to identify variations in the approaches to quality management in different sectors, an advance on the more usual black and white, BS 5750–non BS 5750 distinction upon which most previous analyses have tended to be based. Even more important in some respects, the analysis instead of simply establishing the extent and variation in the adoption of different kinds of quality management strategies, also linked the variations to the internal character of the small firm and external influences from the sector in which it operates.

Size and the use of particular kinds of quality management strategies were examined first but the temptation to explain variations in quality strategies entirely in size terms was avoided. Size reductionism (Burrows and Curran, 1989) is all too easy and all too common in small business research and should always be treated with suspicion since size by itself can never be the complete explanation of the occurrence of particular management and organisational arrangements as the analysis of the sectoral variations above showed.

Instead, size effects were integrated with a number of other factors such as the history, organisational characteristics, routine or non-routine character of the product or service produced, the processes utilised in the production of the good or service and customer behaviour. These were combined to suggest why the patterns of non-formal and formal quality controls were as found in each of the sectors. For instance, it was argued that in some sectors there was no historic use of formal methods of quality control but that other kinds of informal quality management strategies had become institutionalised to the extent that they lessened the chances of formal standards ever being adopted.

Sectors such as electronics and computer services, which are the most likely to have adopted BS 5750 or other formal quality strategies, were analysed to show the role of a number of suggested influences on this outcome together with some suggestions on how these influences interact to produce this effect. For instance, the history of technological development in these sectors, particularly in electronics, as realised in specific operational processes, went with formal methods of operating to produce relatively high levels of bureaucratisation and adoption of BS 5750 or equivalents. These tendencies appear to have been reinforced by established industry norms, where customers expect suppliers to have formal quality procedures. In the other sectors, using the same kind of analysis, other patterns of influences produced quite different outcomes. Good examples of these include the general printers and garages where few pressures either from other firms or from private customers appear to exist to push firms towards adopting formal quality management strategies.

It is also necessary to stress that the data does not show any blunt, across the board rejection of formal quality standards such as BS 5750, by small business owners. There need not be anything ideological or psychological about small business owners' rejection of formal quality approaches. Rather, it can be suggested that their enthusiasm (or lack of enthusiasm) is a pragmatic response to the constraints and opportunities they face and the perceived relevance of formal quality strategies to their enterprise in the sector in which they operate.

The explanation offered should be treated as provisional at this stage since it will be developed further in the next chapter when the data from the case studies is examined. Nor should the explanations be taken to imply that just because formal quality strategies such as BS 5750 are so uncommon among most types of small firms in the present research and in other research, they are never likely to be the norm for small firms. The conditions influencing the adoption of formal standards change over time. For instance, marketing pressures may develop in some sectors so that a 'bandwagon' effect evolves influencing firms towards registration. The data presented in this chapter suggests that employment agencies, and possibly paper merchants, may be examples of this trend.

Nor do the influences examined in this chapter exhaust the range of possible influences which might lead small firms to adopt formal quality management strategies. For instance, political pressures may increase in the future so that it becomes difficult for small firms to avoid adopting BS 5750 whether their owners believe it suits their needs not. This has already happened to some extent, for instance, in personal financial services where independent advisers (mostly small businesses) are bound by performance standards monitored by an external agency (the Personal Investment Authority, for example) and a statutory body, the Security and Investment Board, able to sanction firms which fail to maintain the standards. Equally, customer behaviour may change over time. Private consumers, for instance, may come to insist on formal standards if consumer pressure groups can gain sufficient support for imposing such standards even if no statutory regulations are introduced.

In summary, it is possible to identify several themes related to the adoption of quality management strategies including formal methods such as BS 5750. In developing the first steps of an explanation for the particular kinds of quality management strategies deployed by small business owners, the emphasis has been on a multi-causal explanation rather than stressing one influence (especially size) either predominantly or by itself.

5 Small firms and quality: owner-managers' strategies

INTRODUCTION

In the last chapter an overview of the quantitative findings from the 150 telephone interviews with small business owners was offered. In this chapter the quantitative analysis is extended to incorporate qualitative data from the second stage of the research, the 10 in-depth case studies. This data is extremely important in establishing the 'logics'[1] which lay behind the decisions of owner-managers in constructing the range of quality management strategies observed. Without the insights provided by the case studies, the quantitative data would add up to little more than a set of tables showing the patterns of quality management in small firms with little revealed of the reasons *why* the patterns emerged as they did. We have already suggested that size alone as the key explanatory variable for the adoption or non-adoption of a formal quality standard is too simplistic. Instead, we have argued that there are widely varying mixes of influences at work. In this chapter, this analysis is continued in greater detail to contribute to the overall theorisation of quality management in small businesses being developed.

Perhaps the most significant (even if quite expected) finding in Chapter 4 was that the vast majority (just under 90 per cent) of owner-managers, operated informal methods of quality control. Further, three quarters (74.9 per cent) stated they had no intention of adopting or (much less commonly)[2] were unaware of, BS 5750. A crucial issue, therefore, is to explain why so many owners-managers take this stance despite all the pressures, propaganda and support directed at persuading them to adopt a formal standard. Our approach throughout is to avoid the strongly prescriptive tone of so much of the literature on small firms and formal quality management strategies. We are not attempting to suggest small business owners are myopic or mistaken in not opting for BS 5750, still less do we see our role as offering advice on how they might be persuaded to abandon their resistance. Rather the aim is to use the data collected to indicate why the majority of small firm owners consider informal methods more appropriate to their business than formal methods. *A priori*, we assume that small business owner reasoning on quality management is usually (though not, of course, always) rational, informed and market effective for their businesses and their survival and prosperity.[3] In other words, we adopt a different view to much of the previous literature which routinely assumes that formal quality management strategies are always superior to other approaches and that the main problem is persuading small business owners that they are in error in not accepting this 'universal truth'.

More specifically, this chapter examines the types of informal quality control methods used by small business owners, how they operate on a day-to-day basis, how they vary from business to business and why they are considered to be more appropriate by owner-managers. We examine the 'logics' or reasoning offered by these owners and evaluate them against conventional criteria (such as business growth, profit consciousness and efficient resource utilisation) used to assess the effectiveness of any enterprise in a market-based economy. However, since the findings also show that a minority of small firms who operate informal methods have not rejected formal methods out of hand, the chapter also examines why some small firm owners say they may shift from their present informal quality control strategies to adopt more formal methods, even if in a limited way, at some time in the future.[4]

SMALL FIRM OWNER-MANAGERS' EXPERIENCES OF QUALITY AND QUALITY STANDARDS

The implicit assumption in the pro-BS 5750/TQM literature, as noted earlier, is that small firm owner-managers' informal methods of quality control are inadequate to meet customer requirements or agreed quality standards and are becoming increasingly deficient as quality standards rise (Fox, 1991; DTI, 1992; Drummond, 1992). Only by systematically formalising procedures for quality control, it is avowed, can this vicious circle of decline, leading frequently to business failure, be converted into a virtuous circle of rising quality performance. This assumption has already been questioned in earlier chapters.

Owner-managers in the present study discussed and explained in detail their quality management strategies and their reasons for adopting them. Often they compared their strategies with alternatives and especially with formal quality standards such as BS 5750 which, echoing previous research, the majority rejected as unsuitable for their businesses. Moreover, the data showed that their decisions, like the process of managing quality itself, could be re-assessed and changed. Quality strategies, in short, were not simply one-off decisions, taken and then used without further thought.

Owner-managers, in describing how they managed quality, offered abundant evidence that where explicit customer requirements can be specified, they were active in understanding and attaining them. Where they were not, the small firm owners frequently compensated for this by an overkill approach, offering more than they believe the customer expects:

> everything is worked out individually with the customer. If you come in and want a job, you will specify the colour, you will specify the paper, price, delivery and so on. You clarify at the beginning and that's it. It is very cut throat now and if you're not producing the goods, i.e. on time, to the right price and quality, you'll lose the work, it's that simple. You can't get the work back, you'll lose the customers.
>
> (Genprint)[5]

> There's a fairly simple way of how we assess quality. We either get a customer at the end of the day who is satisfied, or he's dissatisfied because he's not getting the service. Hopefully, in the majority of cases, the former is the case; we don't get too many customers that complain about the service that we provide. We do tend to bend over backwards because we're looking for referrals. That's the main reason for doing it. We measure our quality purely by the reaction of our customers.
>
> (Compsys)

> We not only have to produce a product which meets customers' electrical and mechanical specifications, but since we guarantee all parts plus labour for a year, we have to make sure that the product does not fail due to negligent workmanship. We instil in people that they have to get it right first time.
>
> (Transys)

Implications in the literature that small firm owners operating informal methods of quality control are making inefficient guesses about what is required and may not be able, or even attempt to, deliver goods and services in accordance with customer requirements or agreed quality standards, are therefore questionable. They contradict the clear, careful attention given to assessing the quality needs of their businesses by owner-managers in this study. The evidence indicates strongly that small business owners *do* understand that the customer is central to their livelihoods, that they are more than active in trying to deliver what customers require and use a variety of techniques to achieve this goal.

Indeed, owner-managers' methods may have more in common with prescribed formal quality management techniques than many of the advocates of the latter would admit. For example, the owner-manager of Transys talked openly about 'getting it right first time' (a phrase linked closely with Deming (1986) although it is unlikely that this respondent had ever heard of Deming). But rather than treating this notion as some kind of mysterious objective only open to those who have implemented a formal quality programme, many small firm owners see it as a common sense way of remaining competitive by keeping the costs of reworking and returns down.

The owner-manager of Compsys talked about 'bending over backwards' to please customers. This is not too dissimilar to 'going beyond customer requirements', another frequently prescribed message in the quality literature. An implication of the above is that many small firm owner-managers may not need to implement formal methods to adopt many of the basic tenets of sound quality strategies and that advocates of formal quality standards have no monopoly on effective strategies. The owner-managers' approaches may be seen as examples of 'everyday rationality': people in specific situations construct solutions to the problems they experience based on rational assessments often supported by trial and error experiment. Small business owners occupy high risk economic roles and need to solve such problems – in this case quality management problems – effectively in order to survive, let alone prosper.

In effect, owner-managers of small firms are involved in the demystification of quality management strategies. Much of the literature on quality management is an elaboration of every day rationalities born of necessity, applied knowledge and experience. As the discussion in the opening chapters showed, many of the founders of modern quality management were engineers and managers closely involved in devising what were initially informal quality management strategies to fit specific situations. Their printed, formalised versions were often generalisations derived from these experiences. Closely analysed and approached with an open mind, small business owners' use of informal quality strategies very often emerge as a rational way of dealing with customers' needs effectively, relative to the competitive position of the business in the sector and market in which it operates. This is much the same way many formal strategies began before formalisation and elaboration occurred.

CHANGES IN THE IMPORTANCE OF QUALITY

Another main thesis associated with the emphasis on formal methods of quality control, is that quality standards are inexorably rising rapidly as a result of profound changes in the economy. As economies become more competitive as a result of the adoption of, for example, lean production systems or the effects of globalisation and more demanding consumers, it is argued that firms have to raise quality standards in order to survive. In turn, the development and adoption of formal quality standards, become 'push' factors, that is, they become the norm in many sectors, the minimum standard which a business has to meet in order to trade. Yet despite the wide popularity of arguments of these kinds, small firm owner-managers appear reluctant to accept them. For example, asked 'Do you feel that quality has become more important to your business over the last two years?' the following response was typical:

> Not really no. There is a certain standard that you have to adhere to and we try and keep to it . . . you need to carry out a good standard or you don't get work.
>
> (Electromend)

Where changes in quality standards had occurred, they had occurred at a relatively slow rate and respondents believed they had met the change appropriately. Sometimes owner-managers argued that changes touted as rises in quality standards were suspect: some of the changes, for instance, were seen as bureaucratic rather than real. Asked 'In your view has the attitude of your customers changed?', two respondents replied:

> Yes, a lot of them are having to go for BS 5750, this has created more paperwork
>
> (Electromend)

> Yes, its not so much the quality more [the] documentation. The actual quality has never changed, they just want to see that quality documented.
>
> (Transys)

What these mainly very experienced small business owners were suggesting was that minimum (or high) quality standards have long existed in their sectors and they have not necessarily changed greatly in real terms as a result of the introduction of formal methods such as BS 5750. Rather, 'quality' has become associated with increased levels of formality or documentation in many instances, that is, existing quality practices have simply become paper-based with no significant changes in content. Where real increases in quality standards have occurred, they argued they have met these: otherwise they would not be in business.

The tendency to overstate rates of change in modern economies and particularly in the way they affect small firms, has been very common in the 1980s and 1990s.[6] One reason stems from what can be termed the *Tomorrow's World* view of economic change. Here the mass media (such as the eponymous television programme) offer examples of technological and economic changes and present them as if they were already major forces in the economy. In fact, changes of these kinds may take several years to become widespread or major economic forces. One example of the above phenomenon related to small firms is the impact of the Single European Market (SEM). In 1992 the mass media fanfared the arrival of the SEM, suggesting that this would rapidly affect every business in the UK and any business that did not adjust quickly would suffer badly. In fact, for small firms the effects of the SEM appear to have been much more gradual. In 1992, a sample of owner-managers of service sector small firms were asked if they expected the SEM to have an impact on their businesses. Almost two thirds (65.2 per cent) said they believed it would have no impact (Curran *et al.*, 1995: 55). In 1993 respondents from the same sample were asked the same question again. The proportion believing the SEM would have no effect on their business had risen to just over three out of four. Asked the same question in 1995, the proportion of the same respondents who believed it would have no effect had risen yet again to over 90 per cent (Curran *et al.*, 1995). In other words, while the SEM has had an impact which will no doubt increase, for these small business owners it is a very gradual process.[7]

It might be argued, therefore, that the extensive attention given to formal quality management strategies such as BS 5750 is another example of the above phenomenon. The decision by small business owners on whether to adopt a formal quality management strategy is based on a comparison with the alternatives, particularly those already in place, developed out of their close knowledge of the needs of their businesses. It seems from the data in the present study that formal quality standards will often be judged as not having any real superiority over current, informal strategies sufficient to make the investment in change worthwhile. If this is the case, then it is worth analysing the actual quality strategies used by small firm owners in more detail.

SMALL FIRMS AND INFORMAL METHODS

On start-up or entering a particular market, the small firm owner-manager has to decide how to organise to ensure that price and quality requirements dictated by the market are met. The typical response is to develop appropriate informal methods, if only as a first step to adopting more formal approaches, though the evidence indicates that most owner-managers see no reason to proceed to a formal standard. It was suggested earlier that informal methods could be either *simple* or *complex*. These refer to the way quality control is organised: non-paper-based approaches, set and controlled by the owner-manager or structured bureaucratic, that is, systematic approaches again put in place and controlled by the owner-manager. These distinctions refer to the principles upon which quality management is organised rather than to the actual methods devised by small business owners which will vary in individual small firms and in particular sectors.

So what quality control methods or practices are actually used by small firms? In the telephone survey small firm owner-managers were asked 'How do you control quality on a day-by-day basis?' The majority gave a variety of responses, which can be divided into *proactive* and *reactive* quality practices.

Proactive quality practices are those which affect the quality of the good or service *before* and *during* production. For example, an owner-manager who consciously recruits highly skilled staff because he or she believes this is likely to raise quality, is deemed to be proactively increasing the chances of producing a quality good or service.

Reactive quality practices are those which are used to *assess* the quality of the good or service after production. These can take a number of forms but customer feedback is the most obvious. In services, they may involve observing customers' reactions to the service as they experience it but in other sectors they can range from the use of sophisticated market surveys to the use of 'dummy customers' to informal follow up contacts with customers by owner-managers

Owner managers can employ both kinds of practices of course and, in practice, usually will. Which is emphasised will depend on the small business owner, but even more on the sector in which the business operates. Other factors which may influence the mix of practices may be the stage of development of the business and its size, though as stressed earlier, the latter should be seen as one rather than *the* major influence on quality management strategies.

PROACTIVE QUALITY PRACTICES

It became clear that although respondents mentioned a wide range of methods of quality control, proactive methods were highly important with inspection in some form the most important (Table 9). Just over half of the respondents explicitly mentioned this method in response to an open question on quality strategies.[8] Inspection is often regarded as a means of assessing the quality of tangible products in the quality literature. For example, Dale *et al.* (1990) define inspection as the process where: 'one or more characteristics of a product are examined, measured or tested and compared with the specified measurements to assess its conformity' (Dale *et al.*, 1990: 3).

In the early literature on quality control, a good deal of emphasis was put on developing statistical techniques for inspection and these became quite sophisticated but their application was mainly suited to manufacturing activities (Barad, 1996). However, the quality management literature has recently attempted to develop methods of inspection suitable for services activities (see, for example, Øvretveit, 1993).[9] These are much more relevant to small firms because three out of every four small firms are engaged in services activities of some kind.

The type and extent of inspection methods in the firms varied according to the kind of work done and the extent to which established quality standards have been developed for the product or service being considered. In some sectors, such as electronics, where sophisticated quantitative quality standards have been developed, firms are often required to produce products to very precise specifications. In these sectors, it is not usually possible to establish whether standards have been achieved using simple (visual) inspection methods. Instead, specialised test equipment often needs to be used. All the electronics firms used inspection for quality control and nearly four out of ten firms in the sector reported they used specialised test procedures as part of their inspection methods (Table 9).

In sectors where quality standards are not so easily defined, inspection tends to be simpler than in sectors such as electronics. Owner-managers, or whoever is responsible for checking quality, will consider the product, finished or otherwise, against her/his subjective benchmark of the standard to which the product should conform to be acceptable to customers. Inspection procedures of this kind are often still rigorous in the sense that owner-managers (or other delegated persons) often inspect *every* product before it leaves the premises to ensure the firm's products are consistent with the standards adopted. Since they are often highly experienced, the inspection can be exacting:

Table 9 Small firm owners' proactive and reactive methods of quality control (%)

	Electronics	Printing	Advertising, marketing, design	Computer services	Employment agencies	Garages	Plant and equipment hire	All
Proactive methods								
Inspection	100.0	78.6	53.8	69.2	27.3	55.2	53.3	50.5
Test	37.5	—	—	—	—	—	—	2.9
Skilled staff	—	—	46.2	30.8	45.5	17.2	13.3	21.4
Supervision	—	—	7.7	53.8	45.5	72.4	40.0	38.8
Training	—	—	7.7	7.7	9.1	6.9	—	4.9
Checklists	—	—	—	38.5	—	17.2	6.7	10.7
Quality ethic	12.5	7.1	—	—	9.1	—	6.7	3.9
Reactive methods								
Customer feedback	—	—	—	15.4	27.3	3.4	6.7	6.8
N =	8	14	13	13	11	29	15	103

Notes: Responses compiled from open questions. They should not be taken as indicating the full use of each method but of what owner-managers in particular sectors saw as important in terms of their own quality management strategies. This helps explain the absence of mentions of some proactive methods in sectors such as electronics and printing where, for example, skilled staff are taken as given by owner-managers and are therefore not mentioned specifically

> Chris [the other partner] and I [the respondent] do most of the test-
> ing. But also we are signing most of the goods out of the door, we
> load the vans ourselves, and as we're loading, we're checking. Every
> single item is checked.

(Transys)

Visual inspection is also likely to be common in sectors such as printing
and design. Here developing quality standards can be problematic
because of the creative element in many of the products. Quality strategies may therefore combine standard checks on, for example, colour
matching with more subjective assessments of design standards. Creative products pose special problems because subjective assessments
can genuinely vary: the owner-manager's assessment may differ from
that of the customer yet both might be seen as 'right' by other third
parties.

Other methods frequently mentioned in maintaining quality were
supervision and recruiting suitable staff. For example, nearly a quarter
of owner-managers cited employing appropriately skilled staff as
important in relation to quality (Table 9). However, the importance of
this factor is related to economic sector (as Table 9 again supports).
There are two explanations for this. The first relates to the requirements
of the job. To achieve the desired level of quality some jobs simply
require higher skilled employees than others:

> with the work we do, you can only employ people who have been
> brought up in the repair game. It's not like manufacturing where you
> can walk straight in, you've got to be a repair man and know exactly
> what to do.

(Electromend)

This approach can be contrasted with the view expressed by the owner-
manager of another of the case study firms:

> they [the employees] have no retentive memory whatsoever. But for
> the work they're doing it's the only kind of people you can get,
> you're talking drongos really, but you've got to have your drongos.

(Transys)[10]

Electromend requires skilled workers to repair electric motors while
Transys required unskilled workers to perform basic assembly work.
However, the situation may not be as simple as this implies. The owner-
manager of Transys might wish to employ more skilled workers but the
market the firm faces has a price structure which bears down hard on
costs leaving little room for the increased costs of better quality labour.

To use better quality labour would, in other words, make the firm uncompetitive. However, this is not a fundamental problem because the present labour force reaches acceptable quality standards. In other sectors, owners may perceive different choices. For example, a firm may be able to move up market to produce higher value added products and services which may not only allow the firm to use higher quality labour but actually require such labour to successfully exploit the new market opportunities. Alternatively, in some sectors capital can sometimes be substituted for labour in the form of using more sophisticated equipment.

Of course, the calibre of the labour employed and its role in quality management strategies should not be seen in isolation. Even where there is a need for skilled labour, for example, other factors may be seen as even more important. Respondents in the vehicle repair sector which uses a lot of skilled manual labour, nevertheless play down the importance of this in quality management and put much more emphasis on supervision (Table 9). In other words, they take skilled labour as a given since the business could not function for long without it but their replies show they are very conscious of the importance of supervision. This might be seen as arising from the character of businesses. Inspection at every stage of every task undertaken by employees in a small vehicle repairers is difficult, but superior to 'after the event' checks. Completed servicing or repairs may have faults which are difficult to detect without expensive checks requiring dismantling and a lot of time. Owners may therefore feel it necessary to supervise as closely as possible as jobs are carried out, to minimise quality failures.

The general importance of supervision in quality control emerged very clearly. Nearly four out of 10 owner-managers mentioned supervision as a proactive method of quality control (Table 9). This human resource component can clearly have a highly significant influence on the firm's overall quality strategy. Owners need to give continuing attention to employee performance in maintaining quality or ensuring it does not drop below an acceptable standard. But in some kinds of business, this will be more important than others or attention to employee performance will take different forms. Accordingly, the data suggest that the application of supervision varied, not only to the skills of employees, but to the amount of trust placed in them.[11] As human resource specialists have long pointed out, whether the employer adopts a high or low trust strategy in relation to employees makes a considerable impact on the firm as well as the way quality is managed. Owner-managers in different sectors displayed both strategies:

It's an open office. We all know what we're doing. We are aware of our requirements. Everyone monitors their own quality.

(Compsys)

It is down to us sitting in, slapping wrists, we spoon feed people through. These are not exactly over-intelligent people, it is a low tech industry so you get low tech people, but they need spoon feeding on a regular basis and that is what we have to do.

(Transys)

Although this need not be the case in all similar instances, direct supervision was much less necessary in Compsys where employees were skilled and capable of getting on with their own work independently according to the owner-manager. However, in Transys which had less skilled employees, the view of the owner-manager was that supervision was constantly required to achieve the desired quality standards.

A second explanation for the emphasis put on the 'right' labour as a quality strategy, relates to the degree of control employers can exercise over the quality of the final product or service before it reaches the customer. In businesses where the final product is an intangible or where the good or service is produced and consumed instantaneously, owner-managers have fewer effective *reactive quality control* options available to them. There is therefore a greater reliance on *proactive quality practices* which focus on the skills and commitment of employees. These influences may explain why owner-managers in the advertising, marketing and design and the employment agency sectors were the most likely to cite recruiting and employing skilled staff as important quality concerns (Table 9). In design, for example, the skill and creativity of the design artist is crucial to the quality of the final product. Similarly, in the employment agency sector, the skill and conscientiousness of employees who deal with client firms, reflects directly upon the quality standards of the firm. Quality failures discovered after the event – perhaps from customer complaints – may be too late in the sense that the business has already been damaged.

Both recruiting the 'right' people and supervision are therefore very important for quality control in most small firms. It emphasises well the people-based character of the small business as an economic entity which makes it so much less easy to treat as something to which a rational, bureaucratically based quality management strategy can be tagged. The people-centred character of many of the quality management strategies was also shown in other ways. For example, owner-managers frequently mentioned their concern to keep abreast of what was going on in the workplace by adopting 'a hands on' or a 'management by walking' approach. This enabled them to influence quality while production was taking place and this appeared to hold as much in manufacturing as in service activities where it might be expected to be used much more commonly. Moreover, it provided owner-managers with what they saw as opportunities to instil in employees a general 'quality ethic' and their own specific rules in relation to the delivery of quality for their business.

The extent to which owner-manager strategies had the desired effects on employee attitudes or generated a 'quality ethic' in the small firms sampled, is unclear. Whatever the claims made by owner-manager respondents, it is difficult to comment on their accuracy without testing the opinions of the employees themselves: owner-managers are not always the most informed on the views and attitudes of their employees. However, research by Reeves and Hoy (1993) suggests that in firms where management demonstrates a clear commitment to quality and this is recognised by employees, there is a greater chance of this translating into quality as perceived by customers. This implies that management attitudes and actions can influence the quality of the work from employees which, in turn, is converted into positive customer reactions. But is this a result of employers and employees sharing ideas about quality, a 'shared quality culture' of the kind discussed so positively in the writings of quality gurus, or is it simply employers enforcing strict quality standards, causing employees to modify their behaviour accordingly? The evidence from the case studies indicates that both occur but the emphasis is on owner-managers enforcing rules to regulate employee behaviour. However, in firms employing higher skilled workers, owner-managers were more likely to adopt high trust approaches allowing employees more discretion in delivering quality to customers.

Much of the writing on formal quality strategies stresses the training component in such strategies. This is considered essential to instilling a quality ethic as well as to improving employee task performance. The owner-managers in the study, however, did not apparently regard training as a key element in their quality management strategies. Less than one in 20 reported that training was a main constituent in their quality strategies (Table 9). This lack of emphasis may simply be a reflection on their attitudes to training more generally. In the past a good deal of research has reported that small firm owner-managers typically underestimate the importance of training (Manpower Services Commission, 1986; Ajimal, 1987: 13). More recent research (see, for example, Curran *et al.*, 1996a) suggests that while small firms provide less formal training because they are reluctant, or find it difficult, to commit resources, they provide relatively high levels of informal training. Informal training is often under-reported because it is frequently integrated closely with managerial and work activities in general. In other words, owner-managers may not see training as important because it is so much part and parcel of the way employees are managed. It may be, however, that the informal training given to employees, particularly when they join the firm, contributes strongly to establishing the firm's quality practices.

It is important to stress that informal training should not be seen as necessarily inferior to formal training. Abbott (1993) for instance, concluded that informal training is often at least as effective as any formal equivalent in a wide range of small firm environments. It can be tailored closely to the precise needs of the firm and the specific characteristics of individual employees in ways which, for instance, externally provided formal training would find difficult to match. In developing a quality strategy for the firm, owner-managers will aim to mould employee behaviour to suit their desired ends. For this they can use a variety of means – rewards and punishments – to achieve employee conformity and training, and informal training in particular, will be one of these means. Our guess is that the telephone survey data understates the importance of employee training in quality management and the case study data lends support to this supposition.

In the case study firms, the provision of training varied with owner-managers opting for differing mixes of informal and formal provision. The nature and extent of the training reflected the points made in the above paragraph and tended to fit the needs of firms especially in relation to the skills of the employees and the nature of the work tasks undertaken. For example, in Transys, where employees were low skilled, informal training was frequent and based upon a continuous boosting of employee work performance to achieve and maintain required standards. However, where employees are more skilled, training may reflect more ambitious and wider quality objectives:

> I give them a good bit of training, concerning different skills and different repairs, if they haven't experienced a job before then I try and let them do the next job, so that it gives them all further skills. At the end of the day it proves to be better for the company. Then I can send most people out on most jobs and not be reliant on one individual. You've got to give them all multi-skills.
>
> (Electromend)

The owner-manager of Electromend clearly considered improving the skills and experience of his workforce beyond existing levels to be valuable for the business and enabling operatives to cope with a wider variety of work tasks. As a result there was less chance of the business losing customers because there were not enough employees with the right skills at any time. It also helps to boost the morale of employees who are no longer doing the same job every day.[12]

The practice of what human resource specialists (see, for example, Goss, 1994: 28) call 'functional flexibility' which aims at ensuring that employees have a wide range of skills so that they can easily switch between tasks and substitute for each other, is now accepted practice in many large enterprises in the UK.[13] Here we have another example of small firm owner-managers developing strategies which parallel those advocated as good practice in larger enterprises. Yet if the owner-manager was asked 'Do you practise functional flexibility strategies in the use of labour in your firm?' he or she would probably reply that they did not understand the question. In the interviews owner-managers often claimed almost exactly the same advantages for their approaches as claimed for functional flexibility in human resource management texts: it made labour flexible, eliminated inefficient labour demarcation, helped meet fluctuations in customer demand and raised employee morale.

In some sectors training may help meet other needs which affect quality. For example, in sectors which experience high rates of technological change, a main function of training may be to keep employees up to date on new techniques and products. One sector which showed this pattern conspicuously in the present research was computer services where owner-managers stressed that keeping themselves and their employees up to date was a constant battle due to rapid technological change. Yet unless the battle was won, firms would fail to provide a quality service to customers. The owner-manager of Compsys, for example, said he paid a lot of attention to these problems using both in-house, informal training and outside training providers to ensure staff were up to date. Often the firm could only afford to send one or two employees on external training. When these employees returned they passed on the new skills and knowledge to other members of staff in the firm. In this way, all staff become aware of current developments without the costs of formal training for all staff.[14]

Proactive methods of quality control which seek to influence quality practices before and during production, therefore, consist of a number of common elements many focusing on employees. Employing people with the right attitudes and skills, supervision, training and instilling a 'quality ethic' are found in every sector. The importance of each, however, varies depending, first, on owner-managers' approaches to quality management, but, second, and more importantly, on the characteristics of the sector in which the firm is located. The evidence from the telephone survey and the case studies, shows that owner-managers used some or all of these methods routinely and continuously. What was also evident was that some of the techniques they had developed mimicked (usually unconsciously) those used in larger enterprises and advocated in human resource texts and by government policy. Once the distinction between formal and informal approaches is relaxed, the differences between small and larger enterprise quality management strategies may be rather less and small firm owner approaches to quality management may not be as 'unprogressive' as is sometimes asserted.

REACTIVE QUALITY PRACTICES

As defined earlier, reactive quality practices are those used to assess the quality of the good or service after production or where production and consumption occur simultaneously. The most important kind of reactive quality practices were, as noted earlier, forms of customer feedback. The key difference between proactive and reactive practices as we have classified them here, is that proactive approaches anticipate quality issues by seeking to put in place measures which will ensure quality reaches a given standard, while reactive practices are 'after the event' practices which monitor and remedy perceived quality failures or help define new standards.

In services, the kinds of activities in which the great majority of small firms are located, reactive quality controls can be important. This is especially the case in those services where there is no tangible final product and proactive quality controls are more difficult to use. Where production or performance occurs in the customer's presence, this will be linked often with some kind of assessment of customer reaction as the employee performs the service. This may be done by observing customer reaction or by asking customers their views directly or indirectly. Other strategies include follow-up enquiries. For example, customers may be offered a comments sheet to proffer an opinion of the service received. Hotels, for example, often place a questionnaire in rooms asking customers to complete and return it if they have any comments to make on the quality of the hotel's facilities and service.

More sophisticated are the use of *ex post facto* checks such as user surveys conducted some time after the consumption of the service. These may be conducted by the firm itself or carried out by a market research agency. They can include questions on competitors' performances adding to the knowledge upon which the firm's quality management strategies can be developed. Another strategy is the use of dummy customers which is frequently referred to in the literature and, it is sometimes alleged, widely used.

Among firms in the study, customer feedback was not in fact mentioned frequently as a quality control strategy. Well under 1 in 10 owners cited this as an important method of quality control and none of the case study evidence provided examples. All the firms whose owner-managers did mention customer feedback were in the service sector. This lack of mention of customer feedback strategies is somewhat surprising since most of the firms were in services and customer reactions might have been expected to be important in quality management. Of course, owner-managers may rely on observing customer reaction or on informal contacts with customers whenever opportunities arise. Such informal contacts have been shown to be highly important to owner-managers in the past (Bryson *et al.*, 1993; Shaw, 1995). One reason for the low level of usage of more formal versions might be that customers are not all that useful as quality assessors in practice. For example, they may be reticent about complaining about poor quality. If they are unsatisfied they may not provide feedback but simply find another supplier, that is, take their business elsewhere. More formal measuring of customer reactions may also be seen as expensive and ineffective. Using market research agencies, for example, adds to costs and customers' willingness to respond may be limited.

Overall, therefore, *simple informal methods* of quality control can be divided into proactive and reactive methods but on the evidence from the telephone survey and case studies, proactive methods were by far the most frequently mentioned. This might be expected because, as the traditional adage has it, 'prevention is better than cure'. It also accords with much of the professional literature on quality strategies which emphasises 'zero fault' approaches to quality management, stressing that it is cheaper and achieves higher levels of positive customer response if quality control concentrates on 'getting it right first time'. But it needs to be said again that these small business owners arrive at their quality management strategies through devising their own approaches and solutions to quality issues: they are not aping textbook approaches but formulating ways of managing quality based on their experiences and what they define as the quality needs of their businesses.

COMPLEX INFORMAL METHODS OF QUALITY CONTROL

All small firms operate simple informal methods of quality control of the kinds discussed in the previous sections.[15] However, some owner-managers decide that these basic quality approaches are not enough and add bureaucratised solutions to the informal strategies. In other words, they develop written procedures or quality manuals documenting operating and quality practices in a structured or semi-structured manner. Where this occurs, firms can be said to be operating *complex informal* procedures in terms of the typology adopted here. These were defined in Chapter 2 as structured, bureaucratised procedures (that is, written) supervised and controlled by the owner-manager or delegated employee, but with no direct external control or monitoring by second or third party agencies. Approximately, 18 per cent of the sample operated these methods (Table 5, Chapter 4). Given this is a significant percentage, it is worth considering why some small firms are inclined to use these more bureaucratised methods and in what ways these methods manifest themselves.

One obvious argument why small firm owners may be motivated to adopt *complex informal* methods of quality control is that they are a response to the increased difficulties of controlling quality in larger small firms (Churchill and Lewis, 1983), especially in firms with above 20 employees (Table 10). The notion that exerting personal control is easier where the firm has only a small number of employees has been supported by previous research. For example, Scott *et al.* (1989) reported that owner-managers believed it was easier to supervise workers effectively when they were in close proximity. This is much less possible, it is argued, in larger or growing small firms with larger premises. Owner-managers of firms in the present study employing only informal methods of quality control appeared to agree. Over twice as many respondents in larger firms (20+ employees) reported that maintaining quality was difficult than those in firms employing 1–4 people (Table 10).

Table 10 Is maintaining quality difficult? Small firms operating informal methods of quality control and firm size (%)

	1–4	5–9	10–19	20+	All
No	75.0	70.0	69.6	30.8	67.7
Yes	22.7	26.0	26.1	53.8	27.7
DK/NA	2.3	4.0	4.3	15.4	4.6
N =	44	50	23	13	130

Base: All firms in the telephone survey reporting using simple informal or complex informal methods of quality control

Table 11 Small firms' personnel responsible for maintaining quality by firm size (%)

	1–4	*5–9*	*10–19*	*20+*	*All*
Owner-manager	90.9	80.0	56.5	46.2	76.1
Director with special responsibility for quality	9.1	20.0	39.1	46.2	22.3
Quality manager	—	—	4.3	7.7	1.5
N =	44	50	23	13	130

Base: All firms in the telephone survey reporting using simple informal or complex informal methods of quality control

One response to increased size of firm may be increased delegation. That is, other partners, directors or trusted members of staff, may be given responsibilities for a particular operation or for certain employees. There is clear evidence of increased delegation of responsibility for quality in larger small firms in the research (Table 11). Owners of firms with 20 or more employees were over five times more likely to report that somebody else in the firm had responsibilities for maintaining quality than owner-managers of firms with 1–4 employees. Again, it is worth remembering that, as argued earlier (in Chapter 4), size *by itself* is unlikely to offer a complete explanation of this relationship: other factors such as owner-managers' management styles and sector influences also play important roles. Of course, non-size factors may be linked with size but the links may not be simple.

However, owner-managers who operate simple informal methods of quality control may not feel delegation is enough to ensure desired quality standards are met. This may be because they feel that exerting control through other people is less effective than if they continued to manage quality directly themselves or because they wish to ensure that those to whom responsibility has been delegated maintain appropriate standards or both. The result may be the adoption of bureaucratised control procedures or *complex informal methods* which make all staff and procedures accountable to a system. In this way, owner-managers try to keep track of what is going on in the firm and ensure that the quality standards they have set are met. A formal system also helps pinpoint who is responsible for quality failures more easily.

Data from one of the case study firms shows how an owner-manager might decide to implement *complex informal* methods for some of the above reasons. The respondent decided that by introducing more bureaucratised methods, control and efficiency – including quality standards – would be increased. He asserted that he implemented the system to:

> make the company more efficient. Knowing where the company is going, having more information to hand. Also, traceability so if there is a problem it can be traced to where it has occurred.
>
> (Autorep)

The respondent based the system on the BS 5750 format although he had no intention of registering formally. He preferred to cherry pick procedures from the BS 5750 approach which he considered beneficial for his business but ignored others thus minimising the attendant costs:

> I like some of the 5750 procedures because we know where the company is, and we know who's doing what and why they've done it, but actually maintaining the 5750, the cost of it, at this moment in time we won't spend it. I don't think it will make any significant difference to us, from what we're doing now.
>
> (Autorep)

Another reason why small firms may be motivated to adopt complex informal methods, relates to customer pressures. Some customers, especially larger firms, may require suppliers to provide some kind of quality documentation with the final product as supplied. This option may only occur in special circumstances (not all the firm's customers may make such demands) and owners may have no strong belief that formal standards raise the quality of output from the firm. Nevertheless, if customers want such assurances, owner-managers may be willing to document their procedures:

> we have a quality manual which covers everything from how to do a soldered joint, how not to eat acidic fruits near the machines, all that sort of thing . . . If people want it [documentation] we can use it, the systems are there but it is costly, they can pay for it, and we have got a channel for that, but in the main it is just that we're in the middle of it [and it does not affect what we do greatly].
>
> (Transys)

The above examples of the use of *complex informal* methods of quality control do not show any great enthusiasm on the part of owner-managers for formal quality control strategies. Formal elements are added to the simple quality control strategies all firms utilise to overcome problems of larger size, or because formal approaches such as

BS 5750 are recognised to have some useful elements, or reluctantly, because it makes customers happy and may secure an order that might otherwise be lost. Essentially, *complex informal* methods are added to augment other, established, mainly *simple informal* methods rather than replace them.

In summary, *complex informal* methods of quality control were used by just under one in five of the firms in the study. They were operated in addition to the *simple informal* methods all firms use. There was a positive association with size with larger firms being more likely to adopt such methods. Where *complex informal* methods were being employed, the data did not indicate that this was normally a stage in the shift to adopting formal, third party approved quality standards such as BS 5750. On the contrary, those operating complex informal quality control strategies appeared generally as sceptical of formal standards as those owners (the great majority) who used *simple informal* quality control strategies only.

WHY ARE INFORMAL METHODS CONSIDERED MORE APPROPRIATE?

Small firm owner-managers use *simple* or *complex* informal methods of quality control because they consider them to offer an effective and appropriate way of operating. That is, they are effective at delivering the required level of quality and the efficient operation of the firm:

> I can't see how it [the current system] could work any better, we've simplified it, it is easy to work, everybody knows the system, and it works. We've done it for the last fifteen years.
>
> (Electromend)

However, owner-managers are not simply adopting a lazy view of quality management, that is, a view which in effect regards quality management strategies adequate because that is what the firm has always used. They also often have views on how alternative quality management systems – particularly formal management systems such as BS 5750 – might compare with the strategies currently in place (Table 12). Asked their opinion on BS 5750 and why they had not adopted it for their business, the owner-managers suggested overwhelmingly that formal methods lack relevance, are bureaucratic, are costly and time consuming to implement and maintain.

Many small firm owner-managers believe that formal quality control methods such as BS 5750 lack relevance to their specific businesses. One kind of explanation offered related to the internal operation of

Table 12 Small firm owners operating informal methods cited disadvantages of BS 5750, multiple and main responses (%)

| | Simple | | Complex | | All | |
	Multiple	Main	Multiple	Main	Multiple	Main
Not relevant	65.0	30.1	66.7	11.1	65.4	26.2
Costly	61.2	27.2	77.8	37.0	72.3	29.2
Bureaucratic	57.3	17.5	63.0	18.5	73.8	17.7
Time consuming	68.0	17.5	85.2	25.9	71.5	19.2
Other	10.7	1.9	29.4	—	14.6	1.5
D/NA	—	5.8	—	7.4	—	6.2
N =	103	103	27	27	130	130

Base: All owner-managers who use simple or complex informal methods of quality control
Note: The above responses were collected through multiple and main response questions

small firms. Owner-managers recognised that formal methods require small firms to bureaucratise using written manuals and procedures to standardise their approach to quality management. But it is far from clear to many owner-managers in the study why this would be beneficial:

> If we need a motor repairing, we don't need any written information, it just has to be done. The guy who dismantles it, will make a decision on what needs to be done and the work gets carried out . . . You're only as good as the man who takes the electric motor apart, and creating, more paperwork isn't going to make it any better.
>
> (Electromend)

> We don't need to have things documented at every stage to get back to the man in charge of quality. He only knows when something has gone wrong when a ream of papers comes up to him, 'Oh, something's gone wrong here, I'll start the investigation', so he sends reams of papers back down the line, he doesn't actually go in there and start looking.
>
> (Transys)

> Transformers are a low-tech industry in comparison to a lot of the electronics industry, very low tech. It is the basic block of the unit, and therefore it doesn't command the high tech world of BS 5750. You are up-rating yourself to such a degree that you price yourself out of the market.
>
> (Transys)

As the owner-manager of Electromend implies, in many small firms maintaining quality is not seen as an overwhelmingly difficult problem. In his view, employees are aware of what they have to do and that they have to do it properly. If the system is working effectively then there is no point changing it: 'it isn't broken and doesn't need mending' is their assessment of their quality control methods and the reason for the negative attitudes to formal quality management system such as BS 5750.

The owner-manager of Transys made a number of observations on the relevance of BS 5750 to firms such as his. First, he argued that formal methods were designed to cope with control, coordination and communication problems associated with larger firms, but such problems do not exist at all, or to the same extent, in small firms. Second, he pointed out that formal quality control methods are, as Halliday (1993) suggests, more suited to complex forms of production, that is, where the technology used warrants such quality control procedures.

The application of these methods, for example, is more appropriate to high technology industries who see some benefit in documented quality and firms are prepared to pay (as are their customers) the premium for doing so. The overall point which emerges here is that small firm owners were wary of over-engineered solutions to problems such as quality control.

Another reason why many small firms consider formal methods irrelevant relates to external market conditions. As noted previously, there has been a persistent media emphasis on small firms implementing BS 5750 either because their customers demand it or because, without it, they cannot compete effectively. However, as we have argued, for most small firms this is simply not the case. It depends greatly upon the economic sector in which the firm operates and the type of work being done. In Chapter 4, it was suggested that in some sectors, such as electronics, formal quality control standards were likely to be significant in contractual and subcontractual relations between firms. In other sectors, such as employment agencies, BS 5750 appeared to be actively used as mainly a marketing tool.

However, in most sectors neither of the two above influences appear to be pushing small firms to adopt formal quality standards. Large firms in some sectors may use small firms as suppliers but make no demands that they be BS 5750 registered. This may occur even when the large firm insists on BS 5750 certification for some of its suppliers. For example, according to the owner-manager of Genprint, one of the printing firms in the sample, larger customers have not made any demand that they implement the standard. The obvious reason which might be suggested for this lack of pressure is that the large firms realise that it would clearly have no benefit. Existing quality control procedures operated by the small firm are entirely adequate in the opinions of both parties. Another example of how pressures to adopt BS 5750 are countered by small firm owner-managers who believe no added benefit would result to them or to the customer, is provided by the owner of Transys. On being given an ultimatum by a larger customer insisting the firm register for BS 5750, the owner-manager stated:

> We turned round and said that there is absolutely no need because under BS 5750 you can approve us as an 'approved sub-contractor'. Basically, do you want to pay twice as much for your transformers? They said 'no' we'll go to a BS 5750 transformer firm. We said fair enough and they had a look around and they came back and gave us a vendor assessment and we're still producing for them!

> (Transys)

In other sectors where the main customers are private consumers, it was argued it is unlikely these customers would demand that firms from whom they purchase products and services should be BS 5750 registered or be over-impressed when small firms proclaim they are 'BS 5750 approved'. The small garages sector provides an exemplar of the above conditions. The owner-manager of one of these small vehicle repairers, Autorep, reported:

> In the beginning we thought if we don't have it and other companies do, people will spend their money with other companies rather than us, but I don't think that is the case, a lot of our work is done for private individuals. They are not interested whatsoever in BS 5750. It's how much you charge at the end of the day.
>
> (Autorep)

The direct and indirect costs of BS 5750

BS 5750 is not cost free. Even if a small business owner is not particularly impressed by what registration could do for the business, it is not simply a matter of opting for registration in the hope that it might be useful. Small firm owners considered the financial and time costs associated with implementing and maintaining formal quality standards, particularly third party supervised varieties such as BS 5750. Usually the result was to conclude that the costs were too high relative to any benefits that might result.

It was not just the costs of implementing the standard which was scrutinised critically by respondents, although these were a factor. Several owner-managers suggested that the on-going costs (of remaining BS 5750 approved) were more significant in the long run:

> it's absolutely amazing the costs that you don't see immediately. You think it will cost £5,000 to set up and have BSI come down and vet you, fair enough, but it's the on-going costs of having someone administer it ... By spreading the increased overhead cost on to all the transformers, it would throw us right out of the commercial market.
>
> (Transys)

> the cost is quite considerable because in order to have BS 5750 you have to create a lot more paperwork, and you're not necessarily bringing the goods up to any better standard. The goods and the repairs would be exactly the same – all that would alter would be the cost of the paperwork and the cost of a couple of extra workers to deal with it, and I see that as being a bit of a farce.
>
> (Electromend)

These owner-manager opinions are at odds with those offered in the literature. It is argued in the latter, for instance, that by implementing BS 5750, small firms will gain a commercial advantage over their competitors (DTI, 1992). This may happen but is by no means certain and many owner-managers were extremely sceptical. More accurately, competitive advantages resulting from adopting BS 5750 are only likely to occur under specific conditions which may be met only in a limited range of sectors. For instance, where price is an important consideration and technological complexity is low, small firm owners indicated that implementing and maintaining BS 5750 or equivalents had no operational advantages and could easily price them out of the market. On the other hand, if adopting BS 5750 is combined with shifting the business up-market, the investment and running costs of adoption might be more than covered by the additional profits from the market shift.

SMALL FIRMS WHICH ARE CONSIDERING OR INTENDING TO ADOPT FORMAL METHODS

Despite the above doubts about the relevance of formal quality standards such as BS 5750 expressed by a high proportion of owner-managers in the study, about a quarter of the small firms currently operating informal methods (simple and/or complex) are thinking about, or intending to, implement BS 5750. That a quarter of the firms were reported to hold such views might seem to contradict the strong tone of rejection in the reporting of findings in the previous sections in this chapter. This contradiction is more apparent than real. The evidence suggests that owner-managers who assess whether BS 5750 would be beneficial to their business often conclude that no advantage would accrue and do not proceed further.[16]

In Chapter 1 it was argued that owner-managers may be motivated to consider adoption of BS 5750 for one or a combination of reasons. First, they may explore the possible procedural benefits (improvements in the internal operation of a firm or organisation) which could result. Second, they may assess the marketing advantages which could result, especially if adoption can be linked with moving the firm up-market to higher value added outputs. Third, the owner-manager may experience external pressures either from customers or as an emerging element in the competitive ethos of the sector in which the firm operates. They come to see the latter as a need to adopt BS 5750 mainly as a defensive response.

These respondents were asked to think what kinds of reasons might influence them to consider adopting BS 5750 as a possible strategy for their businesses. In line with research by Holliday (1994) and the SBRT (1994a) the possible benefits to the marketing strengths of the firm were an important potential consideration and more important apparently than possible procedural benefits (Table 13).

However, the main reason why small firms in this sub-sample were considering implementing BS 5750 relates to external pressures, mainly to maintain the firm's competitive position. Both these findings were reflected in the comments of one of the case study owner-managers who had thought about whether to adopt BS 5750:

It's [BS 5750] vital. There will come a time in the very near future where if you don't have BS 5750, or the equivalent, you won't get business. Whilst I could argue that it doesn't really apply to us because we are dealing with off the shelf software and off the shelf hardware, so it's someone else's problem, it does apply to us because the quality issue will ripple right through supply, manufacture and the service industry. There won't be an alternative, we will have to comply if we want to continue.

(Compsys)

Marketing image is vital if you are in the selling game. Whilst following the procedures is good from the point of view of running the business, that little standard that says 'approved' opens numerous doors. It's easier for you to knock on someone's door and sell your system if you've got it than if you haven't got it.

(Compsys)

These findings need to be treated with some caution because for most respondents they concerned a hypothetical situation, that is, they were considering what advantages or disadvantages adopting BS 5750 might have for their business. However, the reasons they offered were very similar to those offered by the smaller proportion for whom the question was less hypothetical, that is, those who actually were considering more or less seriously whether to register. External pressures were the most frequently mentioned reasons followed by marketing advantages and then the procedural advantages which might result. Again, however, the above should not be taken to indicate that a substantial proportion of the firms are considering adopting BS 5750, or even likely to actually adopt the standard.

Table 13 Small firm owners operating simple or complex informal methods and their possible reasons for implementing BS 5750 (%)

	Multiple response			Main response		
	Simple	*Complex*	*All*	*Simple*	*Complex*	*All*
Procedural advantages	56.0	75.0	60.6	24.0	14.3	21.2
Marketing image	88.0	87.5	87.9	32.0	37.5	33.3
External pressure	60.0	75.0	63.0	40.0	42.9	39.4
Other	4.0	—	4.0	4.0	—	3.0
D/NA	—	—	—	—	14.3	3.0
N =	25	8	33	25	8	33

Base: All firms in the telephone survey reporting using simple informal or complex informal methods of quality control who were thinking about or intending to adopt BS 5750

CONCLUSIONS

In this chapter the analysis of quality management strategies in small firms has been developed further. More of the data from the telephone survey has been introduced together with qualitative data from the face-to-face case studies. Overall, the same two central issues introduced in earlier chapters have been pursued: why have so few firms opted to adopt formal quality standards such as BS 5750 and what are the 'logics' which underpin the widely varying quality management strategies adopted by owner-managers in the different kinds of small firms in the study?

The analysis revealed a variety of logics behind the quality management strategies used by owner-managers. There was little evidence that the management of quality was random or poorly conceived. The strategies were usually clearly thought out, detailed, based on careful assessments and owner-managers' experiences. Some of the practices echoed those found in the quality literature although the owner-managers often did not use the terminology in the literature. Indeed, they were almost certainly unaware of the latter. For instance, several respondents offered equivalents to such principles as 'getting it right first time' and 'going beyond what the customer required'. Overall, the quality management strategies of the owner-managers arose over-whelmingly out of developed 'everyday rationalities' derived from their assessments of what the businesses needed and their experiences.

The small business owners in the study rejected what might almost be described as the 'quality panic' apparent in much recent management writing on the topic. The latter alleges a very rapid increase in general quality standards, which if not acknowledged by small businesses through the adoption of quality management strategies such as BS 5750 or TQM, will result in loss of market share and even business failure. Owner-managers, on the other hand, took a cool-headed approach, arguing that they recognised changes were occurring – as they always had – but found few problems coping with the quality standards demanded by the market. They were very sceptical of the effectiveness of bureaucratic, system-based formal quality standards such as BS 5750. They believed that adopting such approaches often added to paperwork and costs but offered no great improvements in real quality and could actually lead to problems for the business under some circumstances.

In analysing in greater depth the quality management strategies displayed by firms in the study, the *simple informal* methods which were by far the most common variety found were sub-divided into *proactive* and *reactive* kinds. This analytical distinction is based on the principle of whether the quality control strategy is preventive or 'after the event'. *Proactive* procedures emerged as much the most important: owner-managers, in other words, appeared to accept that prevention was better than cure. A high proportion of the proactive strategies were people-centred. For instance, recruiting the right people, those with the 'right' attitudes and skills were very important in the views of the owner-managers. Once employed, supervision was also important in maintaining quality. Training appeared less important but there was reason to believe that its role in quality strategies may have been understated.

Reactive quality control strategies were less important than proactive strategies but still of some importance. Customer feedback was significant in some sectors but there was not much evidence of owner-managers using systematic or formal methods of collecting data on customers' views through follow up questionnaires or dummy customers. Instead, owner-managers relied on their own informal collecting of customers' views on the quality of the products or services being produced plus information from their normal contacts with others in the sector.

A minority of owner-managers used *complex informal* methods of quality control, that is, paper-based, bureaucratic strategies instituted and controlled by the owner-manager without outside supervision or validation. There was some evidence that the use of such methods was positively related to size of business, but the style of management of owners and the sector in which the firm operated were also important. In some cases, such methods were possibly a step on the way to adopting an externally validated and monitored formal quality standard such as BS 5750, but these were few.

Finally, some firms had contemplated adopting external standards such as BS 5750 more seriously and the main reason was as a response to external pressures, though some thought it might lead to market advantages or procedural benefits. Among the great bulk of firms who had not opted for BS 5750 and had no immediate plans to do so, most accepted that they might have to think more seriously about BS 5750 at some time in the future if it became more widespread. The result might be that they might have to adopt BS 5750 to avoid losing customers. If they did, adoption would mainly be a reluctant, defensive response not the result of a positive assessment of the advantages. Overall, most believed strongly that the quality management strategies they had developed for their businesses were effective and more effective than a third party controlled standard could be.

6 Small firms and formal methods of quality control

INTRODUCTION

As Chapter 4 showed, under 5 per cent of firms in the study operated formal, second or third party controlled quality strategies though a further 9 per cent were implementing such methods. Other research, again noted earlier, reports similarly low levels. This disappoints supporters of formal quality standards but they assert that the trend is upward and will accelerate (DTI, 1994; Pera, 1992). In the earlier chapters, the reasons for the lack of owner-manager enthusiasm for BS 5750 have been examined. But what about the experiences of those owner-managers who have taken the BS 5750 path or an equivalent? Do their experiences bear out the doubts of owner-managers who reject BS 5750?

In this chapter, data is presented on the owners who decided to implement and register for formal methods. It analyses the reasons why owner-managers decide to use this approach to quality management, their experiences of the different ways to prepare for certification, the costs of a formal quality management strategy and, finally, their views on the impact on their business. The latter includes not only their perceptions of the benefits (or disadvantages) of registration but their views on the costs of continuing to be registered.

It will be remembered that Chapter 2 distinguished between two kinds of formal quality management in small firms. 'Second party' controlled systems are bureaucratised, that is, paper-based approaches to quality management which are externally dictated and assessed by firms' customers or suppliers. 'Third party' controlled systems are similar in that they are based on formal, paper-based approaches but the external controls are exercised by bodies such as BSI and other organisations whose prime function is the defining and certifying of quality standards.[1]

SECOND PARTY APPROACHES

The evidence showed that the use of second party controlled methods was very limited among the case study firms. Indeed, only two firms operated these methods (Table 5, Chapter 4). Of these, one firm's quality control procedures were supervised externally by its larger customers while in the other case, control was exercised by its main supplier. Because 'second party' methods are rarely discussed in the literature, more attention is given to them here than their incidence in the study perhaps warrants.

Historically, customers exerting influence on their suppliers' quality strategies is, of course, common. However, the formalisation of such influences, that is, converting them into systematic, paper-based standard procedures imposed on suppliers, is more recent. The most frequently cited influential pioneers of customer defined and imposed quality standards are the Ministry of Defence (MOD) who have developed and insisted on quality standards of this kind since at least the 1960s (Sadgrove, 1994).

Other large organisations in the private and public sector – particularly those who buy goods and services in large amounts – have followed the MOD's example. Bastow in Rock (1992) suggested that around 10 per cent of large UK organisations such as British Telecom, and 80 per cent of local government purchasers, now insist suppliers use a formal quality strategy, either second party controlled or BS 5750 or a similar third party certification, as a condition of doing business. This still does not provide clear evidence on the balance between second and third party controlled systems, however, and almost certainly overstates the importance of second party systems. Many of the second party systems said to be in operation are likely to be relatively minimal compared with third party controlled systems such as BS 5750. Control is often exercised infrequently or through cursory inspections by customers' representatives. The trend has tended towards buyers insisting on suppliers having third party approval (such as BS 5750) rather than going to the trouble of developing and administering their own quality control systems for their suppliers.[2] Indeed, it has been argued that the convenience of third party certification has led to this increased popularity (Sherwood, 1986).

Because customer-imposed quality systems turned up so rarely in the study, the evidence is very limited. Indeed, all the evidence on the operation of this quality control method comes from a single case study firm. Meditron's owner-manager reported that the company was forced to adopt a formal quality system based on the demands of its larger health and medical care customers as a condition of doing business. The system, which he described as 'beyond the requirements of BS 5750' involves a comprehensive formalisation of quality procedures for every aspect of production to ensure customers are confident that the quality standards they demand are met. This is supported by a high level of documentation covering all stages of the company's operations.

The reasons why medical and health care customers are likely to insist on rigorous quality standards are obvious. The overwhelming need for products which reach high standards in this area is often, literally, a matter of life and death. One way of ensuring such standards is to devise and impose a quality standard on suppliers, supporting it with regular monitoring. The common alternative in other sectors of insisting that suppliers have BS 5750 certification, is judged inadequate for a high proportion of medical products. The emphasis on procedures at the heart of BS 5750 which, many argue, do not actually guarantee quality, is simply not considered good enough (SBRT, 1992; Halliday, 1993; Holliday, 1994).

The opposite case, that is, where *suppliers* dictate their customers' methods of quality control is also poorly covered by research, though it exists. For example, research by the SBRT (1992) indicated that around 5 per cent of small firms were affected as customers by formal methods such as BS 5750. Higher levels of supplier controlled quality standards were found in the wholesale, and especially the retailing, sector. Again, the reasons for this supplier insistence are fairly obvious. Suppliers wish to ensure that their products are sold in an environment they see as consistent with the image they want to present of the product or service. For instance, makers of expensive perfumes or cosmetics may restrict the retail outlets from which the products may be purchased so that they are on sale only in surroundings with a luxury ambience. In other words, they believe the quality of the environment is closely related to the quality of the products. An even more common example probably is where suppliers will only permit firms to sell or service their products if they are confident that the latter firms can offer high quality support services to customers. In this study this form of quality control was again rare. It was found in only one respondent firm in the telephone survey which sold computer products including modems, keyboards and line drivers, mainly in North American markets where quality standards are very stringent.

More generally, second party methods appear likely where the supplier (or customer) wishes to impose a quality standard because they believe there are important sector-specific reasons for doing so and/or where appropriate third party methods do not exist. BS 5750 is not sector-specific although sector-based versions can be generated given appropriate conditions such as a proactive trade body widely recognised and influential within the sector. But BS 5750 may not be deemed as a sufficiently effective quality standard in some sectors as the case study firm Meditron exemplifies. In this case a second party system may be set up. In other sectors the result may be that no formal standard is developed, with reliance continuing to be placed on existing informal practices.

THIRD PARTY APPROACHES

The evidence, however, appears to suggest that, for most sectors, the overriding trend is away from second party towards third party controlled methods. Sherwood (1986) suggested the development of third party controlled methods had the advantages of uniformity and consistency in the quality procedures used by firms, making buying decisions simpler for customers. He also suggested that the change in emphasis from second to third party controlled methods may be related to the economic incentives for larger organisations to reduce their quality management costs.

Where third party methods have not been introduced in a sector, large firms may insist on suppliers/customers meeting and documenting compliance standards for quality, subject to their inspection and administration. This means regular assessment of each supplier by the larger organisation. The adoption of a standardised system of quality control has the effect of allowing large organisations to shift the responsibility for quality on to their medium sized or smaller suppliers or customers. This shift to third party controlled quality standards effectively externalises the costs of quality control across the sector.

In a sector where third party quality control methods have been developed, individual firms no longer have to 'reinvent the wheel', that is, devise specific quality control systems for their needs or to impose on businesses with whom they have dealings. A third party controlled system can either be applied across all firms or adapted to the needs of specific firms at a lower cost than setting up a completely new system in each individual firm. Moreover, the knowledge bank on how to ensure and maintain effective quality standards in the sector will be available in principle to all firms.

Several types of third party controlled schemes were reported by respondents in the research. The most popular, as expected, was BS 5750. Thirteen firms were implementing this standard at the time of the fieldwork and five more had already registered.[3] However, some small firms operated separate sector-specific third party quality control methods. An example is the RMI/SMTA Quality Control Programme used in the vehicle repair/garage sector. This scheme is one of several developed by trade associations which are more attractive to firms in these sectors than BS 5750 because they are geared towards sector-specific needs.

However, trade associations have also developed sector-specific interpretations of BS 5750 (Bethell, 1994). One example, is the Construction Information Research and Information Association (CIRAIA) scheme in construction (see Oliver, 1990). Another firm operated in accordance with the Allied Quality Assurance Publications standard (AQAP), a forerunner of BS 5750 which has now been largely superseded by BS 5750 (see, for example, Tisdall, 1990). The most widely recognised sector specific interpretation of BS 5750 is the Tickit scheme (Tickit, 1992). The scheme, sponsored by the DTI and developed by the British Computer Society, is in use in the computer software sector. However, the research picked up no examples of its use in the current sample. Since the original research design was concerned with assessing owner-managers' strategies in relation to BS 5750, the data presented below mainly relate to the BS 5750 standard only, though evidence on other third party methods is introduced where available.

MOTIVATIONS FOR IMPLEMENTING FORMAL METHODS

As the opening chapter indicated, previous evidence suggests several commonly cited motives among small business owners who opt for third party controlled quality strategies such as BS 5750. Three are mentioned most frequently. First, are procedural benefits, that is, benefits expected as a result of improvements in the internal operation of the enterprise following the adoption of BS 5750 or an equivalent. Second, comes marketing benefits. Owner-managers may believe these can be coupled to certification to improve the firm's position in the market relative to its competitors. Third, BS 5750 may be adopted as a result of external market pressures emanating from customers or suppliers or the widespread adoption of the standard by competitor firms.

Much of the previous research on small firm owners' motivations for implementing BS 5750 has been piecemeal and unsystematic. For instance, many of the reports emphasise one particular motivation to the exclusion of others. The SBRT research (1994b), for example, mainly considers customer pressures. Other reports are theoretically and methodologically remiss. For example, a report by Pera (1992) emphasised the importance of 'increasing profit' as a motivation for implementing BS 5750, but did not say *how* the firms in the study intended to increase profits. Was it through increased sales, using certification to shift to higher mark-up products or through reduced operating costs or some combination of these or other profit-related effects? 'Increasing profits' may also be a vague aspiration rather than a well grounded expectation based on careful assessment of the likely results of adoption. As other research on small business owners has shown, major decisions can be made with surprisingly little serious consideration due to time constraints on owner-managers and a reluctance to allow outsiders to have an influence on the business (Curran *et al.*, 1993: 22–23).

Evidence provided by another larger SBRT study (1994a) is more useful. This indicated marketing aspects as the most significant motivation reported by owner-managers. This was followed by procedural aspects or 'improving quality', and finally, by external pressures such as 'satisfying a major customer' or 'holding on to customers'. Here, therefore, marketing advantages emerged as more important than procedural benefits. However, the order of importance of owner-manager motivations depends greatly on the composition of samples in research of this kind. Since sector and size can be important in relation to adopting BS 5750, samples which do not accurately reproduce the sectoral and size distributions of small firms across the economy can produce differing results.

The ways in which questions are asked in research and, even more importantly, the ways in which the results are analysed and presented, can also affect interpretations of responses. For example, in the present research, among small firms currently implementing, or who were already registered BS 5750, the main motivation on one interpretation was expected or realised procedural benefits but if the data is presented in another way, this motive emerges as less important. Three-quarters of the firms' owners mentioned procedural benefits as a motivation but fewer, 45 per cent, suggested it as their *main* motivation (Table 14). An even more striking example of this effect is the differences in the importance of marketing advantages. Eighty per cent of owner-managers mentioned this reason but only 20 per cent stated it was their *main* reason. Neither interpretation should be seized on necessarily as the 'right' one. They offer different perspectives on the reasons why these owner-managers thought BS 5750 would have benefits for their businesses.

In real life, people often have mixed reasons for adopting a particular course of action rather than a single, isolated motive, particularly where

Table 14 Small firm owners' reasons for opting for
formal methods of quality control (%)

	Multiple	Main
Procedural advantages	75.0	45.0
Marketing advantages	80.0	20.0
External pressures	45.0	25.0
Other	5.0	5.0
DK/NA	—	5.0
N = 20		100.0

Base: All respondents currently implementing formal
methods or already registered
Note: Percentages under the multiple column do not sum
to 100 because respondents could give more than one
response

the decision relates to a complicated issue whose outcomes are by no
means black and white. Seeking BS 5750 certification is a complex decision where benefits cannot be guaranteed in advance. As suggested
earlier, the process of achieving the standard can be protracted and
some owners may even eventually decide not to register even though
they adopt a substantial proportion of the procedures which normally
accompany registration. In these circumstances, owner-managers'
motivations may have changed as a result of experiences during implementation with new motivations coming to the forefront.

The qualitative data from the case studies helps us understand in
more depth the complexities of owner-managers' motivations surrounding implementing and adopting BS 5750. An example of a firm
which implemented the standard for procedural reasons was Electrico,
a contract electronics manufacturer with one large firm customer taking
about two thirds of its output. The firm's MD decided to tighten up
quality procedures after losses due to returns on past orders,

In the beginning it [the decision to implement BS 5750] was financial,
we couldn't afford the gamble of having goods returned to us. I can't
afford the risk of our customers beginning to have doubts about us.
We have had a couple of experiences which we said we had to do
something about it.

(Electrico)

Despite the overall importance of procedural reasons, Electrico was the
only case study firm where the MD stated that they were the main

original reason for his decision. Other case study firms' respondents stated that other reasons were initially more important, yet there were indications that procedural advantages were often recognised subsequently. For example, the directors of Beeplant, a plant and equipment hire business, originally decided to implement BS 5750 as a result of external market conditions. But the importance of this motivation receded as other competitive components, such as price, became important in the recession which emerged as implementation proceeded. The respondent director pushed ahead with implementation and eventually intends to register because he believes that the procedural benefits will be considerable.

A similar experience was reported by the owner-manager of Console, a software consultancy. This firm was made sensitive to BS 5750 by some of its larger customers. Console's administrative director stated that she came to accept that the firm might need to respond to the importance of registration as a criterion in customers' buying decisions. However, on examining the standard further, it was believed that adopting BS 5750 would produce significant operational advantages.

The phenomenon of emphasising one reason as the initial motivation to implement BS 5750 but later coming to see other reasons as important, especially procedural reasons, was therefore common. This could be a part of the learning experience accompanying the complex process of implementing and registering for BS 5750. It is, after all, what proponents of BS 5750 have always argued: adopting the standard brings the firm a whole range of advantages even if those deciding to go down the BS 5750 route are not always aware of all of them at the start or have doubts about the claims made.

On the other hand, what the data might be showing is the familiar effects of what social psychologists have long called 'cognitive dissonance' (Zajonc, 1960) or what others might call a 'converts' effect'. Cognitive dissonance occurs where individuals take decisions which are initially inconsistent with their beliefs and values or where the results contain significant features which could have resulted in rejection of the course of action. It is even more likely where putting the decision into effect involved effort and stress. Dissonance produces psychological discomfort and one way of reducing this, it is argued, is to interpret aspects of the resulting experience very positively, confirming the 'correctness' of the original decision. In other words, small firm owner-managers who think hard before deciding to opt for BS 5750 or feel forced by external forces to implement third party prescribed quality controls, may have considerable doubts during and even in the early period after registration. But having gone through what is often a considerable and costly upheaval to implement and put BS 5750 into practice, they then became very positive about its effects even though these may be difficult to demonstrate objectively.

The data shows that of those firms who were implementing or were registered BS 5750, a quarter did so as a result of external pressures. External pressures to go down the BS 5750 route are especially likely to be associated with post-decision dissonance effects. Such pressures can come from two sources. The first and most cited was discussed in detail earlier, that is, large firms and public organisations insisting that suppliers are BS 5750 registered. As explained, this may be due to a growing consciousness of quality standards among large business managers, perhaps reflecting greater competition in the economy, national and global. Their counterparts in public sector organisations have felt a compulsion to imitate the private sector since the latter is now widely seen as the arbiter of good management practice, or have been forced to adopt formal quality standards as a result of government pressures (Kelly, 1991; Kirkpatrick and Martinez Lucio, 1995).

Alternatively, as was suggested earlier, the reasons why larger enterprises have increasingly insisted on suppliers having BS 5750 certification may be more mundane. While insistence may be based on a belief that genuine quality benefits will result, a more persuasive reason might be that it is an expression of purchaser power, shifting quality responsibilities (and their associated costs) on to suppliers (Sherwood, 1986) and/or partly a rationalising of supplier lists (Curran and Blackburn, 1994).[4]

Customer pressures came from a variety of sources according to the telephone survey data. For example, five firms cited large firms, four cited local authorities, four the Ministry of Defence and three central government. Not all these were large businesses or organisations, however. Three firms cited medium sized firms as the sources of these kinds of pressures. Again, it is worth making the distinction between *mentions* of a particular influence and citing it as the *main* motivation for adopting BS 5750. Customer pressures were cited as a main motivation by only four firms (only one of which was a case study firm – Meditron). One reason for this difference was that some respondents saw customer pressures increasing and likely to be more important in the future than currently:

> there will come a time (or it has arrived in many cases) when you will not be able to market manufactured products without BS 5750 approval. All of the large organisations have laid down internal

buying rules demanding BS 5750 . . . as that is passed down to companies like ours [they] increasingly demand BS 5750 or equivalent
capability. Anyone who doesn't have it finds themselves unable to
market.

(Electrico)

BS 5750, is forecast as being the capability that is going to be
required in the nineties, and even more relevant is that our customers
began to demand it, particularly British Telecom were making it very
clear if we didn't have BS 5750 by the end of 1993 then they would
not be able to do business [with us].

(Electrico)

However, the importance of customer pressures should not be overstated. Less than 3 per cent of the total sample were motivated to
implement formal methods of quality management by customer pressures, so its overall influence is still fairly modest, especially in relation
to the amount of emphasis given to it in the media. The latter often sees
customer pressures as the main reason why small firms (and firms in
general) are adopting BS 5750 but clearly on the evidence here, this is
far from the case as yet.

The other source of pressures on small firms to implement BS 5750,
also discussed earlier, is competitive pressures. That is, in sectors where
registration is, or is becoming, common place, small firms may feel the
need to register to remain competitive. Despite the plausibility of this
reason, it turned up infrequently in the research. It may be that this
influence has yet to develop fully since it will be linked with overall
levels of registration in specific sectors and the economy generally. Evidence from the research reveals that of the nine firms affected by
external pressures, eight were affected by customer pressures and only
one by competitive pressures.

The firm affected by competitive pressures, Paperco, a paper merchants, offered case study insights into the motivations to implement
and register for BS 5750, as a result of such reasons. The firm's major
competitors had already adopted BS 5750, making registration a serious matter for all firms in the market. As the commercial director of
Paperco put it,

our bigger competitors have made a big issue of achieving it. Some
of the biggest paper merchants in the country have used it as a very
positive advertising thing. Some of them were on very early (four or
five years ago) and you almost saw that as soon as one of the major

paper merchants had got it, three or four of the other majors were straight in. It has almost been a snow ball effect. There are certain printers who will not deal with you unless you're BS 5750.

(Paperco)

One way in which this motivation might grow in importance is where firms choosing to implement the standard see it primarily as a marketing strategy. For example, as noted in Chapter 4, many employment agencies are already actively using or considering BS 5750 as a marketing strategy. The result has been an increase in competitive pressures for other employment agencies to implement the standard:

> It [BS 5750] has been used as a 'big stick' by these businesses in an attempt to differentiate between agencies, much to everyone's dismay.

(Thompson, 1994: 9)

This strategy is, of course, self-defeating in the long run in the sense that if all or nearly all firms in a sector opt for BS 5750 for this reason, then the end result is that no firm gains an advantage over its competitors once it is standard in the sector.

Table 14 showed that marketing reasons were the most commonly mentioned motivation for implementing BS 5750 but only one in five firms who were implementing or had registered for the standard, did so *mainly* for that reason. Unfortunately, none of the case study data illuminates marketing as a main reason. Holliday (1994, 1995) in her case studies, reports in detail a firm whose owner-manager very clearly exhibited this motivation for registering for BS 5750. What the evidence suggests is that while gaining marketing advantage is a reason for implementing and achieving BS 5750, it is less commonly a prime reason.

In summary, the telephone survey data and case study evidence suggests that small firms usually implement BS 5750 for a mix of reasons. This might be expected for such a complex change in the firms' operations. Often owner-managers offered a *main* reason such as procedural advantages, external pressures, or as a marketing strategy but all the motivations mentioned can be important to some degree in most firms and their relative importance can change over time. Procedural advantages were the most frequently mentioned *main* motivation for implementing BS 5750 whereas marketing strategy reasons were the most frequently *mentioned* motivation overall. Many firms were initially influenced by marketing and external motivations but the experience of implementing and achieving BS 5750 often coincided with increasing value being placed on procedural advantages.

THE IMPLEMENTATION PROCESS AND IMPLEMENTATION EXPERIENCES

Having made the decision to opt for BS 5750, owner-managers then have to embark on the implementation process itself. This, as the discussion below illustrates, is a complex, often time consuming, process which may, in the event, have no clear ending. Owner-managers may, and the data shows this is by no means rare, stop the process at any point abandoning or retaining the stages already put in place. This may simply be a stopping of the clock due, for example, to the owner-manager deciding that implementation is too time consuming and other needs of the business are more compelling. But the result may be that the firm never proceeds to full registration. The owner may decide, for instance, that the already implemented stages provide all the advantages likely to accrue from BS 5750 and full registration will bestow no further advantages.

Although, owner-managers may not approach the implementation process quite so analytically, it can be argued that they are faced essentially with three main kinds of considerations which will determine the nature, and ultimately the impact, of registration should the firm go the whole course. These are:

1 *Objectives*. What do owner-managers want from implementation and registration? This is by no means obvious. The evidence suggests that just wanting 'to improve quality' is much too simple an answer to the question.

2 *Constraints*. What constraints do owner-managers face in attempting to attain these objectives? These can be of many kinds – financial, management and employee skills and commitment limitations, the availability of external advice and the willingness of owner-managers to take advantage of what is available etc.

3 *Methods*. What methods will owner-managers use to meet their implementation objectives given the constraints? There are a very great number of ways in which BS 5750 can be implemented with some being much more effective than others.

Objectives

On deciding to implement BS 5750 owner-managers have to decide what they desire from implementation and registration. It is likely, of course, that much will depend upon the initial motivations for implementing BS 5750. For example, those owners implementing the standard to achieve procedural benefits, may concentrate on the internal effects of each stage of implementation, analysing and seeking to maximise the benefits for the firm's operational efficiency. For them, registration itself would simply be the culmination of these processes. Alternatively, firms seeking to register for marketing advantages or as a result of external pressures, may initially give much less consideration to the internal effects of implementation but concentrate on the image the firm presents to the outside world.

The case study data illustrates the effects of variations in owner-managers' initial objectives. According to their owner-managers, three of the four case study firms (Electrico, Console and Beeplant) implementing or registered for BS 5750, did so mainly to achieve procedural benefits. In each case emphasis was placed on developing a system which enhanced internal processes. The remaining case study firm (Paperco discussed above) registered mainly as a reaction to external competitive pressures. As expected, the owner-managers in this firm appeared less interested in giving the attention needed to develop procedural aspects. Emphasis, indeed, was placed upon *minimising* the impact of the standard on the operational side of the business. They wanted as little disturbance as possible to the way the firm operated because they were sceptical that significant procedural advantages would follow. Such changes might, in fact, *damage* the firm's operational efficiency in their view.

The above presents a somewhat polarised view of owner-managers' objectives in deciding to implement and/or register for BS 5750. In practice, results were often much more mixed. For example, close analysis of owner-managers' statements from the case study tapes indicates that although the owners of Electrico, Console and Beeplant focused on the procedural aspects of implementation, they were still conscious of the potential marketing impact of registration. Similarly, although the directors of Paperco were cynical about the procedural advantages resulting from registration and, indeed, did little to give them a chance of emerging, they still reported improvements in customer complaints procedures as a result of registration. In other words, it might be more accurate to state that while owners had primary objectives, other objectives might be emergent or latent, that is, some objectives could become explicit as the implementation process proceeded and might then affect how the process developed.

Constraints

As well as considering the objectives of implementation, the constraints faced by owner-managers in achieving their objectives in implementing and/or registering for the standard also need to be considered. In a literature review by North *et al.* (1993), these constraints were separated into two distinct groups:

1   the financial and time costs involved in implementing and registering for the standard;
2   the inherent applicability of the standard to the needs, existing methods, personnel relations and market conditions of the business.

Financial and other costs

Small firm owner-managers mentioned costs most frequently in discussing the constraints accompanying implementation and registration (Table 15). The costs of implementing and registering for BS 5750 are difficult to estimate accurately because they are subject to so many influences (North *et al.*, 1993). They will vary according to the size, sector and complexity of the business, the costs of the consultancy support used (if any), the availability of grants and other help, the certification body used and, finally, the time it takes to implement the standard.[5]

For all the small firms in the study who had implemented or regis-

Table 15   Small firms operating formal methods:
problems with BS 5750 (%)

	Multiple	*Main*
Cost	65.0	40.0
Bureaucracy	35.0	25.0
Time	50.0	15.0
Other	20.0	—
DK/NA	—	20.0
N = 20		100.0

Base: All respondents currently implementing formal methods or already registered
Note: Percentages under the multiple response column do not sum to 100 because respondents could give more than one response

tered BS 5750, data on the different financial costs and time spans of implementation were recorded. The range of costs was extremely wide and fully bears out the difficulties that advisers have in offering guidance to those considering registration or those attempting to assess the economic advantages and disadvantages which might result. Respondents reported that implementing and registering BS 5750 could cost anything from £2,000 to over £20,000 (Table 16).[6]

However, it became clear that the expected relationship between firm size and costs of implementation/registration was not quite as close as might be thought. Smaller firms (those with less than 10 employees) never spent more than £10,000. On the other hand, it was not the case that larger small firms always reported total costs at the higher end of the range. Larger firms reported expenditure over the range £2,000 to over £20,000. It was not possible to make a full assessment of the relationship between cost and the complexity of the business because this was beyond the capability of the telephone survey.

Subjective opinions among the owner-managers on the overall cost of implementing BS 5750, that is, whether it was considered 'high' or 'low', varied. Most owner-managers believed that while costs were 'high', they were often necessary:

> It's a lot but you've got to think about the net benefit. I think that it is the problem with small companies. OK you're out there to earn

Table 16 Small firms operating formal methods: total costs of implementing BS 5750 (%)

£	%
2,000–2,499	5.0
2,500–4,999	10.0
5,000–7,499	15.0
7,500–9,999	10.0
10,000–19,999	25.0
20,000+	5.0
DK/NA	30.0
N = 20	100.0

Base: All respondents currently implementing formal methods or already registered
Note: Respondents' estimates of costs are based on 1993 or earlier £ values

money but also you've got to get the business up and running
properly.

(Console)

One form of cost stressed in respondents' replies was not the direct
financial costs involved but the opportunity costs of the time of
owner-managers and staff devoted to achieving implementation. These
costs were mainly incurred by owner-managers or other senior staff.
The opportunity cost in the form of owner-manager hours lost, was an
especially large burden for some firms but other staff might also be
involved. The managing director of Meditron estimated that the firm
invested somewhere between £5,000 and £10,000 in staff time, and
between £40,000 and £50,000 in lost business. The administrative director of Console estimated that it may have cost between £50,000 and
£60,000 in staff time and lost revenue. As noted earlier, these costs are
approximate because of respondents' difficulties in estimating precisely.

Next came consultants' and assessment fees. Here the case study data
is helpful. Of those case study firms who had used a consultant, expenditure varied from around £3,500 at Beeplant (with further costs possible
because they had not yet finished using the consultant) to £4,500 at
Paperco and £8,750 at Console. These figures indicate that, even after
Department of Trade and Industry funding – which all three used – a
consultant can be a significant cost. None of the above commented
upon third party registration fees, since they were not sure what they
might be at the time the case study interviews took place. However, their
preliminary estimates were that they would be around £2,500. Expenditure on documentation was also mentioned, although respondents
were unable to provide costs or estimates for this item.

The time taken to achieve full implementation, can be significant and
was mentioned as a problem by half of the respondents (Table 15). Pera
(1992) estimated that small firms took, on average, about 15 months to
implement the standard. In our sample, the firms estimated taking
rather less time on average, just under 11 months (Table 17). But
respondents were unhappy about the amount of time involved:

I don't think I personally envisaged the amount of problems there
has been. At the start we set up a budget of how much it would cost.
We didn't anticipate in man hours and man days, how long it would
take.

(Console)

it took a lot of physical time, really from me to start off with, so as
an overall small business we were not able to pursue some of the

Table 17 Small firms operating formal
methods: time span for implementing BS 5750

Months	%
1–6	25.0
7–12	25.0
13–18	15.0
19–24	15.0
24+	5.0
DK/NA	15.0
N = 20	100.0

Base: All respondents currently implementing formal
methods or already registered

normal business activities which we would have had. In other words,
I was not pursuing the sales side of the business and certainly not
pursuing the engineering side of design work because I was occupied
with the quality system, so I'm sure the business at that time did dip
in terms of sales, invoices going out of the door.

(Meditron)

As with financial costs, there was no direct clear relationship between
firm size and estimated time taken to implement the standard. While no
smaller small firm (less than 10 employees) took more than a year to
implement the standard, larger small firms (more than 10 employees)
sometimes took no more time than smaller firms. Overall, larger firms
took anything from under 6 months to over 2 years.

Post-registration costs

On implementing and registering for BS 5750, small firms face further
financial and human resource commitments in maintaining registration. Firms have to be prepared to undergo regular, usually
unannounced, inspection to ensure that their operating procedures
matched those formulated and approved in their initial registration.
Moreover, firms are expected to maintain BS 5750 documentation in
accordance with the requirements of the standard. Where changes
occur in procedures or in the products and services produced, this will
usually require revision of their manuals and further inspection. This
will incur additional costs and staff commitments. None of the case

study firms were able to produce accurate costings for this post-registration phase of BS 5750 because none had sufficient experience. However, the consensus among the respondents was that annual re-registering would cost about £500. This may be an underestimate since it was clear that these estimates assumed no major revisions. Nor does this cost take into account the post-registration administrative costs involved in maintaining the standard, which are thought to be significant.

Methods

While the objectives of implementing and registering for BS 5750 and the constraints firms face having adopted these objectives, are linked closely to the methods by which certification is won, the methods should be seen as analytically separate. In other words, whatever the objectives and constraints, there are a number of methods firms can use in achieving BS 5750. The data shows that firms used a variety of methods.

Often the methods chosen represented a compromise between the objectives of seeking BS 5750 certification and estimates of the costs, direct and indirect, involved. Somebody in the firm has to take responsibility for the implementation process once the decision to opt for BS 5750 has been made. Around 85 per cent of firms implementing or registering for BS 5750, gave responsibility to one person to implement the standard. In most cases this was an owner-manager or director. However, 40 per cent of the firms subsequently appointed a specialised quality manager. Only 30 per cent (six firms) employed extra staff to implement and maintain the standard.

One key decision which firms have to make in the implementation process, is whether to employ a consultant. As one respondent put it:

> you either employ a consultant who advises and does a lot of the labour work for you which is obviously going to be quite expensive or you go for the other expense which is your time and effort, so either way its quite expensive to the company. It perhaps would be easier with a bigger company where you can say to one person, 'right you specifically can try and implement the system and you're overall responsible for it'. But for us and I'm sure for small companies generally, everyone within the company does a multi-function of jobs. So perhaps pulling one person away to try and concentrate on getting a quality system together can be quite painful to the small company.
>
> (Meditron)

Small firms use external sources of advice, especially consultants, to support the internal person responsible. Despite the criticism of consultants in the press, especially in relation to the Department of Trade and Industry subsidised Quality Consultancy Scheme (Rock, 1992), 11 firms used a consultant in the implementation process. The reasons for this were, as expected, related to the owner-manager or director (or whoever was responsible for implementing the system) either being unclear on how to proceed without guidance, or simply not having the time:

> I think BS 5750 is just too deep a subject, we couldn't do it without a consultant. It is far too deep and complex a subject, for someone like me or plant hire people to go through. It's knowing the buzz words, once you've got the buzz words it's easy to go through. It's all jargon, you know. They call jobs 'modular tasks' and crap like that.
>
> (Beeplant)

> Realistically, time is always a prohibitive factor in a business of our size, particularly last year when we were very busy and I think it would be ridiculous for us to take the time out to write the manual ourselves. We wouldn't have done it. These guys [consultants] they know the way through, what the trip up points are so to speak.
>
> (Paperco)

Research by Blackham (1992) suggested that there was no connection between using a consultant and achieving benefits from registration but this tells us little about the difficulties that owner-managers encounter trying to achieve registration without specialist help. Bailey (1992) suggests that some consultants use pre-written manuals regardless of the client firm's specialist requirements causing the system to fail subsequently as normal working practices gradually reassert themselves. In other words, the firm achieves registration on the basis of a system which is not integrated with the firm's actual operating procedures. However, the case study evidence suggests that firms are sensitive to this problem. For example, the commercial director of Paperco suggested:

> we said to the consultant, 'As far as we're concerned this is a smooth running business that is quite tightly controlled, therefore we can't see why [we can't] put the manual around what we've already got.' And he was in agreement with us, and therefore he didn't feel it necessary to make any major sort of changes, and he developed the manual from there.

Other respondents were not so impressed by consultants and used other methods:

> I've been around a long time, I've seen a lot in the world of manu-facture and consultants come and go, they charge exotic fees and in my experience they are to be avoided.
>
> (Electrico)

Instead, Electrico made use of a training scheme,

> we employed the services of a government scheme guy to do some shovelling for us at the front end, spade work. A training agency asked us if we could find use for a guy, and it is not uncommon for us to take advantage of those situations. In this situation, we had a very capable guy who spent six months with us. He was going to get into 5750, he wanted to do it and a lot of leg work was covered in those six months..
>
> (Electrico)

A further four firms, who had implemented or were registered BS 5750 at the time of the case studies, took external advice from local training and enterprise councils, trade associations and chambers of commerce. These bodies often run training courses which are frequently cheaper than using a consultant (Bethell, 1994). Another advantage of this approach is that the owner-manager or designated responsible person in the firm, is forced to have hands-on involvement in the implementa-tion process. This increases the chances that procedures will be directly geared to the firm's needs (Fox, 1991: 1). However, this is not necessar-ily cheaper at the end of the day than using a consultant since it is likely to be time consuming and may keep the owner-manager or employee away from their normal commitments.

For example, a number of case study owner-managers reported they had difficulties understanding and interpreting the paperwork accompanying the standard:

> it's almost as if they are trying to set some exam traps. It says it all, but you have to read it all! Then read it again and again. A lot of it is trite nonsense but it obviously is a global procedure. But it would be very hard for it to be definitive in terms of all our interests, so you have to try and interpret that document in terms of your application of it.
>
> (Electrico)

However, the severity of these reservations can hinge on whether the owner-manager is familiar with working with formal methods. This can depend on the sector, for example, since some types of economic activities are much more paper-based than others and/or inherently more bureaucratic. Where owners were more comfortable with paper-based administrative systems, they were less likely to find the implementation of BS 5750 problematic:

> I didn't find it too bad to understand because, bearing in mind, I've been through all the quality procedures, some of the other people within the company couldn't make head nor tail of some of the sections, so it wasn't clearly worded, but yes to me I understood it.
>
> (Meditron)

Agreeing with the fears expressed by Bannock (1991), many small firm owner-managers who had implemented, or registered, BS 5750 were concerned that by introducing the necessary formal procedures, they were making their firms more bureaucratic in undesirable ways. For instance, they worried it might make their firms less responsive to everyday problems or changes in market conditions (Table 15):

> the main reservation was that we were going to get bogged down in paperwork for paperwork sake. Initially, you got the impression they wanted forms for everything without getting any real work done.
>
> (Paperco)

> actually detailing what you do, writing the procedures. There is a resistance to being told and learning again.

Interviewer: Do you consider the standard to be bureaucratic?

Respondent: I can't see the value of this guy [the consultant] with Mo [the managing director] upstairs. I mean they must have had a whole week so far just sitting discussing things. It's a very hard business and I would rather have Mo down here chasing money, but that's what I do and I see the balance sheets and the figures every day. I don't need all that nonsense. We're running a business, [let's] get on with it, get on with real work.

> (Beeplant)

Thus, a number of case study respondents considered paperwork and bureaucracy to be constraints. Whether this issue is a lasting hurdle may be doubted. As owner-managers become more familiar with the implications of the standard, this constraint may become less important. In support, a number of owners reported that the problem had become less significant over time. Some also stated that their apprehensions about the bureaucratising effects of adopting BS 5750 were less than first feared, that is, it is possible to implement the standard flexibly and in ways which keep the negative effects to a minimum.

Another sectoral concern, discussed earlier, is the standard's relevance to service based organisations and this was voiced by some owner-managers. BS 5750 was originally developed with large manufacturing firms and, it is argued, the standard may be less relevant in services and especially for small service sector firms (Bannock, 1991; Jack, 1991; Pengelly in Rock, 1992; North *et al.*, 1993). The data from the telephone interviews reflected this since manufacturing firms were over twice as likely to operate formal methods as service firms (Table 7, Chapter 4). A respondent who spoke for Paperco, the paper merchants who had adopted BS 5750 reluctantly, said that the manufacturing origins of BS 5750 were very apparent and while there were few problems in implementing the standard, it was of questionable operational relevance and certainly of limited benefit to service firms:

> you can tell it was set up for manufacturing firms. In fact the assessor couldn't touch us, you could tell he was unsure.
>
> (Paperco)

Not all service firm owners in the study found the manufacturing origins of BS 5750 much of a problem. Console and Beeplant, for example – both service sector firms – implemented the standard mainly for procedural reasons. The owner-managers of both were enthusiastic about the benefits. It may be that owner-managers' opinions about the relevance or over-rigidity of the standard are determined less by sector or its origins and more by their motivations and attitudes.

Employee reactions

Another aspect owner-managers need to manage in implementing BS 5750 is the attitudes of staff. Change always tends to promote resistance among those affected, whether they are employees or the owner-managers themselves. (Some of the high proportion of negative attitudes to BS 5750 recorded in the telephone survey probably stemmed from the same familiar psychological root.) Organisational behaviour texts frequently discuss the problems of resistance to change and how to manage change effectively (see, for example, Huczynski and Buchanan, 1991: 532–545), but there appears to be no easy solution. Most of the documented resistance to change concerns workers in larger firms but small firm owners are likely to experience similar behaviour:

Most of them [the employees] couldn't give a toss, if you want the truth ... I had to be involved I had to make it quite clear [to the employees] we were going to do it, even though we might grumble and complain, we had to keep soldiering on and meet the targets that we set. They were not always appreciated especially when there were other more pressing targets like meeting customer orders and so they were not always appreciated ... We promoted it and we promoted their interests in it and a lot of them became quite proud when we'd done it. In fact, some of them are very proud that we've done it, others became proud, but the majority asked 'how much do I get out of it?

(Electrico)

On the other hand, small firms may have advantages over larger firms in that the small scale of the enterprise may make it possible for staff to be more easily involved in change processes such as adopting BS 5750: [7]

I think [all people in the firm were] pretty enthusiastic, we all realised that in order for the company to grow we needed to achieve that. Being a small company everybody knows what is happening within the business, perhaps a bigger organisation who has got many departments and borderlines between them might struggle, but certainly everybody here was keen on implementing, and we had no problems at all.

Interviewer: Did they participate in the implementation process?

Respondent: Yes, we got everybody involved, everybody knew what was happening, we asked for suggestions, we always ask for suggestions for improving different methods of production. We don't specifically have a suggestion box, but its something I'd recommend to any company. To actually listen to the people who do the jobs.

(Meditron)

It can be seen from the above that owner-managers' experiences of employees' reactions to introducing BS 5750 can vary. These differences may relate to a number of factors. First, owner-managers' attitudes to employees are an important determinant to employees' attitudes towards implementation, a message constantly reiterated in the quality management literature supported by findings from research (see, for example, Reeves and Hoy, 1993), whatever the size of firm. Second, the tightness of work schedules and urgency of production may have an effect. Small firms often operate at near full, or even over, capacity with little slack to cope with out of the ordinary events or demands. Implementing BS 5750 can push staff and capacity over the limit in a busy firm so that staff resistance easily occurs. Third, like some employers, employees may find it difficult to appreciate the competitive advantages, or even necessity, of implementing the standard. This may be because of poor communication between employers and employees or, again like some of their employers (including some of those implementing BS 5750) they have genuine, well informed doubts about the wisdom of adopting a formal, externally controlled, quality standard.

A key part of the implementation process is developing the quality manual, the 'bible' of the firm's operating procedures. Again, most case study firms were careful to ensure that the practices detailed in the manual were an accurate reflection of the way the business operated, but owners also wanted to minimise the changes (and disruptions) needed to implement the standard. For example, as one respondent suggested,

> we didn't have to do a lot, we had to dovetail a few things, but when we set up the manual we virtually set out what we did. We've only really made a few adjustments but they're very minor really.
>
> (Paperco)

Not all firms can make the changes as easily and smoothly, however. Other case study firms experienced teething problems before the manual could be finalised:

> [Originally] we wrote a quality manual which was an ideal picture at that time. But we were not doing it that way. There is no harm in changing standards . . . but now we've got to go back and change the manual so that we get a quality product at the end.
>
> (Console)

> It [the quality manual has] been adjusted a bit here and there . . . they never are right to start with. It doesn't matter how well you write it, someone will always offer a different interpretation. Even as it stands now its not correct because an assessor can come along and look at the terminology used in the 5750 standard, and he will say, 'just a minute, your manual doesn't quite comply'. But there's nothing seriously wrong with that because very often that's all they can find to gripe about. When the quality man comes along, it's no good leaving nothing to find because he will spend a whole day looking. He's got a form to fill in, and he's got to say he's found this, that and the other, otherwise there would be no point in being there.
>
> (Electrico)

REGISTRATION AND POST-REGISTRATION EXPERIENCES

After the quality manual is finalised, the firm may then apply to register for BS 5750. In research by Pera (1992) the most popular third party certification body was BSI Quality Assurance. At the time of the research only two case study firms had registered for BS 5750, with one just about to register. Two of these firms had used, or were intending to use, BSI. However, Paperco registered with Bureau Veritas Quality International (BVQI) after investigating BSI and a number of other options:

> About 9 months ago we wrote to about three of them [certification bodies], but we talked to the consultant and he said BSI is expensive. Also BVQI, this was their line of work, they're geared to the paper industry specifically . . . [but] . . . for two and a half days work they were definitely expensive but BSI are dearer.
>
> (Paperco)

Case study owner-managers' assessments of the services provided by the third party certification bodies were mixed. Paperco were pleased by their chosen certification body despite the costs:

> They hardly touched us, the consultant was delighted. They got us for eight [points] . . . and they were nothings.

It is interesting that the respondent's comments show more relief about registering quickly than opinions about the service itself. This may reflect a view that sees third party certification bodies as quasi-official – akin to organisations such as Customs and Excise – whose approval is a matter of formal recognition rather than of perceived benefits.

The MD of Electrico was less enthusiastic about third party certification bodies but also reinforced the interpretation that they are regarded as similar to government licensing bodies:

> Bloody expensive, but alright apart from that. They have joined the likes of the tax man, the VAT man and whoever else who comes in our factory and inspects. They've all got to go home with their brownie points.

After registering small firms have to decide how they will maintain the standard, that is, who in the firm will be responsible for the ensuring that procedures are adhered to and maintaining contacts with the certification body. In both Paperco and Electrico this was the responsibility of a senior manager:

> I do most of it. If I find anything wrong I'll go and talk to them [employees], but that rarely happens.
>
> (Paperco)

The technical director is responsible for quality and always has been. The responsibility for quality should not be with someone who is involved in manufacturing, but with someone else. I don't think that's just my way of thinking. I think its common practice, someone who can say independently 'yes its good enough' or 'no you've got to re-do it'. So he was heavily involved.

(Electrico)

Holliday (1994) cites an example of a firm which adopted a very relaxed application of its BS 5750 procedures in between assessor visits because the owner-manager was not convinced of any likely procedural benefits: the main motivation for registration had been gaining market advantages. But when the assessor's periodic visit was due, the firm 'rediscovered' its BS 5750 working practices and put on a show for the assessor. Assessors' visits are supposed to be unannounced but in practice this does not always happen. In the case of Electrico the assessor visited several firms in the locality, so typically owner-managers could receive warnings from either other firms or even the assessor about an imminent visit.

Costs of maintaining BS 5750 registration

In addition to the costs of registering there are also the costs of maintaining BS 5750 registration. As Table 18 shows these can vary greatly.

Table 18 Small firms operating formal methods: total costs of maintaining BS 5750

£	%
Up to 999	15.0
1,000–1,999	5.0
2,000–2,999	15.0
3,000–3,999	20.0
4,000+	5.0
DK/NA	40.0
$N = 20$	100.0

Base: All respondents currently implementing formal methods or already registered
Note: Respondents' estimates of costs are based on 1993 or earlier £ values

Despite most of the figures in the table being estimates (hence, the high proportion not offering any figure at all) it appears firms can pay from under £1,000 to over £4,000 to maintain and re-register for the standard. Size of firm, sector and the complexity of the procedures embodied in the firm's BS 5750 documentation can all cause such differences. So also can the certification body used. Some are more conscientiousness than others in monitoring firms apparently, and the fees charged may reflect this difference.

OUTCOMES – FORMAL METHODS OF QUALITY CONTROL IN PRACTICE

The two alleged main advantages of adopting BS 5750 offered in the literature, are procedural benefits and marketing advantages. Other commentators, however, have argued that implementing BS 5750 may have negative impacts. For example, increased bureaucratization arising from documenting internal procedures may lead to decreased internal efficiency through reducing the firm's flexibility and ability to respond to the market, as well as demotivating staff. Evidence from previous research supports both of these assessments. Adoption of a formal quality control standard approved and monitored by a third party can be both beneficial and non-beneficial depending on a variety of factors. Research by SBRT (1994a) notes that a significant number of respondents reported 'reduced scrap'[8] and increased sales. But over half of the respondents stated that adoption had led to additional administrative problems and 12 per cent reported lower productivity. However, on balance, previous research suggests positive outcomes are more common.

Post implementation effects on costs

The quality management literature devotes a great deal of attention to procedural benefits in the form of operational cost savings and improvements in efficiency that can result from implementing formal quality control methods (see, for example, Fox (1991) and Tickit (1992)). However, whether such results are experienced in small firms will largely depend upon their ability to digest the implementation, maintenance and registration costs as well as the attitudes and management skills of owner-managers.

Case study evidence demonstrates that while all the respondents were aware of the overheads associated with implementing and maintaining BS 5750 and their effects on efficiency, its impact on the business was subtle and could vary. Being registered involves extra costs which add to the normal costs of production. These can be neutralised, of course, if the benefits of registration are sufficiently high. Respondents, however, often recognised that adopting BS 5750 incurred a financial premium associated with the standard:

> we have locked in costs, there is no way we can do things on the cheap. You can't run an outfit which is BS 5750 approved that doesn't have certain levels of capability. You've got to have a managing director, you've got to have a quality controller, you've got to have clean toilets and other essentials, so therefore, there are certain overheads. You can't run it from your bedroom, back of the garage or anywhere cheap.
>
> (Electrico)

> I have heard it suggested that BS 5750 may improve costs from 5 to 15 per cent in large firms, and I said to the consultant 'don't be stupid, if we were losing 5 per cent through inefficiency we wouldn't be here!'
>
> (Paperco)

> it will push our prices up, but it's not going to be the biggest thing. If we had been registered in the recession, 5750 or not, we would have had to absorb those costs, because there was no scope at all for pushing prices up. BS 5750 will cost a certain amount of money a year but I believe that the money it will save when implemented far more outweighs the £500 for maintenance. £500 that's three nights out with a good client.
>
> (Beeplant)

The financial director of Paperco suggested that many of the estimates offered in the literature are out of line with sensible business practice, especially in competitive markets where overheads have to be kept to a minimum anyway. Conversely, the managing director of Beeplant suggested that once the costs of implementation and maintenance are digested, the potential for cost saving would be far greater. However, it must be noted that Paperco had registered, whereas, Beeplant was still implementing the standard at the time of the research.

There are costs, therefore, which can be attributed unambiguously to registering for BS 5750. If, as appears likely, these have a non-reducible lower limit, it is possible that the ability to digest the costs becomes less easy as firm size reduces. In other words, there may be economies of scale related to registration which do not help small firms. This is similar to the problem of compliance costs more generally for small firms. Meeting legislative requirements for a wide range of issues is more expensive for small firms than large firms (DTI, 1996b: 29). This strengthens the argument that many small firms will not be able to afford these costs, making BS 5750 not worthwhile on cost grounds alone.

Effects on efficiency

Even more difficult than estimating the costs of registering for BS 5750, is estimating the overall effects on the efficiency of the business. Respondents often found it difficult to define and assess 'efficiency' in ways which allow comparisons between firms or with some objective standard. Asked 'Has implementing BS 5750 affected efficiency?', half of the case study respondents considered it too soon to be able to offer a sensible answer (Table 19).

As Table 19 reports, two of the twenty case study firms reported *reductions* in efficiency, while four reported no change. Only five reported improvements so far. These assessments need to be treated with caution.[9] Not only is 'efficiency' a slippery concept but the impact of BS 5750 may well vary over time. Initially, there may be few real improvements or even a drop in efficiency as the new quality control system beds down. Later, efficiency effects might become manifest but equally there is no guarantee they will be permanent. The impact of the changes may decline over time as owner-managers and staff become less conscious of the need to adhere closely to documented procedures. One function of the periodic re-assessment of registered firms is to ensure that the firm is keeping to the standard, but this need may not occur if the re-assessment process is not sufficiently thorough (Holliday, 1994).

Table 19 Small firm owner-managers' assessments of the outcomes of formal methods in practice (%)

	Quality	Efficiency	Sales
Reduced	—	10.0	—
Stayed the same	35.0	20.0	45.0
Improved	20.0	25.0	5.0
Don't know	45.0	45.0	50.0
$N = 20$	100.0	100.0	100.0

Base: All respondents currently implementing formal methods or already registered

Effects on employees and training

One aspect of the impact of BS 5750 on efficiency is its affect on employees and training. Small firms are very much people-centred economic entities. Despite their market-based character and the influence of hierarchical structure reflecting the powers of ownership in market economies, small firms frequently operate as quasi-egalitarian structures with the owner-manager as *primus inter pares*, particularly in smaller small firms. How adoption of a formal quality control strategy affects employees, therefore, is important to assessing its overall impact.

The quality literature frequently discusses the relationship between BS 5750 and staff training (Fox, 1991; O'Rourke, 1993). It is argued that the standard makes training a requirement of registration and is likely to raise levels of training overall. Rather than relying on informal methods of training, common in small firms (Abbott, 1993; Curran *et al.*, 1996a), BS 5750 requires a more formal approach (Felstead and Green, 1993). Again, these issues are not simple. Whether BS 5750 actually raises overall training levels in small firms requires investigation as does the kinds of training that follow the decision to implement and register for the standard.

In line with some of the previous evidence (see, for example, Holliday, 1994), the present research found, that although 75 per cent (15 firms) did increase employee training as part of the registration process, training was mainly still informal. This should not, however, be seen necessarily as a failure of BS 5750 to live up to the promises made on its behalf. Abbott (1993) has argued that informal training may be as, if not more, suitable for small firms than formal training. Even so, a problem remains. There is a distinction between training required as part of the implementation process and training to add to employee skills (Jackson and Ashton, 1995). The evidence from the present case studies is that most of the training is directed towards understanding the procedures attached to the standard rather towards enhanced skills. The MD of the firm manufacturing medical components highlighted the importance of training linked to the procedures of the standard:

> if people weren't familiar with, for instance, the paper-work, it could be filled in wrong, and the wrong information would be forwarded on, and so people have to be trained in the respect of completing documentation. So training is very important . . . We found it easy to do internally because of mine and my partners' knowledge of what we were trying to do. It would have been difficult to convey that information to an external person, [for him/her] to then try and train people within the company. We thought that an external training

organisation would perhaps miss things more specific to our company. I think the smaller the company is, the more specialised needs they actually have. You can't clearly define borders like you can with perhaps a bigger company where a quality system is perhaps relevant to one department. And if that department is doing nothing but machine tooling, it is perhaps easier to bring in an outside person to train all the people in that department.

(Meditron)

Undoubtedly, adopting the standard can lead to training over and above that required to implement and operate the standard but it is not a necessary result of implementing the standard.

Apart from training, BS 5750 is likely to affect employees in other ways as the system attempts to ensure accountability of employees to the final product or service. Blackham (1992), supporting much of the literature promoting BS 5750, reported that employees in BS 5750 registered firms experienced increased motivation and participation. However, Holliday (1994) reported more pessimistic results, arguing that de-motivation is inevitable as employees are increasingly supervised and inspected to check their adherence to the system's rules. The case study evidence from the present research gives a fairly positive appraisal overall of employee responses to BS 5750:

With a couple of people it has made them aware of the intricacies of service and a little bit more careful. If you have a complaint, they're a bit more with it. It might have had to happen with the growth of the company anyway, but the people in the sales office have a better overall awareness.

(Paperco)

In some areas, in terms of our quality team – yes [motivation has improved], in terms of the general assembly work, I think it's questionable. I think they were fairly careful anyway. I don't think it would be fair to say they were shoddy before. It's part of the nature of our company to be careful and to have pride in our work. It sounds [a] paean, I know, but in a certain size company you can actually pull together . . . if someone produces something bad, it's very clear they've let everybody down.

(Meditron)

However, there are two caveats to be entered concerning this evidence. First, these are employ*ers'* assessments not those of their employees. Second, the fact that employers' positive opinions of the standards' effects on employees are favourable, may relate to greater managerial control over staff behaviour as a result of registration, rather than employees reacting in a favourable manner to the new system. It is difficult to be certain on these points since the research did not seek employees' opinions. However, research by Rees (1996) on employee reactions to quality initiatives in larger firms shows how complex these reactions can be, and that not all of them are positive. Third, as the above quotations imply, employee motivation and participation may be more related to the quality of the pre-existing work culture than the result of a new quality control system.

Market advantages and sales

A much promoted advantage of BS 5750 is improved marketing performance. BS 5750, it is argued, leads to increased sales and/or allows the firm to shift to more profitable areas of the market (DTI, 1992). Table 19 shows that while none of the case study firms reported sales being hurt by BS 5750, as with assessments of efficiency, a high proportion of respondents felt unable to offer a view or believed it had made no difference. Again, the caveat needs to be kept in mind that most firms were still at the implementation stage and it was probably too early to assess whether market advantages had resulted.

Case study respondents were conscious of the marketing implications of BS 5750 registration:

> it may all come down to that marketing banner, but there are a lot of things the small company has got to do to make itself credible, especially if you're working in the city.

> (Console)

Console decided to register for BS 5750 as a means of making itself look bigger to potential customers, to compete with larger, well established businesses. But BS 5750 may be used as a marketing strategy in a different sense. Meditron were considering registering for BS 5750 so they could enter a different market where registration was already a competitive necessity. This was despite the owners' claim that its current quality system was 'beyond BS 5750'. However, all the owners suggested the main advantage was not so much in winning new customers but rather in keeping old ones. This perhaps explains why only one respondent reported the firm had gained sales by registering for BS 5750 (Table 19). The rest either claimed sales had remained the same or were unsure.

THE RELATIONSHIP BETWEEN BS 5750 AND QUALITY IN PRACTICE

As a great deal of the literature critical of BS 5750 has made clear, the relationship between the standard and quality is not always direct or obvious. The proponents of the standard are of course keen to make the link. They argue that BS 5750 entails being systematic about the firm's operational procedures from answering the phone to dealing with customer queries to raising levels of quality consciousness among all staff from owner-manager to the lowliest operative. These are bound to improve the quality of products or services offered by the business, it is alleged. But as the earlier review of the literature indicated, commentators have argued that putting in place bureaucratised quality management strategies even though they are externally controlled and monitored, need not automatically result in genuine quality improvements.

Respondents in the study also had doubts when asked whether they thought implementing or registering BS 5750 had an effect on the quality of their products or services, a substantial proportion (45 per cent) were unsure since it was too soon after implementing BS 5750 to tell (Table 19). Not a single firm reported a reduction in product or service quality but 35 per cent (7 firms) reported that they could detect no change. Only 20 per cent (4 firms) reported an improvement. Putting the results in a slightly different form, of those respondents who felt able to offer an assessment, only a little over a third (36.4 per cent) were confident that implementing registration had led to an improvement in quality.

This certainly does not indicate that third party controlled formal quality strategies are a sure way to improve quality according to the small business owners who felt confident enough to offer an evaluation. From the data collected, the reasons for these somewhat equivocal judgements reflect the kinds of reasons discussed in the opening chapter on the difficulties of establishing clear quality definitions against which the firm's BS 5750 performance can be assessed. Where customer requirements can be explicitly formulated and documented, the insistence built into BS 5750 is that these requirements shall be consistently delivered. Here quality can be seen to be achieved where it is defined as consistently meeting customer requirements (or quality standards) measured against specific criteria. The problem is that clear definitions and criteria against which quality performance can be judged, are not easy, or are very difficult to establish for many kinds of economic activities.

Earlier it was noted that benefits could be unexpected but nevertheless observed and welcomed. Electrico's management used the standard as a means of tightening up on quality. The firm had bad experiences concerning the return of faulty goods and expected that BS 5750 would help. In the event, the respondent was pleasantly surprised:

> Our quality has improved, and I thought we were good before. We've had one customer complaint in the last year which we were able to deal with by traceability. In the past there would have been many more.
>
> (Electrico)

It should be noted, however, that this highly commendatory view had been achieved in a firm where circumstances favoured positive results from registration. Electrico not only operated in a sector where customer requirements can be explicitly formulated but had an owner-manager highly committed to making quality improvements through registration.

Other firms had other approaches even where the circumstances were favourable to positive results. Paperco as noted earlier operated in a market where customer requirements can be explicitly formulated, for example, paper weight, size, colour etc. However, the directors, it will be remembered, decided to implement BS 5750 as a result of external competitive pressures. They decided that the internal impact of the standard was to be minimized because quality standards were high enough already. However, one of the respondent directors reported that quality improvements had occurred though he doubted whether they were worth the investment required to register:

> There is only one area where I think there has been an improvement, complaints. We were a little bit lax, but I think it [BS 5750] has made us give it more attention. When I find out how much it [BS 5750] cost, I will then be able to tell you whether it was worth it for that one thing, and I think I know my answer.
>
> (Paperco)

In other words, what the findings show on whether quality improvements have resulted from BS 5750 registration is a mixed and uncertain picture. BS 5750 *can* be used to, and can actually, improve quality where customer requirements and the corresponding business processes can be explicitly detailed *and* where there is a positive commitment on the part of the owner-manager or whoever is responsible for quality strategies. But BS 5750, on its own, does not guarantee improved quality as the findings from this research show, echoing the results from previous research.

CONCLUSIONS

This chapter concentrated on the minority of firms who had decided to implement and register for BS 5750. Devoting a whole chapter to this minority was justified on two main grounds. First, there has been intense concentration on the alleged benefits of BS 5750 coupled with frequently expressed surprise at why so few small firms have adopted this quality management strategy. The firms that have adopted BS 5750, even though they are a minority, are a test bed for deciding whether the benefits are so clear cut or that the scepticism declared by so many small business owners on the likelihood of beneficial results, are warranted. Second, if, as is claimed, the proportion of small firms who will adopt third party controlled quality management strategies is liable to increase greatly in the future, then an examination of the practicalities of the processes revealed by pioneers among small business owners will be well worthwhile.

In reporting findings on the likelihood of adopting externally controlled and monitored quality standards, the findings showed that while second party approaches occurred, the great majority were third party controlled with BS 5750 the most popular. Second party approaches might occur where quality control had to be exceptionally high as in the production of medical equipment products. Here BS 5750 standards might be seen as not stringent enough. They might also be used where relations between the customer and supplier were close or in sectors with a long history of formal quality control standards predating the emergence of BS 5750, though the latter might replace these earlier approaches.

The analysis suggested that there could be economic advantages in adopting BS 5750. For all firms, quality management standardisation reduced the need for firms to devise their own standards. For customers, BS 5750 or a similar externally controlled quality standard, shifted some or even nearly all of the cost of quality control on to suppliers. For public sector bodies it is an easy way of demonstrating to government and the public that they are quality conscious and business-like in their dealings with the private sector, thus protecting taxpayers' interests.

Motivations for adopting BS 5750 or other externally controlled quality management approaches by the minority of owners implementing and/or registering were very mixed and not easy to untangle. The research design used allowed the main reason claimed for adoption to be distinguished from the total mentions of any specific reason. Thus, procedural advantages (benefits to the operational processes of the firm) were much the most frequently mentioned for adopting BS 5750 but only a minority reported that these were the *main* reason. Slightly easier to understand were those adopting BS 5750 due to external pressures from, for example, customers though even in these cases other motivations might play a part and vary between firms and over time. For instance, the recognition of procedural benefits might come late in the process, eliminating initial doubts about any such benefits on the part of the owner-manager.

Overall, there was a well demonstrated fluidity in the reasons (including the main reasons) for adopting BS 5750 over time as more experience was gained and assessments of the likely effects changed. These changes could occur during implementation or after actual registration. In some cases this could lead to the implementation process being halted or frozen. An owner-manager could abandon the whole strategy or, more likely on the findings from the study, halt it at a point where the results were seen as positive but further stages of implementation and registration were judged unlikely to produce further benefits.

The fluidity of the reasons might also be related to other factors. For instance, it was noticeable that some respondents exhibited a 'late convert' pattern, that is, they claimed to have discovered benefits of BS 5750 registration only after the event and in some cases after having had considerable doubts at the start. While this might be due to clear benefits emerging after registration, it might also be an example of cognitive dissonance. When people go through a protracted, difficult and expensive set of processes to achieve a goal which they may have had some doubts about initially, they are likely to exaggerate any benefits they perceive after completion in order to persuade themselves, and others, of the value of their decision. This is, of course, difficult to verify but the pattern of responses and the way the experiences are described by respondents lends itself to such an explanation.

The data on the experiences of implementation were analysed in terms of the owner-managers' objectives, constraints experienced and methods used. The fluidity and common lack of a clear main motivation for adopting BS 5750 were partly explained by the assortment of objectives reported by respondents as having driven, or as still driving, their strategy to register. As expected they ranged from the negative (registration undertaken very reluctantly as a result of external pressures) to a highly positive assessment of the likely benefits. In some cases, the respondent seemed ambivalent about exactly what the objectives were having embarked on implementation more in hope than clear expectation.

As might be expected, costs were the most mentioned constraints. Costs were not only financial. Respondents often found that time and opportunity costs arising from the need to devote managerial and staff resources to implementation, were even more important. The other kind of cost mentioned frequently was lost production. When owner-managers and employees have to take time away from their normal commitments to support implementation, output is usually lost. In some cases managerial and staff time losses were reduced by using a consultant. But consultants cost money also and owner-managers and staff still need to liaise with the consultant. Not all consultants were considered effective.

Other constraints were rather less obvious. One set of constraints related to the inherent problems of implementation and adoption of BS 5750 in particular sectors. In some sectors these problems can be severe. This is a particular problem in services or knowledge based businesses where the 'product' and the processes which lead to its production are not easy to separate, especially when the firm offers bespoke products or services. Defining lucid procedures which will clearly result in quality benefits and/or ways of measuring the effects of any procedures can sap the confidence and will of owner-managers in sectors which throw up these kinds of difficulties. Constraints can also halt the whole process. Where a firm was running at near full capacity in a busy dynamic market, owner-managers and employees could find implementation the straw which finally breaks the camel's back.

Employees have to be persuaded of the benefits of registration. Where this means extensive changes in procedures or where they doubt the reasons for the changes, problems can result. If owner-managers are not particularly committed to registration because they are adopting BS 5750 for negative reasons or are not effective communicators, these problems are likely to be even more pronounced. Yet unless employees can be persuaded of the positive aspects of registration, the chances of winning the potential benefits of BS 5750 will never be high and may decline over time. Enthusiasm, as proponents of BS 5750 stress, is required from every member of the firm if the new quality control strategy is to be effective.

Finally, findings on *the* key question were considered: did registering for BS 5750 actually enhance the quality of the firm's goods or services in the opinions of those who were in the process of registering or had registered? Here views were mixed again. Almost half of those asked the question reserved their judgements: they were unsure as yet. Most felt it was too early to give a firm opinion. Among those with an opinion, none stated that the effect had been negative, that is, BS 5750 had led to a decline in the quality of the firm's products or services. On the other hand, less than half reported increases in quality and the majority reported that they could detect no difference.

Success in implementing second or third party controlled quality strategies is clearly not easy as measured by the difficulties respondents encountered and the likely incidence of clear positive outcomes. In a sense, both sceptics and enthusiasts for BS 5750 and similar approaches to quality, are right. As the findings from the study show, second or third party controlled quality strategies are not easy options with guaranteed results in terms of clear quality gains. Success in implementing formal quality standards tends to depend greatly on the following. First, owner-managers' motivations for, and attitudes towards, implementation. For example, if owner-managers are keen to achieve procedural improvements, BS 5750 gives the scope to do so, especially in relation to issues such as quality and employee training. However, the exact scope for reducing operating costs and increasing efficiency is never certain. There is always a considerable element of doubt on the precise outcomes. It is also possible to register without considering these issues, concentrating instead on registering to satisfy marketing or externally imposed requirements. In these circumstances, failure to attend to procedural issues may lead to problems in realising the potential benefits.

Second, success depends on the difficulties of defining and implementing a formal control strategy in particular sectors. Some sector characteristics make adopting a formal quality control strategy difficult especially for small firms with limited resources. Finally, there is the point that small firms, especially the very smallest (those employing, say, under five people) which are the most common, may not be able to gain much from registration for logistical and cost reasons. Because they are small, there is little headroom for greater internal efficiencies based on formal methods or opportunities to make market gains sufficient to offset the costs of implementation and registration. In this sense, the caution shown by small business owners in relation to second and third party controlled quality management strategies in many sectors could well be fully justified.

7 A theorisation of quality management strategies in small firms

INTRODUCTION

The increasing importance of small firms in the UK economy is now widely accepted. Government, support agencies and academics seeking to understand the economy, need to be concerned about how small enterprises perform if effective policies are to improve the UK's place in the global economic league. Quality is equally accepted as key to improved economic performance. Over the last decade or so, the favoured solution to raising quality standards in Britain has been adopting BS 5750, and government boasts that almost half of the world's ISO 9000 certificates are held by British businesses (DTI, 1996b: 52). This, it is claimed, gives UK businesses a competitive advantage, ahead of businesses in other countries.

On the other hand, although small businesses have contributed very positively to the economy, the message from government, support agencies and many academics, is that they could do a lot better. Whatever the undoubted entrepreneurial flair of Britain's small business owner-managers, their managerial skills are often seen as poor. Lack of time, suitable support and training and an awareness of what better managerial skills could do for their businesses are, it is alleged, holding Britain's small businesses back from realising their full potential. If their importance continues to grow, this weakness could become more serious for Britain's economy in the next century.

The weakness of small business owner-managerial skills is sometimes seen as illustrated by how they approach the management of quality. They appear, it has been argued, to be very reluctant to be professional, and assume that there is little more they need to do: quality and quality standards are not apparently seen as serious problems by the majority of small business owners. These kinds of attitudes, it is sometimes argued, are illustrated by their seeming refusal to adopt BS 5750, the professional approach to quality management used by business owners who are serious about the performance of their enterprises. Even after mammoth information campaigns pushing the advantages of formal quality standards and plenty of cheap consultancy and resource support, the adoption of BS 5750 by small business owners has been lethargic at best.

In this book views of the above kind have been challenged. First, the basis of BS 5750 has been examined, emphasising that it is *not* a quality standard in the sense of guaranteeing the quality of any good or service produced by a business with BS 5750 certification, but rather an indicator that the operational procedures of the business conform to some set of externally validated precepts. Second, the notion of 'quality' itself has been subjected to close scrutiny exposing the inherent vagueness of common applications and suggesting an alternative, more economically literate approach suited to a market economy which also highlights the dynamic, shifting character of 'quality' in different economic activities over time. Third, based on a careful empirical examination of small business owners' approaches to quality management, a theorisation has been constructed which not only explains the low take-up of BS 5750 among small business owners but how their quality management strategies are, in fact, far from simple, unsophisticated or ineffective.

Small enterprise quality management strategies in this theorisation are contingent upon a wide range of factors – size of firm, sector, its history, the character of the product or service, internal and external organisational relations, the labour market profiles of employees and owner-manager's managerial styles and strategies – resulting in many different approaches to managing quality. No single strategy is superior to all others: different strategies are effective in different contexts. Generic strategies, on the other hand, especially formalised, across the board approaches such as BS 5750, may be effective under some conditions but the evidence indicates that such conditions are likely in only a limited number of small business contexts.

The theorisation of small business quality management strategies arising out of the study upon which this book is based, has considerable implications for policies to promote higher standards of quality management and quality outputs in the UK economy. At its simplest, the message to government and others promoting quality standards is that generic solutions, imposed from above, which endeavour to offer quality strategies for all businesses, simply fail to take account of the complexities of small businesses and their situations. Even the increasing examples of BS 5750 which take account of sector and/or size of firm, cannot escape the basic weakness which arises from the generic foundation of the standard.

NOTIONS OF QUALITY AND THEIR APPLICATION

Chapter 2 argued that management writings and policy pronounce-ments often treated quality as a 'taken for granted notion', that is, its meaning was typically assumed rather than defined. This was coupled with the assumption that quality was universally understood and that there was agreement on its meaning. The fundamental flaws of these assumptions were easily demonstrated. 'Quality' was shown to be a complex, unstable and highly problematic notion about which produ-cers and consumers could easily be uncertain and confused. The impli-cation of much of the conventional discussion of 'quality' is of some kind of absolutist standard – 'the best there is', 'customers demand and deserve the best' etc. – but analysis of the notion showed that 'quality' is always relative, always a function of price, taste, technology, informa-tion and negotiation in the market.

The lack of clear thinking is just as evident in the specialist literature aimed at raising management and business performance. For example, as Chapter 2 showed, there is much talk of the modern business needing to be 'customer driven', giving customer definitions of quality primacy in strategically developing the business. Only in this way, it is argued, can the business hope to prosper. But, again, it is easy to expose the economic illiteracy of propositions of this kind. Of course, customers often have clearly defined wants and notions of quality but equally often their ideas are poorly informed and vague while businesses seek to shape customers' ideas in order to maximise profit. Businesses are not passive suppliers of what customers want – even where the latter are clear about what they want – they are also powerful players in the market whose goals may conflict with those of others, including those of customers, and override them.

The chapter then outlined an alternative approach based on the idea that 'quality' in any context (economic or non-economic) is relative and socially constructed through a process of implicit or explicit negoti-ation. 'Quality' in this formulation is a joint construction by producers (to include owner-managers, employees and others whose inputs are used) and others external to the enterprise (to include customers, actual and potential, competitors, commentators such as consumer pressure groups, the media and the state through its regulatory activities). While all involved may want and work hard for positive outcomes (the busi-ness wants to survive and prosper: customers want their demands met) there is no guarantee this will happen. Negotiation is easily subverted by poor or false communication, asymetricalities of information, the abilities of the parties to process information, differing notions of what is acceptable at a given price and the intervention of third parties such as the state.

In practice, quality is often negotiated successfully: suppliers and customers engage in market exchanges approximating to quality standards they find acceptable. However, neither conditions nor the relevant actors' views are stable. Tastes change, new technology affects product or service content, existing suppliers may change the conditions under which they are willing to supply the good or service, new suppliers may enter the market, consumers may receive more or new information and the state may change relevant regulations. These stimulate renegotiation between the parties and new notions of quality relevant to the good or service will emerge. Quality, in other words, is dynamic, changing and unstable. Fixed standards of quality, however well intentioned or helpful to suppliers or consumers, are always under actual or potential threat.

The alternative approach to 'quality' outlined above provided the conceptual foundation to the analysis of the data reported in the book. The analysis showed the explanative value of quality seen in this way. Not only did it provide a clearer notion of what 'quality' should be taken to refer to but it provided a much better fit with the data than any absolutist approach. For example, it furnished a basis for explaining why small business owners have been so reluctant to adopt BS 5750 in so many sectors. It also helped in developing distinctive, sector-based interpretations of the quality management strategies operated by owner-managers in the seven sectors covered by the research.

QUALITY MANAGEMENT STRATEGIES IN SMALL FIRMS

The quality management strategies of small business owners were divided into two main types, each with a further subdivision:

1 *Informal methods of quality control*
   (a) *Simple informal methods.* Non-bureaucratised, rule of thumb approaches implemented on a day-to-day basis.
   (b) *Complex informal methods.* Structured, bureaucratic or semi-bureaucratic approaches using paper-based systems set up internally and controlled entirely by owner-managers themselves.

2 *Formal methods of quality control*
   Predetermined, defined procedures for controlling quality assessed
   and monitored by bodies external to the enterprise. They may be
   either:
   (a) *Second party assessed.* Where the definitions and assessment
        are controlled by customers/suppliers; or,
   (b) *Third party assessed.* Where the definitions and assessments
        are controlled by a body whose main or sole function is quality
        assurance such as the British Standards Institute.

What is important about this typology is that it recognises a fundamental element in the analysis of quality management. Put simply,
this is the point that quality standards existed long before present
debates or the introduction of formal standards such as BS 5750.
This might seem obvious, even banal, but much of the debate on
quality management implies that firms paid little attention to quality
until recent debates started and/or quality standards cannot be
implemented without some kind of formalisation such as BS 5750.
The typology opens the way to nullifying both points. The findings
reported in the preceding chapters show, in fact, that quality
management is a major concern of small business owners, that
informal strategies can be highly effective, indeed that they can be
as, or even more effective, than formal standard-based strategies
such as those being pushed hard by government and proponents of BS
5750.

The data from the research demonstrated that virtually all small
business owners are aware of BS 5750. Ignorance therefore is not the
reason why they are so reluctant to adopt this approach to quality
management. Under 4 per cent of firms in the study were fully BS
5750 certified. However, a further 9 per cent were in the process
towards certification. While this might indicate a future increase in
small firms adopting externally dictated formal standards, this conclusion might be premature. As the data shows, some firms start the
process of acquiring certification but never complete it. They either
decide that it is not for them after all or stop where elements of BS
5750 have been incorporated into their quality management strategies
but conclude no advantage would be gained by proceeding to full
registration.

BS 5750 is always in competition with existing quality management
strategies in small firms. Owner-managers assess the advantages of a
formal standard against their existing strategies. Two main sets of
advantages for BS 5750 are posited:

1   *Procedural advantages.* These are possible gains in operational efficiency which follow the adoption of BS 5750 which proponents are keen to emphasise. They argue that a systematic, manual-based, externally assessed and monitored approach to quality management will always be superior to informal approaches.

2   *Marketing advantages.* Becoming BS 5750 certified, it is argued, enables a business to gain market advantage because customers will find its products or services more attractive and/or because it helps a business to move into more profitable markets.

In addition, for some firms the 'advantage' of implementation can be staying in business or maintaining current market share. This happens, for example, where customers insist that suppliers are BS 5750 registered if they are to continue to do business with them.

Against registration, are the costs of becoming certified and maintaining recognition. These vary greatly but for many small firms, particularly smaller small firms, the costs can be significant. Indeed, the costs may be substantial enough for the owner-manager to recognise that the firm will gain no advantages. For instance, some owner-managers in the study believed their businesses were already so leanly managed that procedural advantage gains would be few or even negative. Adoption could also slow the firm's responsiveness to the market, lowering operational efficiency. For many this assessment was coupled with an appraisal that no market advantages could result from certification big enough to offset the additional costs.

Of course, owner-managers could be wrong in the above assessments and be forfeiting the advantages from certification. But the detailed analysis of owner-managers' reasons for refusal to seek formal recognition, showed their thinking to be based on a careful consideration of the pros and cons which, to an outsider, appear rational and convincing. Market advantages from BS 5750 provided the easiest means by which to objectively evaluate the advantages and disadvantages of the standard. For instance, owner-managers in several sectors, where customers were mainly or solely private consumers or other small businesses were not registered for BS 5750, argued that certification would achieve little market advantage because their customers would not be impressed. It is difficult to argue against this verdict. With more data, it would be possible to estimate the correctness of claims about procedural advantages more fully one way or the other. However, what is clear from the data is that BS 5750 is no *guarantee* of quality improvements and/or internal efficiency etc., and therefore, its position as British *Standard* for quality management systems is undermined and its credibility is questionable.

What was especially striking about the quality management strategies employed by the owner-managers in the study was how they varied. By definition most were informal or informal combined with some complex informal elements though the variation remained considerable. A key aim of the study became developing an explanation for this variability. One reason suggested by previous writers was that the level of formalisation of quality management strategies was positively related to size of enterprise. The data from the present study did indeed find such a relationship. Among firms with 20 or more employees over a third were either third party registered, or in the process of possibly acquiring registration. Among the smallest firms, those with one to four employees, the comparable proportion was under 3 per cent.

However, size-based explanations of differences between firms have to be treated with caution. Size, by itself, says little about *why* owner-managers opt for one kind of quality management strategy rather than another. The obvious explanation linked with size is that as firms become bigger, owner-managers find it more difficult to personally oversee all the operations of the business and maintain high and consistent quality standards. To overcome this problem they resort to some kind of bureaucratic mechanism to fill the gap. A paper-based, quality audit trail, for instance, can require a signature at the completion of each stage of production and delivery to the final consumer. Failures to reach acceptable standards can then be traced to the point where they occurred. Adopting BS 5750 is simply procedures of this kind taken to further levels of formalisation.

While business size is undoubtedly linked with the adoption of formalised quality strategies, it is far from a complete explanation. Even among the largest firms in the study, those with 20 or more employees, well over half are not even in preparation for third party certification. In other words, factors other than those related to size are likely to play a part in influencing owner-manager quality management strategies. Any explanation of small firm quality management strategies therefore needs to incorporate these non-size based factors. In this study, it was shown that in some sectors or under some conditions such factors were actually more important than size.

THE INFLUENCE OF SECTOR

In Chapter 4 the analysis showed how sector was related to the kinds of quality strategies typically employed in small firms. For each of the seven sectors, the analysis incorporated the history, culture, employee characteristics and customer attitudes in the sector. The likelihood of adopting third party certificated formal quality strategies was shown to be related closely to these sector-based influences. The analysis showed how the influences were patterned and functioned in each of the sectors:

Electronics

Electronics emerged as the sector where small firms were most likely to opt for third party certificated strategies such as BS 5750. One reason for this was that manufacturing is associated with products amenable to quantitative quality standards. But perhaps even more important was the historical links between this sector and the defence industry. The Ministry of Defence helped originate the first externally imposed formal quality standards which were a model for the later BS 5750 standard. Another reason is the sector's high level of subcontracting producing a need for controlling quality *across* firms jointly involved in manufacturing final products. Historically, these factors have combined to help create a culture of formal quality, that is, new technology is translated into production processes designed with built-in formal quality strategies, perpetuating the formalisation of quality management.

Computer services

Another high tech sector – often linked with the electronics sector above – had the second highest proportion of firms operating formal quality control strategies. Yet the level operating second or third party quality management strategies was significantly lower than in electronics. One reason suggested for the difference was that the sector had a much larger non-manufacturing, non-routine component made up of firms involved in software design, application and customer services. For these activities establishing formal quality standards is much more difficult and, just as important, many customers are unlikely to demand such standards or regard them as important. Their customers, for example, are frequently other small businesses not BS 5750 registered or not knowledgeable enough to be able to interpret technical standards.

Employment agencies

In contrast with the above sectors, the level of formalisation of quality management strategies is low among employment agencies but the evidence also showed that over half of the firms were considering or preparing to adopt BS 5750. The agencies provide business services so there is no easy quantitative basis for formalisation and their main markets are not among manufacturing firms but in the expanding service and professional sectors. What appears to be pushing firms towards BS 5750 in this sector is market advantage. In the absence of any widely recognised, sector-based quality standards, agencies use BS 5750 certification to convince customers that they are professional in their approach. There are indications that other sectors with similar characteristics may be opting for a similar strategy.

Printing

What stood out in the findings from this sector was the sheer lack of resort to BS 5750. None of the general printing firms had adopted the standard and only one was even considering doing so. The analysis of this lack was linked to historically developed sector-based quality strategies. The traditional powerful role of trade unions in maintaining craft-based quality standards for both employees *and* employers together with the importance of public technical education provision and suppliers' support were all argued to be important. All functioned to generate a comprehensive set of sector-based quality standards widely accepted even by professional customers. Quality standards, in short, have become embedded in the processes of production and the sector's subculture over a long period of time. These rendered more recent quality strategies such as BS 5750 largely redundant for this sector. The exceptions to the above were the two paper suppliers in the sample. One had opted for BS 5750 and the other was considering doing so. Here the incentive was competitive pressures from other larger paper suppliers who had adopted the standard, a pressure not faced by the general printers.

Advertising, marketing and design businesses

This sector has close links with the above sector and is equally unlikely to have adopted BS 5750. On the other hand, firms in this sector were much more likely to have adopted complex informal methods of quality management. The interpretation of this pattern emphasised the difficulties of formalising quality standards for a sector where originality and creativity are so highly stressed. Customers are not seeking standard solutions but original solutions tailored to their needs. On the other hand, operationally there are considerable in-house difficulties in managing the 'production' of such outputs. Except in the smallest firms, owner-managers will have difficulties in maintaining tight control over every project as it progresses from original specification to final presentation to the client. Yet failure could hurt the business badly because individual projects are often of high value, contributing significantly to the firm's turnover. Each project is different, each requires creative inputs and a necessary delegating of responsibility to those involved in the project. It was suggested that informal complex controls might be attractive to owner-managers because they could help reduce in-house uncertainties by formalising the management of the more routine components of the production process.

Small vehicle repairers

All but one of the small garages operated informal methods of quality control and only a minority were considering BS 5750. This was surprising at first sight. This is a sector where quality standards are important if only for safety reasons. Motor vehicles are technologically sophisticated and maintaining them requires skill even allowing for recent developments in IT-based test equipment. They are also expensive and owners are often very emotionally attached to their cars as well as very reliant on them for day-to-day transport. The lack of the use of formal quality standards in the sector was attributed mainly to customers' lack of insistence. However important their vehicles are to them emotionally and practically, consumers are usually poorly informed and/or technologically illiterate despite all the magazines, newspaper attention etc. devoted to the motor vehicle. True, consumers are often critical of the service they receive yet clearly they do not see BS 5750 as a solution. While this lack of pressure continues there is little or no market advantage for small vehicle repairers to formalise quality management.

Plant and equipment hire

Owner managers in this sector again showed little enthusiasm for second or third party quality control strategies but did have a slightly higher than average propensity to use complex informal methods. This pattern was seen, first, as a result of the very mixed set of products handled by firms in the sector. Even so, much of the equipment for hire has manufacturers' specifications which govern its quality performance. Hire customers/users are mainly familiar with these specifications so there would be little point in small equipment hire firms adopting further standards. Where skills are required for the operation of the equipment, customers/users are responsible for these unless the plant and equipment firm supplies an operative. On the other hand, keeping track of equipment can be much more difficult since it is often hired for varying periods away from the firm. There is also the relevance of health and safety factors. Construction and other equipment is complex, sometimes dangerous for operators and, as a result, all involved need to be aware of the risks and the regulations which seek to minimise the hazards. The regulations, for example, often specify statutory periodic inspection and maintenance standards and, in a sense, are substitutes for product quality standards. Complex informal quality strategies could help solve the problems of keeping track of equipment, operator efficiency and meeting health and safety standards. This mix of influences, therefore, might help to explain both the lack of second or third party strategies but some favouring of complex informal strategies by owner-managers.

These sector-based influences on the kinds of quality management strategies employed by small business owner-managers are argued at the very least to be as important as, or even sometimes override, size influences. They help explain both the reluctance of small business owners to adopt BS 5750 as well as the distinctive variations in quality management strategies found in the study.

LOGICS OF QUALITY MANAGEMENT

The above section concentrated on *between sector* explanations of the variation in quality management strategies found among the owner-managers. But as the data also clearly showed there were also plenty of intra-sector variations. Some of these can be attributed to prosaic factors such as new firms or firms which have recently moved into a sector who have yet to embrace non-informal quality management strategies but who will later develop complex informal or adopt externally dictated quality control strategies. Others, although in a particular SIC category, are in niche markets or are so highly specialised that adopting a second or third party controlled quality management strategy simply would not occur to the owner-manager as sensible.

However, the findings from the face-to-face interviews which formed the basis of the case studies, also showed how even owners of firms in the same sector with similar markets could develop differing 'logics' of quality management. Owner-managers, as stressed earlier, were very conscious of the need to ensure the quality of the products or services produced by their businesses. But quality management issues can be solved in a variety of ways. There should be no *a priori* assumption that there is a single best way, even for firms in the same sector. Although owner-managers worked out their own solutions to managing quality, one of the key findings was that very often they arrived at approaches which had many of the elements of the quality management strategies formalised in the management literature. For instance, some used phrases such as 'getting it right first time' or 'we always put customers first' but this was not out of any familiarity with the quality literature but simply the result of their own approach to running their businesses.

In effect, the owner-managers were demystifying quality management as formalised in so many quality management texts. Based on their rational assessment of the best way to run their businesses and maintain sound customer relations, they devised flexible, effective strategies with low levels of bureaucratization suited to the needs of the firm. The results were often quality management strategies without any unnecessary bureaucratic elaboration, a 'lean production' approach to quality management appropriate to the specific circumstances of the firm. Frequently, this resulted in quality management practices economically and organisationally superior to any formalised approach such as BS 5750 for the particular firm.

Of course, not every firm with informal and/or complex informal quality management strategies should be seen as having an optimum strategy. Quality management is only one of the many responsibilities of small firm owner-managers and not all can get it absolutely right. But then as was demonstrated earlier, not every firm, small or large, with BS 5750 can be assumed to have an optimum quality management strategy either. Quality management, given all the internal and external factors that can influence its results, is too complex for simple recipes or for every responsible manager to arrive at the optimum solution. BS 5750, for instance, is now accepted as no magic way to solve quality management problems.

Proactive and reactive strategies

The findings from the research and especially the case study data showed, as expected, that owner-managers used a mix of proactive and reactive strategies to manage quality. Proactive strategies seek to anticipate problems while reactive strategies assess at the point of consumption or after delivery to the customer. Proactive strategies were much the most important of the two but both were employed. Owner-managers sought to prevent quality failures from occurring and the strategies used were often very rigorous. In texts on quality control, product sampling is often mentioned as a basis for quality. Large firms, whom the texts are aimed at frequently, have to rely on sampling to control quality for cost reasons. But in small firms inspection is often total: every product or service delivery is inspected at every stage. Again, in their approaches, small firm owners were implicitly emphasising the wisdom of the quality management literature and its concern with 'zero defects' and 'getting it right first time' but again arrived at through personally devised management strategies not textbooks.

What stood out in the analysis of quality management in the firms was how reliant it was on people. Time and time again, owner-managers mentioned how important staff were in their quality management strategies. Skilled, committed employees are an obvious basis for high quality yet how a firm acquires and retains such employees, and how they are managed, are more problematic. Recruiting and retaining the 'right' people is a frequently mentioned management headache by small business owners. In some sectors, firms typically rely on unskilled or semi-skilled workers, sometimes out of choice and sometimes because of economic constraints. Low cost entry, highly competitive sectors are often low profit sectors and therefore managers need to be very cost conscious. This includes labour costs and owner-managers may find building a highly skilled, committed labour force far from easy. Quality management strategies will need to take this into account.

Even where firms find it easier to recruit skilled and committed employees this does not automatically produce high quality products and services. Much will depend on owner-managers' attitudes to staff. A distinction can be drawn between high trust and low trust labour management strategies. Some owner-managers are committed to high trust employment relations giving employees a lot of freedom to make decisions and decide how best to do their jobs including taking responsibility for quality. Other employers in similar sectors and kinds of economic activities maintain a low trust work environment, offering employees little leeway in how they do their jobs and impose a centralised, often bureaucratically based quality control. So while sector and external constraints may greatly influence quality control strategies, owner-managers also have choices in how they use people in their quality management strategies. Whatever the choices made, people are central to the resulting quality management strategies.

Business size and quality management strategies

There were differences between how small and large firms might be expected to maintain quality. Quality management texts, for instance, often stress the importance of formal training in both raising skill levels and instilling a commitment to quality in their labour forces. The small firm owner-managers in this study were much less enthusiastic about formal training. One reason for this is the problems small firms have in meeting the costs of training and coping with the problems of people being away from the job. Instead, small firm employers concentrated much more on informal training but this was often an important element in their quality control strategies. Moreover, the indications were that it was also effective. It could be tailored to the needs of the job and the characteristics of the employee to maximise its usefulness to the firm and quality control.

Another difference between large and small firm practices suggested by the findings from the study is in the use of customer feedback. Quality management texts frequently suggest that businesses ought to give resources and attention to assessing customer reactions to their products and services using market research and other formal strategies. The small firm employers in the study rarely used such techniques. They relied much more on informal feedback often collected rather unsystematically but nevertheless part of the close relations maintained with customers. Aside from the costs of formal customer research, the main reason for the lower level of reactive quality strategies among small firm owner-managers was their heavy emphasis on monitoring quality *before* the product or service reached the customer. Their frequent near-total control of quality at this earlier stage reduced the need to devote resources and time to customer follow-up.

Summarising, small firm owner-managers construct logics of quality management suited to the scale, resources and needs of their businesses. In some ways they echo management text approaches to quality management, often achieving higher standards than would be possible in larger enterprises. In other ways they depart from some of the precepts of quality management and particularly from the much advocated systematic bureaucratisation of quality control which is crystallised in formalisations such as BS 5750. What is clear from the analysis, however, is that reliance on informal strategies is far from inferior as a method of quality control in small firms even if they might be much less effective in large enterprises.

QUALITY MANAGEMENT OUTCOMES

The majority of the owner-managers in the study reported that maintaining quality was not a great problem for their business. Among those who operated informal quality control strategies only, just over two out of three reported that maintaining quality was not a problem. Among the smaller firms (1–4 employees) three quarters offered this response.

As size increased firms were more likely to use complex informal methods and, less frequently, second or third party assessed quality controls. Owner-managers were also more likely to share responsibilities for quality with other managers and staff in larger firms. These shifts towards formalisation and delegation, however, were not entirely successful. Respondents in firms employing 20 plus employees were over twice as likely to report that maintaining quality was a problem than those with firms employing 1–4 employees.

An interpretation of the above is that, in practice, quality management strategies are always to some extent a compromise. Notions of zero fault quality strategies operated by totally committed owner-managers and employees are idealisations which do not happen in real firms. Owner-managers are committed seriously to quality as the findings from the study demonstrated and they seek to ensure staff help realise this commitment. But the everyday reality of running a business in a market economy means that many other kinds of requirements intrude. Production is always at a price, customers are sometimes vague, inconsistent or insist on difficult-to-deliver conditions, employees have varying skills, experience and commitment levels, owner-managers have many demands on their time besides maintaining quality and, where the firm is larger, quality management will frequently have to be shared with others or bureaucratised to some extent. In some firms, quality management will be easier to achieve than in others because some of the above conditions are more favourable but a quality management strategy always has to cope with adverse conditions.

Advocates of formalised quality management strategies such as BS 5750 sometimes counter the above by arguing that the solution is not to adopt half measures such as complex informal strategies but to positively embrace a full third party based approach. The owner-managers in the study and, as other research has shown again and again, are resistant to this option. Their resistance does not appear to be simple prejudice against such systems. The case study respondents offered reasoned assessments for their reluctance. A main reason was that fully formalised third party quality control strategies such as BS 5750 were over-engineered for the purpose. Externally monitored paper-based quality controls, for instance, have start-up and running costs and add rigidities to operating procedures as well as consuming management and employee time. In the views of many owner-managers the extra financial and time costs would not lead to increases in business performance and quality sufficient to offset them. They therefore rejected the BS 5750 approach on rational grounds.

Complex informal approaches might be selected as compromise solutions to the problems of maintaining or raising quality under certain conditions. They add to costs, introduce additional procedures in the production of goods or services which may slow the whole process down, take up management and staff time and run a risk of slowing response to the market. But the costs of introducing complex informal strategies will, in the view of owner-managers who adopt this approach, be lower than a third party controlled quality management system and offer a superior solution to quality management problems given the circumstances faced by their particular firms. Evidently such circumstances are experienced by small firms in a wide range of sectors. They may presage later adoption of a third party controlled system if owner-managers find their current quality management strategies do not meet their needs but, as the data indicated, relatively few owners seem to find this necessary.

However, owner-managers' attitudes to BS 5750 were not necessarily cast in concrete. Although, contrary to media accounts, few had experienced customer pressures towards adopting BS 5750, some respondents stated that if customer pressures increased they would be prepared to register. Others mentioned that if a high proportion of firms in their sector became BS 5750 certified, they would have to consider doing the same. Some saw this as a very real likelihood in the future because of what they saw as an inexorable trend towards third party based quality control in the UK. A small proportion were actively working towards registration at the time of interview. The key criterion in all these decisions was what the owner-manager considered best for their business.

Those firms which had adopted BS 5750 were generally positive about the change. The main advantages claimed were external benefits – marketing advantages of one kind or another – but procedural benefits were also mentioned. Often the latter were unintended benefits of registration: registration was originally externally prompted but procedural benefits followed and were welcomed as a bonus. Although costs were seen as significant (both the initial and the after-registration costs of maintaining the standard) those who had registered considered that, on balance, the firm had gained. There were some indications that these assessments contained elements of *ex post facto* rationalisation. Adopting BS 5750 as a quality management strategy is often seen as expensive, time-consuming, a strain on management resources and difficult to fully implement and maintain: admitting it was a poor decision, on the other hand, might reflect badly on the decision-making skills and reputation of the owner-manager.

CONCLUSIONS

Pulling together the findings and interpretations presented above and in the earlier chapters, it is clear that quality management strategies in small firms are complex and show a high level of variability. The enormous attention given to BS 5750 in government policies to help small firms as well as in the management literature generally, distorts proper consideration of these issues. Quality management is a permanent aspect of managing any enterprise, small or large, and was not invented by recent debates on the importance of quality in economic activities. Nor are small firms simply large firms scaled down. Quality management strategies for large firms, now the subject of a voluminous literature, are solutions to large enterprise quality control problems. Small firms have different problems and solve them with distinctive strategies, mainly what have been termed in the theorisation presented here as 'simple informal quality management strategies' but often with additional elements of what were termed 'complex informal' strategies.

The reasons for the differences in approach to quality management in small and large firms are related to their differing organisational characteristics, management approaches and market situations. The quality management strategies of small firm owners also vary greatly depending on the size, sector, employee characteristics and managerial outlooks of owner-managers. Just because the quality approaches typically employed by small business owners are mainly informal does *not* mean they are necessarily inferior or less effective than the bureaucratised approaches more commonly found in larger businesses and organisations. On the contrary, small business owners devise quality management strategies based on experience, experiment and rational assessments of what they believe is most likely to be effective for their businesses and their economic livelihoods. Usually, the result will be some form of informal strategy while bureaucratised approaches whether internally or externally controlled, will be rarer.

The widely reported rejection of BS 5750 by UK small business owners is not based on a lack of concern for quality or prejudice or ignorance but on an assessment of the likely pluses and minuses of adopting an externally controlled and monitored quality management system. For most small business owners the minuses outweigh the pluses when BS 5750 is compared with the quality management strategies already in place in their firms. This is not to say that small firm owner-managers are infallible on what are the most effective quality management strategies for their enterprises. But on the basis of the research presented in this book, the indications are that small business owners are largely correct in their assessments. They know their businesses, they assess the strategies likely to help them stay in business and perform well, and act accordingly. Remember, the penalties for managerial mistakes by small business owners are severe. Business failure rates are high among small firms. The consequences of failure can be harsh. They can include not only the capital invested but frequently the family home and the owner's self-esteem and the consequences of letting others, particularly employees and family, down. Quality management like other key managerial functions such as financial management, marketing and personnel management which have the potential to make or break a small business, is unlikely therefore to be treated lightly.

POLICY IMPLICATIONS

The results of the research reported in this book have important policy implications. The thrust of government policy attempting to help small businesses achieve high quality standards has been to concentrate on promoting BS 5750. The theorisation and supporting evidence presented in the book suggest that this is a mistaken policy. These mistakes largely explain why the policy has been so ineffectual in the past and why it is unlikely to be any more effective in the future. Flaws in the policy approaches to helping small firms achieve higher quality standards in their operations parallel those in several other initiatives designed to support small scale enterprise in Britain.

The first ground on which government policy promoting higher quality management in small firms fails is that it seeks to impose a solution based on large firm approaches to quality management. Encouraging small firms to adopt BS 5750 assumes that the kinds of solutions evolved to solve quality management problems in large organisations should be adopted as 'good practice' by small firms. As the opening chapters pointed out, the literature upon which teaching in the business schools on quality management developed arose historically to cope with the problems of larger enterprises. The resulting bureaucratised approaches such as BS 5750 or the currently fashionable TQM, assume that what is supposedly effective in large firms will be equally effective in small firms. But small firms are organisationally and managerially different to large firms and face different kinds of external environments. The result of these differences, as the evidence in this book shows, is that large firm quality management strategies do not translate well to the small firm situation. They are over-engineered and expensive for the small improvements which can (but by no means certainly) follow their adoption.

Second, solutions which offer single, straightforward answers to problems faced by small businesses are attractive to government and support agencies because they are administratively simple to implement and cheap compared with, for example, support initiatives designed for different types of firms or localities. They can be delivered as standard packages through TECs and Business Links and are relatively easy to evaluate in terms of the number of firms persuaded to participate in the programmes. But the great variety of sectors in which small firms operate makes it very unlikely that generic solutions will be suitable to all. Indeed, the great risk is that because they are generic they will fail to appeal to many small firm owner-managers because they are seen as too general or too distant from the needs of their businesses.

Third, helping small firms improve their quality standards needs to take account of the quality management strategies small firms already have in place. Small firms are not vacuums where quality management is absent. Small firms are represented in virtually every kind of economic activity in Britain so their quality management needs and strategies will vary enormously. Being aware of the content and range of small business quality management strategies is a first requirement for effective policy formation. Policy has to start from what is the case, that is, what small business owners actually do in relation to promoting quality and build on the practices which are the results of their knowledge, experience and thoughts on how best to run their businesses. Listening to small business owners rather than talking down to them as if they know little or nothing about quality management, is important if policies are to be effective.

On the basis of the research reported here, how can small business owners be helped to improve quality management in their enterprises? If policy assumes, unlike in the past, that small business owners are frequently competent at designing quality management strategies for their businesses, then the aim of policy and support agencies ought to be to help strengthen their strategies. There are several obvious ways in which this could be achieved. Below are eight suggestions prompted by the results from the present research:

1 no single owner-manager has a monopoly on effective quality management strategies and policy ought to provide ways of spreading good practice. But this needs to be bottom-up and sector-based rather than generic. Across the board practices are likely to be too general and too top-down. Data on effective and new quality practices developed by small firms in specific sectors needs to be collected and disseminated. Trade magazines, one of

the commonest sources of information used by owner-managers, are one possible channel for disseminating such information;

2   trade associations, with government funding and support, could fund experiments in quality management strategies which could test, refine and package successful results for wider use by small firm owner-managers. This would promote new thinking on quality management and firms agreeing to be guinea pigs would have the costs of participation covered to avoid any losses;

3   public sector education and training for those likely to be employed in small enterprise sectors such as hotels and restaurants, should make quality strategies more central to their courses. These should highlight two key elements – quality management strategies for the small business owner and quality consciousness for employees. Seeing how important striving for quality is from both sides benefits would-be small enterprise owners and those who will be employed by them;

4   policy and funding should support the establishment and publicising of quality standards or benchmarks to which small firms can orientate their products and services. This already happens in many sectors but small firms (and consumers) are often left out of the processes which set the standards allowing larger enterprises to tailor the results to their needs only;

5   even more important is educating consumers, particularly the general public, about the existence of quality standards and what they can expect of firms who produce goods and services to specific standards. At the moment BS marks on goods, for example, often mean very little to consumers beyond a vague indication that they have an official blessing of some kind;

6   small firms prepared to tender for contracts from public and private sector customers should be subsidised to help introduce appropriate quality controls to meet contract quality standards. This would level the playing field when they compete for contracts with larger firms. They would be able to introduce formal quality standards where required without incurring high compliance costs;

7   support agencies such as Business Links, TECs and ITOs should offer cheap or subsidised 'quality audits' which small business owners can take advantage of to test the effectiveness of their quality management strategies. This is already available in some areas but an up to date version would be staffed by people with a proper knowledge of the sector who would not simply advocate some neo-BS 5750 approach to all firms as 'best practice'

regardless of their specific needs. Building on the firm's existing practices should be the key guiding principle;

8 the DTI could fund 'market profiles' of sectors in which small firms are well represented to report on how the market is segmented, what quality requirements are specific to different sectors and what kinds of quality practices are practical for small firms to deliver to appropriate standards. Attention should also be given to anticipating future market opportunities and how quality management strategies could be developed to allow small firms to grab a share of the new business.

In these and similar ways, policy support for better quality standards in small firms could be promoted more effectively than currently. At the moment the great policy reliance on BS 5750 has not proven effective in raising quality management in small firms because so few small firm owners have been persuaded that BS 5750 is right for their businesses. Moves are being made to make BS 5750 more small firm friendly (see, for example, DTI, 1996a: 52) but it is the contention of the analysis from the research reported in this book that such changes will not remedy its fundamental weaknesses as a quality management approach for small firms.

SOME FINAL REMARKS

The research which prompted this book started out to discover why small business owners were so reluctant to adopt BS 5750. The research was designed to test the wisdom of a national quality strategy based on a single generic standard as well as the assumption that small business owners' approaches to the management of quality might be weak. As it progressed, the focus of the research changed to concentrate on the much more fundamental issue of how quality was managed in small firms. The results led to the conclusion that small firm owner-managers were not only quality conscious but had developed quality management strategies based on clear, well thought out appreciations of the needs of their particular businesses. BS 5750 shifted from being central to the research to being seen much more as contextual: it became one kind of approach to quality management which might have some relevance to owner-managers of small firms and their strategies for managing quality. The result, as the previous chapters demonstrated, was a much more complex and detailed picture of quality and its management in small firms with implications for small business support policies.

Like most researchers, at the end of the research and the writing up of the results, we feel we would have done the research rather differently if we had known what we now know at the start. (Of course, we recognise the obvious absurdity here, that such knowledge would remove the need for the research in the first place.) Again like most researchers, we realise that the answers from one piece of research raises further questions which will need to be answered by further research. For example, the present research suggests a number of issues for further study: other sectors than those in the present research require attention to determine what further variations in quality strategies developed by small business owners occur; we need to know more about the role of employees in raising and sustaining quality standards than our results could offer; future research needs to look more closely at the day-to-day practices of small business quality management rather than simply on the strategies reported by owner-managers; and, the importance of information and advisory sources in the environment – from suppliers, customers, trade bodies as well as TECs and Business Links – in influencing small business owner quality strategies should receive more attention than our research design permitted. It is the destiny of all research projects never to be completed: most business research opens up as many new questions as it answers. What we hope is that the findings and analysis in this book will be seen as a contribution to removing some of the fog enveloping the understanding of quality management in the small business and stimulate further research on the topic.

Appendix: the case studies

INTRODUCTION

As Chapter 3 described, a key element in the research design was the analysis of 10 case study firms. These were selected because they reflected the different types of quality management strategies found in the telephone survey. The case studies provided essential qualitative data fleshing out the quantitative findings from the telephone survey and added greatly to the depth of the overall analysis. Some of the data from the case studies has been introduced earlier in constructing the theorisation of small business quality management presented in the book. In this appendix, the case study data is presented in detail.

In each case study, the firm was visited by a member of the research team who discussed how quality was managed and how quality management strategies had changed over time. Where firms had implemented BS 5750, a detailed account of the processes involved were sought together with an assessment of the results of adopting the standard. The data was collected mainly from a key respondent, normally the owner-manager or a senior partner or the managing or other director. In some cases more than one key respondent was involved. Care has been taken not to over-interpret the views offered or attribute views and actions to people not interviewed. This avoids a common weakness in the case study approach of accepting the views of key respondents as the only possible interpretation of what happened or is happening in the enterprise, or accepting their accounts of the views and actions of others such as employees as accurate beyond challenge. As experienced researchers, we know that the above is unlikely to ever be true. Nevertheless, accepting these limitations, the case studies provide valuable insights into how quality strategies function and are developed in small firms, and especially how variable the experiences of different firms can be.

Case Study 1: Genprint Printers

INTRODUCTION

The quality management strategies used in Genprint illustrate well the use of a *simple informal* quality control system, typical of the other general printers in the study and of a large proportion of all small firms in the UK. It also shows how efficient such strategies can be under appropriate conditions and how more formal quality strategies would add to costs but little or nothing to overall quality either procedurally or in terms of any market advantage.

HISTORY, PRODUCTS AND MARKETS

Genprint is a small general jobbing printer with two partners and two employees and an annual turnover of between £100,000 and £250,000.[1] The senior partner started the firm in April 1980 after being made redundant from a position as print manager in a large firm. The majority of the firm's business is typical of the kind of products produced by small general printers: letter headings, business cards, other business stationery such as invoices and delivery notes, and leaflets. The firm's customers are small firms and local, within a five mile radius. But Genprint does have a few larger customers including Max Factor and Procter & Gamble for whom it does small jobs.

According to the senior partner, the main quality concern of Genprint is making sure that customers get what they ask for. Customers and Genprint negotiate fairly precisely what the final product should be: 'everything is worked out individually with the customer. If you

---

[1] Turnover data on all the case studies provides an indication only. It is based on a question asking respondents to select a category within which the previous year's turnover fell. Respondents were not asked for exact figures because they were not needed for the purposes of the research and some would have been reluctant to provide such information.

come in and want a job, you will specify the colour, you will specify the paper, price, delivery and so on. You clarify at the beginning and that's it'. However, the negotiation is always worked out in terms of Genprint's capabilities as a small general printer. For example, Genprint cannot do full colour work.

THE APPROACH TO QUALITY

The firm operates a *simple informal* quality control strategy. The senior partner has assumed total responsibility for quality in the firm. He also supervises the two employees who deal with the finishing side of operations (collating, folding, stapling). This is not difficult since all operations take place within one small room. Contacts with customers are close. Customers come to the firm either with their own design or an idea which they talk through with the senior partner which could be the basis of a design. In the latter case, the senior partner puts the work out to a local design studio. When the work is returned, he checks back with the customers for approval.

Each order has a job-card which lists all the design and technical details needed for its fulfilment.[2] This specifies the type and size of the paper to be used, ink colours etc. It is common in printing to use a standard colour system which allows customers to define precisely, and the printer to print, each of 500 pre-determined colours. The senior partner then prepares the plate, and prints the number required. Once the print run is completed the two employees finish the product as specified. There is then a final inspection. However, the respondent said errors very rarely remain undetected this far into the production process because of the thoroughness of earlier checks. Once completed the order is delivered to the customer. Delivery is another important quality consideration.

OPINIONS ON FORMAL QUALITY CONTROL SYSTEMS

The senior partner stated that though he was a little unsure about the precise details of BS 5750, he felt it was unlikely it would ever be applicable to Genprint. He argued that there was little organisational or economic sense in changing from the firm's current quality control system.

---

[2] Technically, a job card implies some form of bureaucratisation. But given that this covers only one area of the firm's operation, it is felt that the system used in the firm should still be classified as *simple informal*, rather than a *complex informal* quality control system.

Organisationally, he stressed, current methods provided the simplicity and flexibility required:

> it's all physical, it's check as you go . . . It's not like mass production, every job is different. You run a quality control check as you are doing it. If they're [customers] not happy with the quality they wouldn't accept it. So basically, it has got to be right . . . At the end of the day, if I lose a customer then you will be worried, and I have never lost customer for that [quality] reason.

The respondent said that implementing and maintaining BS 5750 demands a significant amount of financial and time resources, especially in a small firm. But he believed the return from such an investment would be minimal for his business. For example, in his opinion, Genprint does not have the capacity to exploit the benefits of having any extra customers registering BS 5750 might bring: 'we are a very small business and I've got enough customers. I couldn't handle any more. If I had any more customers coming in, I would start letting down those customers I have already got'. Nor had he been able to detect any demands from customers that the firm should register for BS 5750. He stated that one large customer had registered BS 5750 but so far Genprint had only been asked to complete a questionnaire on its quality control procedures.

THE FUTURE

The senior partner believed that Genprint would only ever seriously consider implementing BS 5750 if its main customers demanded it. However, this appeared to be unlikely in the foreseeable future. The firm intended to carry on much as it is now and would probable stay at its present size. The quality control system now in place, therefore, would continue to serve its needs and those of its customers. Overall, therefore, Genprint offered a textbook case of a small firm where *simple informal* quality control strategies worked very effectively, and moving to a third party controlled quality management system such as BS 5750, would offer few or no advantages to offset the additional costs.

Case Study 2: Compsys

INTRODUCTION

This case provides an example of a *simple informal* quality control strategy in a knowledge-based service firm. It shows that firms in sectors which have emerged relatively recently as a result of new technology can operate effectively with simple quality control strategies. However, the owner-manager expects to shift to a formal, third party controlled quality management strategy in the foreseeable future. This is not because he feels the firm needs such a system to support its operations internally: he believes the present informal system works well. But the change will be the result of external influences, namely the widespread adoption of such systems by other firms attempting to gain market advantage.

HISTORY, PRODUCTS AND MARKETS

Compsys is a small computer consultancy firm with nine employees and a turnover of between £250,000 and £500,000 a year. The MD originally worked for another firm in the industry but decided to launch his own business in 1988. The firm markets and sells computer aided design (CAD) systems and 'off the shelf' hardware and software packages. It offers consultancy advising customers on the best package to meet their requirements plus training, installation and after sales telephone and other support. More recently, the MD said the firm had begun to diversify into geographical information systems: computer-based mapping systems which could be used in a variety of economic activities. This shift was to counter sluggishness in the firm's present markets which he described as 'over-mature'.

Since the firm does not develop its own software or hardware, it has to compete almost solely on the quality of service provided: 'there's a fairly simple way of how you can assess quality. We either get a customer at the end of the day who is satisfied, or he's dissatisfied because he's not getting the service'. To achieve customer satisfaction the MD stated that he aimed to provide a level of service beyond what the customer normally expected. In this way, the firm was attempting to differentiate itself from competitors by presenting a 'quality image' to customers. This, he believed, was the most effective method of attracting new customers in what he saw as a highly competitive industry. Moreover, computing technology was changing rapidly so that customers had to update frequently and repeat business could be won by a good quality image.

THE QUALITY SYSTEM

At the time the case study was undertaken, Compsys was operating a *simple informal* quality control system. This was maintained and controlled by the MD himself. In his view there were two main facets of the firm's quality concerns. First, was deciding in which markets the firm would compete: these choices determined much of the content of the firm's quality strategies. Second, there was the internal procedures required to ensure quality was adequate and maintained. Broadly speaking, this involved choosing the most marketable software and hardware for the needs of the kinds of customers the firm served, and ensuring that employees were well versed in the capabilities and applications of the products, the sales procedures, and after sales support.

The MD solved part of the problem by dealing mainly with one supplier with whom he believed he had developed a good personal relationship. He pointed out that there was a large range of software packages on the market but felt there was an advantage in specialising in one supplier so that he and his employees could develop a very thorough understanding of the products, and how they could be best applied to the needs of customers. At the moment, Compsys's specialism was CAD packages, but it was moving into the other areas mentioned above.

Even though the firm was linked closely with one supplier it was thought essential to be aware of new software developments. The MD spent a lot of time monitoring the technical journals to be up to date, and was also helped by information provided by his supplier. But the firm also deals with hardware, a market which the MD described as 'extremely volatile'. Technology and prices are constantly changing and, therefore, it was equally important that he was aware of developments in this area also.

The MD stated that a major problem was ensuring quality was linked closely to employee performance. Though he described the firm's staff as 'quality conscious', he said it took a lot of effort to ensure employees were up to date and able to meet fully the firm's quality aims in dealing with customers. Training was essential. First, employees had to be fully acquainted with the software packages and hardware offered, and how to operate and demonstrate them to customers. Each employee was trained to know two packages but would be a specialist in one of them. Training was initially provided by the original supplier to the MD and perhaps to one or two employees. They would then train the other employees. In this way knowledge permeated through the whole firm. The MD also emphasised training related to selling and after-sales customer care.

The other key quality concerns according to the MD, centred on the day-to-day operation of the firm. Although, he always kept an eye on the overall operation of the business and employees' performances, his daily day-to-day role tended to be minimal. In other words, much of this level of quality management was delegated to staff:

> it's an open office. We all know what we're doing. We are aware of our requirements. We have a small number of customers, and there-fore, we can handle their requirements and know where we are from a progress point of view. Everyone monitors their own quality.

THE FUTURE

The MD stated that quality management strategies, in the sector in which the firm operated, were being pushed towards formalisation by larger firms. In CAD more and more larger firms were becoming committed to BS 5750 registration. The result, in his view, was that registration would become a competitive necessity:

> there will come a time in the very near future where if you don't have BS 5750, or the equivalent, you won't get business ... Quite often now we receive a document from a potential customer asking for a statement from ourselves on what our position is as far as BS 5750 is concerned. Do we have it? If not, what are our intentions? That has become quite the norm.

The MD suggested that although BS 5750 has relevance to the operational side of the business, its main value was in marketing:

marketing image is vital if you are in the selling game. Whilst following the procedures is good from the point of view of running the business, that little standard that says 'approved' opens numerous doors. It's easier for you to knock on someone's door and sell your system if you've got it [BS 5750] than if you haven't.

He believed that the rate of firms registering for BS 5750 would increase even though, in his view, the only real advantage would be a marketing one. Eventually, he argued, BS 5750 would lose much of its marketing value when most firms had registered: everybody would have the standard so no firm could argue it was superior to others on this count.

The respondent expected to register the firm within the next two years to make sure it was not at any disadvantage compared with other firms who had registered. But he envisaged few problems in achieving certification. He claimed significant experience of BS 5750 and formal quality standards because of his experiences of implementing the standard in another firm. However, he reiterated his previous views that the standard was over-complicated, over-bureaucratic, costly and time consuming to implement. If, he argued, the standard could be implemented while Compsys retained its operational effectiveness and flexibility, BS 5750 could generate sales growth for the firm. It might also have some procedural advantages, especially if the firm grew, but he saw this as much less important than the possible sales gains.

Case Study 3: Transys

INTRODUCTION

This case illustrates a small firm in a sector where quality controls are more complex compared with some of the other case studies. The firm uses both *simple* and *complex informal* quality control systems, but the *complex informal* quality system has many of the elements of what has been called in organisational analysis,'mock bureaucracy'. That is, the firm offers a quality control system for customers who demand it, but adherence to the system is ritualised in the sense that the customer gets the same level of quality as customers who do not demand such quality controls. The respondent partner believes that the *simple informal* system is highly effective but is happy to meet customer demands for a more bureaucratised system if they request one. He has no intention of adopting a formal system such as BS 5750 believing it would have no advantages for the business.

HISTORY, PRODUCTS AND MARKETS

Transys is a transformer manufacturer with 22 employees and a turnover of over £500,000 a year. It was started in 1991 when the owner-managers of two similar firms decided to join forces. The firm produces transformers for applications in a wide range of sectors, but most tend to be used in the communications and automotive industries.

According to the respondent partner, Transys operates in a very competitive market. He suggests that quality is a basic concern and key to the firm's approach in the market:

> we not only have to produce a product which meets the customer's electrical and mechanical specification, but since we guarantee all parts plus labour for a year, we have to make sure that the product does not fail due to negligent workmanship.

However, price and delivery considerations are equally important and this can sometimes produce cross-pressures that affect quality:

> there is a pressure to produce [on time]. When you are working on tight margins and you're working like the clappers to get something out of the door, the temptation is to say 'oh that will be alright'.

More recently, the partner suggested, customers have been putting more emphasis on 'quality'. However, the emphasis is not on product quality *per se* but rather on formal quality procedures: 'the actual quality has never changed, they just want to see that quality is documented. We get reams of vendor questionnaires, and we fill them in and send them back, never to see the light [of day] unless a problem occurs'.

TRANSYS'S APPROACH TO QUALITY

In the respondent's view Transys has the capability to produce competitively priced, well engineered, reliable units using *simple informal* methods of quality control. However, it is prepared to produce equivalent units for customers who demand more bureaucratised quality controls, though they will be more expensive as a result. Where the latter is required, the firm has developed quality procedures incorporated in a quality manual, but most customers do not specify this option. This is not a problem for the business though since: ' everything that is in the quality manual is in our heads'.

The above encapsulates Transys's approach to quality. Quality issues are determined on a day-to-day basis according to the skills and experience of the partners: 'that is how we work, we're a small company. We're not sat up in the ivory tower. We're actually down there getting stuck in. We're seeing it first hand and we keep people on their toes'. For each customer's order, the firm has to design and build a prototype unit. The partners begin by analysing the theoretical and mechanical elements of the customer's specification. They then build the unit and test it under normal working conditions. Once this is completed, Transys sends the prototype to the customer who performs their own tests. Once approval has been received, normal production begins.

For each order, the firm has to purchase the necessary raw materials and components. To perform this effectively, the partners have developed several procedures. For example, they have developed their own 'preferred supplier list'. It contains the names of 'suppliers who can service us with the cheapest price, the fastest delivery and the best quality'. The respondent partner suggested that on some occasions they can be forced into a trade-off situation. For example, if

Transys feels an order needs high quality components, it may be forced to accept longer delivery times. However, the respondent suggests that since the firm only usually deals with reliable firms who can offer traceability of their products, difficulties of this kind are not common. Materials and components received from suppliers will occasionally be inspected but only for specialised products or where it is clear there is a problem. In this sector, the norm is that materials and components normally undergo stringent quality tests before being supplied.

Transys's employees perform all the assembly work. Employees are recruited with the basic skills required, but because of the nature of the industry (low tech assembly work), not too much is assumed about their abilities to perform individual jobs. Therefore, they are trained to perform individual tasks on a day-to-day basis:

> we are forced to employ people who do not have the intelligence to understand quality, as such. They are shown a job one bit at a time, and they will do it, one bit at a time . . . You can't say 'go away and do this job' when it has twenty or thirty operations in it because you know full well they haven't got the scope in their brains to be able to hold all that information.

The two partners constantly supervise all employees' work, dealing with problems as they arise. However, the respondent stressed that the firm (and its employees) could not afford to make mistakes, and failures had to be dealt with resolutely:

> if they [employees] make a mistake once that is fair enough. Everyone makes mistakes. If they make a mistake twice then it is starting to get a bit iffy. If they make a mistake three times then they're out. It is that ruthless. It is too costly.

After all units are finished they are physically inspected and tested by one of the partners and then checked again before they leave the factory:

> we [the partners] are signing most of the goods out of the door, we load the vans ourselves, and as we're loading we're checking. Every single item is checked. You give it a quick visual and then pack it in the box . . . If it leaves us, it is working.

Transys's quality control system, therefore, is based on the partners' coordination and knowledge. They directly oversee all design, testing, production and final quality. In the respondent's view this system is relevant to their needs and highly effective: returns are reported to be very low. The *simple informal* quality control system is low cost compared with alternatives such as *second* or *third party* quality control systems making the firm highly competitive.

THE FUTURE

The respondent believes the quality control strategies employed by the firm are effective and can see no operational reasons for change. It has responded to customer pressures for more bureaucratised quality control systems and they can be activated for any customer who demands this level of quality control and is willing to pay the added costs. Yet the respondent did not believe that this would produce any real increase in the quality of the products produced.

Case Study 4: Electromend

INTRODUCTION

A lot of Electromend's quality controls are *simple informal* since they are delegated to employees' discretion. This delegation is necessitated by the character of the business. Employees are often away from the firm servicing customers' equipment on site so it is impossible for owner-managers to oversee all work. Moreover, the work is highly varied, much of it with a one-off character, which again makes any formal specification of quality standards difficult. Yet at first sight, Electromend could be described as having a *complex informal* quality control system in place, but in some ways it is more apparent than real. Electromend has a written quality manual which potential or actual customers can see but, operationally, the manual has little relevance to the day-to-day operations of the business.

HISTORY, PRODUCTS AND MARKETS

Electromend is mainly a small electric motor repairers with 12 employees and a turnover in excess of £500,000 a year. The business was started in November 1979 by three partners who became tired of their existing jobs and decided to put some capital together and start up their own business. Apart from repairing electric motors, Electromend also repairs pumps, mechanical gear boxes and provides a related service for electrical breakdowns and repairs. It also stocks and sells new electrical motors. A majority of Electromend's customers are general maintenance businesses but it also provides maintenance for other businesses directly. For example, it services individual branches of *Barclays Bank* and worked for the government's Property Services Agency.

QUALITY CONCERNS

The main respondent stated that Electromend operates in a very competitive market. Price and quality of the service are key considerations. However, for this business, 'quality' can have a number of differing interpretations. While some customers are technically able to assess the quality of the repairs and maintenance services, others are much less able to judge the quality of work on these criteria. The latter customers are prone to judge quality on more obvious characteristics such as price, time taken and the final presentation of the repaired unit. Of course, the technical quality of the job is important for these customers: if a unit breaks down soon after repair, then the firm would be less likely to receive repeat business or keep a contract. As the respondent put it: 'you need to carry work out to a good standard or you don't get work'.

THE APPROACH TO QUALITY

To meet the above concerns, the firm employs *simple informal* methods of quality control. The firm does have a quality manual but it has been produced mainly to show to potential or interested customers and is not used or adhered to on a day-to-day basis. Quality standards are controlled ultimately by the partners but they delegate a lot of the responsibility to employees:

> as far as the quality of repairs are concerned, everybody has a different part to play on the repair, so it will get dismantled, it will go to the machine shop, and to the winding shop and they will do their bit.

In the view of the respondent, quality is highly dependent on the skills and attitudes of employees. This means that employees' experience and training is crucial. Consequently, the respondent stated that Electromend only employs individuals who have had previous experience of the kind of repair work undertaken by the firm:

> with the work we do, you can only employ people who have been brought up in the repair game. It's not like manufacturing where you can walk straight in – you've got to be a repair man and know exactly what to do.

The senior partner stated that the firm was very keen to add to the experience of employees by providing further training, especially training which widens employees' skills to undertake repairs and maintenance:

> If they haven't experienced a job before then I try and let them do the next job, so that it gives them all further skills. At the end of the day it proves to be better for the company, I can send most people out on most jobs. You've got to give them multi-skills . . . Nobody wants to do the same thing every day.

Training employees is not overly problematic since the rate of technological change in the sector is slow. The firm has bought no new machinery in the last two years and much of the technology used has been around for about thirty years. But the respondent stressed that training also involved instilling a sort of 'quality culture' in employees. Employees were made aware of the importance of doing a 'good job', of 'doing it right first time' and being aware that 'the customer is boss'. For example, to remind employees of the importance of these principles, those who made mistakes return to the site and make good the defect themselves. On a day-to-day basis, employees are encouraged to use initiative in their work. However, the respondent stated that while the firm strived to reach the above ideals, reality is often different and it is often necessary for the partners to supervise employees directly to ensure high standards.

Responsibility for the quality of in-house repair work is also delegated to employees. They are responsible for testing and inspecting the finished unit. In keeping with the partners' beliefs that the appearance of the unit is important, after final external inspection it is then painted:

> when we repair something it is in quite a bit of a state and though it doesn't look like we've done a lot to it, in fact we have. But it doesn't look very good, so we give it a coat of paint.

Perhaps the most important quality consideration of all, according to the respondent, is delivery. Customers want the units mended and returned as quickly as possible since their operations may be seriously held up if a motor or other piece of equipment is down. The firm ostensibly offers a 24 hour service but has its own interpretation of what this means:

> we do a 24 hour service, which doesn't necessarily mean we'll get it back in 24 hours, it means we'll work on it 24 hours and if it is possible we'll have it back before then. It may not be possible but we'll try our hardest.

Overall, the respondent is happy with the firm's approach to quality:

> over the last year we have had very few complaints, and those have been silly ones or through no fault of our own. I can't see how we could work any better. We've simplified it, it is easy to work, everybody knows the system and it works. We've done it for the last fifteen years.

OPINIONS ON FORMAL QUALITY CONTROL SYSTEMS

The respondent sees no benefit in implementing a formal *second* or *third party* controlled quality system for the firm:

> if we need a motor repairing, we don't need any written information, it just has to be done. The guy who dismantles it will make a decision on what needs to be done and the work gets carried out.

The respondent's views apply especially to BS 5750. He suggests that by implementing the standard:

> you're not necessarily bringing the goods up to any better standard than what they [customers] are expecting at the moment. The goods and repairs would be exactly the same. All that would alter would be the cost of the paperwork and the cost of a couple of extra workers to deal with it. I see that as being a bit of a farce.

The respondent's only reason for opting for BS 5750 would be to avoid losing work. But to date, the firm has experienced no external pressures to implement the standard from customers. Indeed, it had developed its own quality manual to counter just this problem:

> we typed it four years ago and not one person has asked for it. So what these customers have said to us is that we have a proven track record of our repairs and our capability, so we have recognition on their accepted list.

In his view BS 5750 tends to be an issue only for larger firms in the sector tendering mainly for larger contracts with big organisations. Electromend does not have the capability to go for these contracts generally so there is little point registering for this reason. BS 5750 is not therefore an issue for the firm.

THE FUTURE

On the evidence from the senior partner of Electromend, the firm's present quality controls work well. They consist mainly of a *simple informal* system with the capacity to meet any demand for bureaucratised *complex informal* quality controls should a customer ask for this as a condition of doing business. There appears to be no likelihood of moving to a formal system such as BS 5750 in the foreseeable future but clearly the firm could do so if customer pressures increased.

Case Study 5: Autorep

INTRODUCTION

This firm uses a *complex informal* quality management strategy. It switched to this from its previous *simple informal* system after embarking on changes intended to culminate in full BS 5750 registration. However, in the process of developing a formal system with the help of a consultant, it was decided that despite the perceived advantages, registration would not bring any further benefits. The system, as developed up to the point where it was decided not to register, was retained as a *complex informal* system of quality management. The respondent felt there were clear benefits and could see no reason for changing the decision not to register.

HISTORY, PRODUCTS AND MARKETS

Autorep is a small repair garage business but it also specialises in engine machining, retailing motor parts, MOTs and car dealing. The firm was set up in 1984 by two partners and has two employees with a turnover of over £500,000 a year. The firm's customers are mainly the general public, though it also does repair work for the local authority. The senior partner suggested that the main way quality is achieved is through high standards of employee workmanship to ensure there is no or little remedial work: 'the job should be done once, done correctly: that's how we judge quality'.

THE QUALITY SYSTEM

Initially the firm had a *simple informal* quality strategy. However, after becoming aware of BS 5750 through links with a local college, the respondent was led to believe that implementation and registration of the standard was a way of winning customers in what he saw as a very competitive market. He and his partner therefore began to implement the standard. But after several months they concluded that the standard would have no effect on sales:

> we've done work for the council . . . [and other customers and] . . . none of them have come to us and said, 'if you've not got BS 5750 your not going to work for us' . . . [Also] . . . a lot of our work is done for private individuals, they are not interested, whatsoever, in BS 5750. It's how much you charge at the end of the day . . . there is no external benefit of registration.

But the respondent and his partner still believed there were potential procedural benefits from BS 5750 so instead of dropping the new procedures, they decided to continue implementing the system, but without registering. The respondent partner considered the firm's previous working procedures to be inadequate and a new system was required:

> to make the company more efficient. Knowing where the company is going, having more information to hand. Also, traceability so if there is a problem it can be traced to where it has occurred.

Besides the low likelihood of additional customers, registration was also considered to be too costly: 'remember those firms that have BS 5750 cannot charge more for their products than those who don't have it'. The owners also initially wanted to formalise their quality management procedures to provide a structure for development and growth. For example, this led to job cards, warranty job cards and internal work orders, which were seen as more suitable to the needs of a growing firm. After discussions with business colleagues and a consultant, it was decided by both partners in April 1992 that the firm would implement a system based on BS 5750, but only use procedures considered relevant to the everyday running of the business.

IMPLEMENTING THE QUALITY SYSTEM

Though the respondent had not felt there were any real problems in understanding BS 5750, it was nevertheless decided to employ a consultant. The consultant was not operating under the DTI scheme so the business had to pay all his fee. However, this was still attractive to the respondents who agreed a deal with the consultant so that he would only come in when required. The respondent felt this met the firm's objectives better, as he believed there were 'too many strings attached' to the DTI scheme, and suggested that 'somebody [the consultant] is getting their pocket lined' when the DTI approach is used.

The consultant's background was in electronics and he had little experience with garages. On the other hand, he had recently helped a number of local firms implement and register for the standard. Together, the senior partner and the consultant began developing and writing procedures based on BS 5750 for those areas of the business considered relevant. The result was a radical change in many existing procedures: 'for example, with engine reconditioning, actually labelling everything that comes into the building with the correct labels. Something that we didn't do before'.

Once completed, the new procedures were compiled into a quality manual. However, the respondent stressed care was taken to make sure that the documented procedures were kept simple to avoid restricting the flexibility of the firm.

None of the firms' employees directly participated in the implementation process. No extra training was provided to allow employees to learn about the new methods of working. Rather the respondent said they would 'have discussions on it' where appropriate. Not surprisingly, the respondent reported that the employees' attitude towards implementing the quality system appeared largely indifferent. He suggested that this was the main problem of implementation: 'a lot of things had to be changed round. It's very difficult to pull them [the employees] all together, that's the thing ... just getting everybody to do what is required'.

OPINIONS ON THE QUALITY SYSTEM

Though the firm had only partially implemented the BS 5750 system, in the view of the senior partner, benefits had been realised. The respondent believed that the quality of service had improved under the new system: 'we now have notes on the job cards, we now have records. This always helps when we go back to a job. I'm very impressed from that point of view'. The respondent also believed that efficiency has increased. The main benefit in his view was 'internal, we know where things are, we know where things have come from, we know who has done what'. Indeed, the respondent suggested that the associated cost savings had offset the cost of implementing the system up to the point where it was finalised. However, employee participation in the system was still, in his opinion, a problem.

Full BS 5750 registration was deemed unnecessary for several reasons. First, there was no external pressures from the market for the firm to become registered: the majority of customers were not interested in the standard. Second, the overheads associated with maintaining and registering for the standard would, in the view of the respondent, push prices above those allowed by the market, rendering the firm uncompetitive. Finally, by not registering, the firm had only formalised those operating procedures which were considered to be relevant, avoiding over-bureaucratisation.

THE FUTURE

The respondent stated that the firm would only consider registering for BS 5750 if external market conditions dictated. He could see no reason for this to happen in the foreseeable future. At the moment, the firm's *complex informal* quality system worked well producing clear positive benefits in operational efficiency. The advantages of the new system over the old *simple informal* system had been achieved without the costs and bureaucratisation associated with BS 5750 registration which would have been uneconomic in the market.

Case Study 6: Meditron

INTRODUCTION

The firm operates in a sector where, literally, quality can be a matter of life or death. It operates a *second party* externally controlled system which is in effect also a *complex informal* quality control system. The main respondent claims that because of the characteristics of the market in which the firm operates, its quality standards are higher than would be required for BS 5750 registration. Although medical safety concerns dictated the relatively strict quality standards used, in the view of the respondent the firm gained considerable procedural benefits also.

HISTORY, PRODUCTS AND MARKETS

Meditron is a small electronics consultancy and manufacturing business with eight employees and a turnover of between £100,000 and £250,000 a year. It started in early 1985 as a consultancy offering design services to other businesses. In 1987, after a number of requests from customers, the firm began to manufacture to specification and has now launched its own products. Meditron produces high quality technically specific products for the medical and health care sectors. The firm's major buyers tend to be health trusts and authorities, individual doctors, consultants and research establishments in the UK, Europe and, most recently, Japan.

In health and medical markets quality is an obvious key consideration. There is little scope for errors where the reliability and performance of, for example, a pace maker is at stake. As the MD of Meditron suggested, this requires a far-reaching, exacting approach to quality: 'our aim as a company is to provide the customer with what they actually want, and to achieve that, quality goes right across the board from a design point of view to manufacturing and testing'.

To the MD and his fellow directors, the implementation and operation of a quality system was nothing new. They had all previously
worked in large organisations and were used to working with formal
quality systems: 'we've never been comfortable with design work on the
back of cigarette packets, or doing everything by word of mouth, we've
always put things down in writing'. In other words, the motivation to
adopt more formal quality strategies was embedded in Meditron's
management culture which, in turn, reflected the characteristics of the
sector in which it operated.

THE QUALITY SYSTEM

Formal methods of quality control were introduced early in the business's life. Though Meditron is not registered BS 5750, the MD believed
the standard is very much in line with the firm's way of operating.
Indeed, the firm would probably have implemented BS 5750 if it had
not had a quality system imposed on it by its customers. The system is
used by customers to check the quality of the firm's manufacturing
capability and, ultimately, the product received, and is described as
'beyond BS 5750'. It enables problems to be quickly resolved through
traceability of all materials, equipment and employee work through all
stages of production. This, suggests the respondent, is 'beneficial for
time and for quality', that is, it has efficiency, as well as product quality,
benefits.

The quality system adopted is based on the requirements of several
large electronics firms and health authority customers. To avoid argument about whose procedures should dominate 'the manual', the firm
'went beyond everyone's requirements'. This, suggested the MD, has led
to a two way process with many customers changing their own ideas
about formalising quality as a result of the firm's approach. The
respondent was enthusiastic about the system and keen to ensure high
quality standards. They have subsequently implemented the system in
areas of operations where it was not directly required, namely sales and
administration. The respondent also believed that employees were
enthusiastic about implementing the system. He suggested that they
were conscious of the company's need to grow and that implementing
the quality system was part of that process. Moreover, by adopting
the quality system, Meditron has raised itself into a reasonably secure
market position.

on the medical side there is really nobody who will tackle the contracts we do. It's usually large firms who want to mass produce for

contracts of a million pounds upwards, whereas we will look at contracts from a pound upwards. As long as it is profitable we don't mind.

IMPLEMENTING THE QUALITY SYSTEM

The MD was responsible for implementing the quality system in all areas of the business. This included researching and writing the relevant procedures as well as their implementation. He had not found it necessary to employ a consultant since advice and support were received from customers. The MD was also keen to involve employees who were seen as essential to the success of the system. For example, he welcomed and was quick to act upon employee suggestions. Internal training was used to familiarise employees with the system and its paperwork.

Implementing the system had been a gradual process: 'we've built up a system probably over several months, possibly a year or so, and we're still updating it, it's not stationary' Initially, the adoption of the system was determined by the need to incorporate new customer requirements. The system was then developed to incorporate in-house solutions to problems in everyday operation. By adopting this mainly gradualist approach, financial and time costs of implementation were kept to a minimum. However, the time costs were seen as a significant burden and higher than initially expected. As the respondent suggested:

> I was not able to pursue some of our normal business activities . . . I was not pursuing the sales side of the business and certainly not pursuing the engineering side of design work because I was occupied with the quality system. So I'm sure the business [suffered] at that time, we did dip in terms of sales invoices going out of the door.

The respondent estimates that the costs of management and staff time have so far mounted to between £5,000 and £10,000 plus between £40,000 to £50,000 in lost business. Though the respondent felt this had been a problem for the firm, he suggested they may be even greater for smaller small firms which have few resources to cushion the changes associated with implementation.

MAINTAINING THE QUALITY SYSTEM

Though the MD is ultimately responsible for maintaining and updating the quality system, responsibility is also delegated to other directors and employees. Indeed, this approach is implicit in the quality system:

documentation follows every contract around the company so everybody knows specifically about the contract, that documentation [needs to be] . . . updated as it goes around. If there's a problem with quality at that particular point in the work program, it's the responsibility of that person in the section to try and correct it there and then, report back on what procedures are used to improve the quality or to carry out the repair.

However, unlike the comments of many other owners on the time and financial costs of maintaining a formal system, the respondent argues that this degree of bureaucratisation does not adversely affect the everyday operations of the business: 'because it's [the quality system] now part of the overall philosophy of the company. I don't think it would take any longer for someone to fill in the paperwork than it would to have a discussion'.

OPINIONS ON THE QUALITY SYSTEM

The firm implemented the quality system to access a potentially lucrative niche supplying manufactured medical equipment to the health and medical care sector. According to the MD, its impact has been far reaching: sales have increased, quality improved, overheads reduced as failure rates decreased. However, the system is still considered to be time-consuming to operate even if the benefits are clearly considered to outweigh the time costs.

THE FUTURE

Accessing new clients in the medical sector will probably mean amending the quality system again, especially for clients in the United States where quality requirements were said by the MD to be 'peculiar'. He is also considering developing the industrial side of the business to reach a wider range of customers. In his view this will probably mean applying for BS 5750 registration. Given the firm's experience with its present quality systems, this should produce few problems. The MD was familiar with TQM but said the firm has no intention of implementing it, because he believed that the business already had many of the virtues implicit in TQM.

Case Study 7: Beeplant

INTRODUCTION

This is a firm implementing BS 5750 after doing so originally as a result of customer pressures. The recession of the early 1990s reduced customer pressures and the firm's management reported that the main motivation was now to realise longer term procedural advantages for the firm. It has taken a long time to achieve registration and, at the time of the case study, the firm's MD estimated that it could take up to another six months.

HISTORY, PRODUCTS AND MARKETS

Beeplant is a small plant hire business. It started as a building business in the nineteenth century but was converted into a plant hire firm by two of the present directors. The firm has nine employees and five working directors with a turnover of between £250,000 and £500,000 per year. Beeplant hires out a large range of site equipment as well as a significant amount of small tools. The firm, like others in this sector, hires out a wider range of equipment than it actually has by borrowing equipment they lack from other firms in the sector. This kind of cooperation is typical in the plant hire sector. The firm's customers are mainly builders, ranging from small one-man operators, to large building contractors.

Beeplant operates in a very competitive industry where quality is important. The financial director defined quality as 'equipment going out to the customer as required in a correct and safe working order'. This, he argued, is essential for ensuring repeat business from customers which the firm relies on greatly. Therefore, the firm's quality systems are tailored to reflect this aim.

Originally, quality management was based on a *simple informal* quality control system. However, on converting to plant hire and joining a plant hire trade association, the firm felt forced to consider more formal methods. A main concern was the effects of health and safety legislation and ensuring that all the firm's equipment complied with the law. The trade association offered a twice yearly assessment to members to confirm they were operating in line with recommended operating procedures and the relevant legislation. Beeplant decided to use this support to develop a more formal quality control strategy. A first requirement of this process was ensuring all staff had appropriate training to confirm that the firm was operating to the required standards: 'all the fellows on the counter have been on sales courses, the fitters go on safety courses and if new equipment comes out, they'll go to the factory to learn about it'. The financial director said that he and his fellow directors were pleased at the results of this shift to a recommended quality control strategy.

In early 1991 Beeplant decided to formalise its procedures further by implementing BS 5750. However, the original motivation for implementing the standard was not gaining further operational advantages. The financial director stated that the decision had resulted from external pressures: 'I can't have a customer come to me and say 'you're not registered, I can't use you' ... [and] ... I'm not going to let customers go by not being registered'.

However, the effect of the early 1990s recession, which had a very noticeable negative impact on the construction sector, reduced the external pressures from bigger customers. Like smaller firms in the sector in the recession, the respondent said that larger firms became more concerned about survival than insisting on BS 5750 registration from suppliers. But by this time, the firm had got to grips with the requirements of BS 5750 and decided to press ahead with implementation. Beeplant is still implementing BS 5750 based on the belief that it will gain further procedural benefits from full registration.

IMPLEMENTING BS 5750

The change in the motivation to register for BS 5750 altered the approach to implementation. When customer pressures were the main motivation, the respondent said that a quick registration was regarded as a priority. But the change in motivation signalled a change in approach, as the MD suggested: 'I could have found out the easiest way of registering. Now if that's all we wanted we could have done it in seven months'. Instead, it was decided to take more time over implementation to produce a system more suitable for the long term success of the business.

The MD decided to use the DTI consultancy sponsorship scheme to support implementation. He believed that since the firm is not big enough to employ a full time quality manager, using a consultant would be the only way to implement the standard effectively. Otherwise, he believed, too many management hours would be lost trying to interpret and implement the system: 'I think BS 5750 is just too deep a subject. We couldn't do it without a consultant'.

Beeplant chose a consultant with previous experience of working with plant hire businesses. He explained what the system required and what he saw as the best way to achieve it for the firm. The MD then went away and wrote draft operating procedures and quality documents for the firm. The consultant amended the MD's work to suit the requirements of BS 5750: 'we're the horse and he's [the consultant] the jockey. He will guide us in the right direction and put us over the jumps'.

However, the MD said he was aware of claims that many consultants have been implementing standardised and 'jargonised' quality manuals for firms regardless of the firms' actual requirements. He was therefore determined to develop the quality manual around Beeplant's precise needs: 'I'm running BS 5750 not the bloody consultant! I tell him what I want . . . If you hit a nail with a hammer, you hit a nail with a hammer and that's what we put down . . . the kiss principle, "keep it simple stupid"'.

As a result, the firm has not attempted to alter dramatically its operating procedures. Rather, BS 5750 has been seen as a means of honing and formalising existing ones. The respondent said the firm had been keen to involve employees. For example, he arranged meetings to explain to staff the motivations for, and the requirements of, BS 5750. Though employees are usually very busy, the respondent indicates that they will continue to receive BS 5750-related training and be involved in the writing of working procedures.

Beeplant has taken its time over preparing for BS 5750 certification and the writing of the quality manual has still to be completed. The MD states that so far the main problem has been finding the time to write and implement procedures. He estimates that the cost has been over £7,500 but this is not seen as a major problem.

THE FUTURE

The respondent estimates that it will take another three to six months to implement the standard. During this time he intends utilise his employees' contributions further and is considering further ways of implementing the provision for training. After completing the manual, Beeplant intends to apply for registration with BSI. However, it has taken a long time to get to this stage and this extended timetable is probably not typical but apparently reflects the effects of the early 1990s recession.

Case Study 8: Console

INTRODUCTION

This a knowledge-based service business which is implementing BS 5750. It has completed virtually all the pre-registration stages. The decision to register has been driven by one of the firm's directors but the other four directors have supported the decision and been involved in the preparation for registration. Employees have also contributed but have had difficulties in finding the time, for instance, to write their work profiles for the preparation of the manual. Overall, although the firm has not yet registered, the firm's main respondent believed gains have already been made and she was optimistic that the other expected main advantages would be realised too.

HISTORY, PRODUCTS AND MARKETS

Console is a consultancy business with 18 employees and a turnover of over £500,000 a year. It was established in 1986 by a group of employees who had previously worked for a large software house mainly as computer programmers. The firm specialises in computer software and hardware problem solving packages for large financial and communications firms. It has one central office which is run by an administrative director (the respondent) with supporting administrative staff. All other employees are specialist consultants who mainly work out on site. Console competes with a number of larger consultancy organisations. The respondent argued that being smaller, quality is essential for developing a reputation and securing repeat business and she believes strongly in offering 'excellence'.

THE QUALITY SYSTEM

The respondent considered formal quality procedures integral to the development of a quality service for customers. Therefore, Console had decided to implement BS 5750 as a result of her thinking and decision. This was seen firstly as means of tidying up existing procedures: 'we had this loose structure of quality standards which applied to our technical projects, but there was nothing internal to formalise it, there were no internal procedures'.

Implementing BS 5750 was also seen as a way of managing growth. The administrative director suggested that it was becoming harder to control quality as employment grew. Formalising procedures would, in her opinion, enable the firm to combat this problem. However, though the procedural motivation for implementing the standard was significant, Console could not, in her view, ignore market influences: 'there's always a nagging thing isn't there? Certain companies won't use contractors who do not have BS 5750, so it [implementing BS 5750] was very much from a marketing and sales point of view as well'.

She viewed implementation therefore as a means of increasing credibility with customers. It was seen as a means of competing with larger rivals and particularly as a way of making the firm appear larger to the outside world. The administrative director did not foresee many problems in implementing BS 5750 apart possibly from employees finding the time to contribute to the development of the system.

IMPLEMENTING BS 5750

Console began implementing BS 5750 in 1990. It was decided that the best route would be to use a consultant. This, it was felt, would take the mystique out of the standard and methods of implementation as well as reduce the burdens on employee time. The firm managed to reduce consultancy costs by using the DTI sponsorship scheme. After initial training at a weekend conference organised by the firm, Console's employees were asked to write the 'work instructions' applicable to their own position. These were incorporated into a 'procedures manual' by the administrative director. The consultant then edited and amended the manual around the requirements of BS 5750.

Writing the procedures manual took about six months in total. This was a difficult time for the firm, especially for the respondent and consultant who spent a lot of time motivating and encouraging employees to give less time to their normal duties and write their contributions. After developing the first draft of the procedures manual, the firm utilised its five strong team of directors to make final evaluations and then formulate the quality documents, such as the quality manual.

The administrative director reflected that though implementation had been very time consuming, the final drafts of the quality and procedures manuals reflected well the existing organisational structure and working methods. The directors felt that these were efficient and wanted to ensure they were not lost after implementing the new system. The respondent felt they had been successful. They had retained Console's flexibility and registration would not, in her view, constrain innovation or growth. Though making a total cost estimate is slightly premature, she reckons that the firm will have spent between £50–60,000 in implementing and registering for the standard. This includes staff hours and revenue lost during this period because staff had to be away from their normal duties. However, the cost is seen as justified: 'It's a lot but you've got to think about the net benefit. I think that it is a problem with small companies. OK, you're out there to earn money but also you've got to get the business up and running properly.'

THE FUTURE

The administrative director feels that through implementing BS 5750 the firm has already realised some of its aims. The benefits already gained from formalising procedures, for example, include improvements in quality and efficiency. She is also optimistic about the commercial impact of registration and believes the firm will gain new contracts and be less likely to lose existing ones. However, the time taken in maintaining and monitoring the system is likely to be a big problem in her view, especially as the firm is keen to accurately reflect its constantly changing methods of operation in its formal written procedures.

Case Study 9: Electrico

INTRODUCTION

This is one of the largest case study firms. It originally used *simple informal* methods of managing quality but the MD became dissatisfied with their effectiveness partly because of the difficulty of applying them in a firm of this size (34 employees) but mainly because customers were insisting on registration as a condition of continuing to do business. The firm had embarked on implementing BS 5750 and registered in April 1992.

HISTORY, PRODUCTS AND MARKETS

Electrico is a contract electronics manufacturer with an annual turnover of over £500,000. The MD started the business in 1983 after being asked to do some design work outside the scope of his existing position in a previous company. The firm does contract manufacturing work and occasionally designs electronic components for businesses who either do not have the capability to produce for themselves or do not have the time or desire to do so. About two thirds of the Electrico's work is for larger businesses such as British Telecom.

According to the MD, the inherent quality of Electrico's products are not, and have never been, an issue. Rather, the main issue is 'quality' as defined in textbook terms of 'consistently giving the customer what they want'. Attaining 'quality' in this sense is seen as a means of ensuring repeat business, developing a reputation, and also, a means of minimising costs:

> Without consistent quality going out of the door you are likely to encounter situations where the goods are returned to you because they've failed someone else's quality audit. That is an expensive pastime. You don't want to be in a position where goods are returned to

you because economically, it is a nightmare. This is an issue that made us take quality very seriously.

THE QUALITY SYSTEM

Initially the firm operated *simple informal* quality control methods based on test and inspection procedures. However, the MD said that such methods had proved ineffective. For example, it was not uncommon for sub-standard goods to slip past these controls. They were then detected by the customer and sent back to be reworked and re-inspected. This was very costly for the firm. He had decided therefore that Electrico would implement a more formal quality system and register for BS 5750. But he also believed that BS 5750 was absolutely necessary to compete successfully in the market in the 1990s particularly when large firms like British Telecom were making it clear that they will cease to trade with non-registered firms. The other directors realised there would be problems regarding 'cost, time and size of the task' but accepted his view that registration was the only option.

IMPLEMENTING BS 5750

Electrico began implementing BS 5750 in 1989. The MD was not involved in the practical side of implementing the quality system. Indeed, he considered much of the standard's wording to be 'trite nonsense'. But he did not wish to use consultants who he suggested 'charge exotic fees and in my experience are to be avoided'. Instead, the quality manual and procedures were largely written by an ex-engineer working on a temporary basis in the firm as part of a training placement. The MD's role was more as final decision-maker. For example, he suggests:

> I would not except any bull-shit or contrived documentation that wasn't strictly necessary. Our policy was that BS 5750 should be as light weight as we could possibly make it, and there is plenty of capability to do it if you are determined. There is enough flexibility in BS 5750 to be able to do that but you've got to be very aware not to stitch yourself up.

He also saw himself as involved in motivating employees, a majority of whom in his opinion 'couldn't give a toss' about BS 5750. He accepted that this was due in part to their concerns with meeting customer's orders on time. He believed, however, that staff should put the extra effort needed for BS 5750 implementation regardless of any other demands on their time. However, it appeared that no extra training for staff to support the shift to a formal quality control system was provided.

Maintaining the firm's flexibility was a key aim of the MD who wanted the quality manual moulded around existing business procedures rather than forcing any radical changes. After a few amendments, the quality manual was completed at the end of 1991. The MD decided to apply for registration with BSI which he considered to be the most suitable from a marketing point of view. Despite finding a few minor problems with the manual, the inspectors insisted that very few alterations had to be made and Electrico registered for BS 5750 Part 2 in April 1992.

Though time costs were a definite consideration, the financial costs were expected to be, and emerged, as the biggest problem associated with implementation. The respondent estimated that the firm had spent around £15,000 over the three years it took to implement the standard; £10,000 on general costs and documentation and £5,000 on registration. This did not take account of the costs of lost hours by staff involved in implementation.

MAINTAINING BS 5750

The quality system is maintained by the firm's technical (and quality) director. The MD said that this role had been given to a director not connected directly with the manufacturing part of the business. This was to ensure an independent assessment of quality issues without the person responsible being influenced by constraints associated with manufacturing processes such as minimising production lead times to meet customer deadlines. Day-to-day quality problems were isolated through the manual-based quality control procedures and, according to the MD, sorted out immediately. More serious problems were dealt with at meetings where quality procedures could be amended.

The quality system, like all BS 5750 systems, is also subject to a periodic (half yearly) assessment, in this case by BSI. The MD stated that it was impractical for assessors to perform spot checks so he is often warned by managers of other businesses that the 'assessors are in town'. However, he claimed this offered no scope for laxity in maintaining the BS 5750 documentation:

> You can't change your history. In between one visit and the next you have to maintain your documentation. It's part of the system and

you can't do it all in a week. It's the first thing he [the assessor] looks at. Have you maintained the programme in the way your quality manual says your going to?

The cost of maintaining BS 5750 was much higher than he had originally anticipated. There is a re-registration fee of a 'few hundred pounds' as well as a fee of £250 per half day for the assessor's time. The MD suggested that overall: I think the annual cost of belonging to this wonderful brotherhood is about £2,000.'

OPINIONS ON BS 5750

Electrico implemented BS 5750, according to the MD, mainly to establish an image as a 'quality supplier' but also to avoid the financial problems associated with returns due to failures to detect faulty work before it left the factory. The latter aim, reported the MD, has been achieved very clearly: 'We've had one customer complaint in the last year which we were able to deal with by traceability. In the past there would have been many more.'

But he also repeated the view that without BS 5750, Electrico would have been at a serious competitive disadvantage in the market. However, he also said that the costs of being BS 5750 registered were significant: 'We are qualified, we have locked in costs. There is no way we can do things on the cheap. You can't run an outfit which is BS 5750 approved that doesn't have certain levels of capability . . . so there are certain overheads.' In one sense, the MD said that costs had increased: there were now more overheads to achieve the same output. But he balanced this by saying that, overall, there has been financial benefits because the amount of re-work had been reduced.

THE FUTURE

The MD sees BS 5750 as essentially for survival in the 1990s. Yet he says he would only consider implementing further quality initiatives 'if circumstances change'. The respondent is aware of TQM but considers it inappropriate because Electrico's existing organisational structure exhibits many of the characteristics of TQM – team-working etc. – but 'without the need for prescribed labels' or added formality.

Case Study 10: Paperco

INTRODUCTION

Although this business is classified in the study as a printing firm, it is a paper merchants supplying all kinds of papers to general and specialist printers. Again unlike the firms in the sample directly involved in printing, it is BS 5750 registered. The main reasons for registration according to the main respondent were as a response to market pressures and as a preparation for growth.

HISTORY, PRODUCTS AND MARKETS

Paperco is a small paper merchant with 14 employees and a turnover of just over £500,000 a year. The MD had worked in the paper trade and eventually managed to get financial backing for his own business which started in 1971. Paperco began slowly, dealing originally in paper but also somewhat oddly in garden furniture. It now concentrates exclusively on supplying paper to commercial printers, serving major publishers and magazines.

Simply stated, Paperco receives an order from a customer (mainly by telephone), contacts a paper mill who directly supplies the paper to the buyer. Paperco judges quality in terms of 'giving the customer what it wants'. According to the commercial director: 'we have to supply what the customer wants, as a specific we can't deviate at all . . . We don't cut corners or anything, what they want is what they get'. More precisely, Paperco has to consider not only the quality of the products in which it is dealing – the correct paper, paper weight, size and colour – but also the quality of service they are delivering, chasing customers' requirements until they are eventually fulfilled. Both are seen as essential to achieving competitive success.

THE QUALITY SYSTEM

Originally, Paperco had no formal system for maintaining quality. The commercial director suggested they got by using simple 'commercial sense ... [and by knowing] ... how it happened', a *simple informal* quality control system in other words. The financial director argued that formal methods were unnecessary at that time since Paperco's system worked well while the business was still small.

The main motivation to implement BS 5750 resulted from external market conditions according to one of the directors. Many paper merchants had registered and this was an obvious concern: 'I think we were worried that if we didn't get it [BS 5750] ... we might just lose a few jobs. If it is a 50/50 choice between us and someone else and they had [BS 5750] and we didn't, then we might have lost out.' However, the directors were also concerned that quality standards might slip as the firm grew. Paperco was once in a position where all members of staff knew how to do all, or most, of the jobs in the firm but as it grew and employee numbers increased, this no longer remained true. Quality was becoming harder to control. The directors considered it would be a good time to implement some more formal procedures. In short, it was felt that this would have occurred eventually regardless of what was happening in the market.

However, some directors were concerned about shifting to formal quality control methods: 'the main reservation was that we were going to get bogged down in paperwork for paperwork sake. Initially, you got the impression they wanted forms for everything without getting any real work done'. The directors stated that they had got the impression that implementing BS 5750 meant scrapping their existing working procedures entirely and implementing a new system specifically set up for paper merchants. This, the financial director reported 'was a little bit of a misconception'.

IMPLEMENTING BS 5750

Paperco began implementing BS 5750 in early 1992. It was decided to take advantage of the DTI sponsored consultancy scheme. The commercial director argued that using a consultant was necessary since existing members of staff and especially the sales team, were always busy so the firm would not have the internal capacity to prepare for registration without help. The financial director also said that an initial examination of the standard suggested that it would be difficult to interpret and implement without specialist help. Compared to these problems the costs were less of an issue. The DTI recommended a consultant who had experience of implementing the standard in similar firms and he was promptly chosen to help.

The financial director was keen to get all employees involved in the implementation process. The commercial director suggested that though their initial reaction was negative, employees eventually became positive, realising that it was an important step in the development of the business. The financial director worked with the consultant drawing up the procedures and eventually the quality manual. According to the commercial director, the consultant was effective because he went along with their request to try not to change the business fundamentally:

> we said, 'if you see something that sticks out like a sore thumb which will obviously lead us into trouble then you've go to tell us about it, but as far as we're concerned this is a smooth running business that is quite tightly controlled. Therefore, we can't see why [we cannot] put the manual around what we've already got'.

On seeing what the consultant produced, the financial director said his task was to 'knock out all things that were irrelevant' and tighten up other procedures that were not quite correct in his view. The outcome, the respondents believed, was a quality manual which was an accurate reflection of the way the business operated.

The manual was completed in October 1992. Shortly after Paperco applied to be registered with Bureau Veritas Quality International (BVQI) since this third party certification body had already registered similar paper merchant businesses. Other third party certification bodies were considered but deemed too expensive. BVQI assessed the manual against Paperco's business practices and was registered in June 1993 with, according to the respondents, very few problems: 'they hardly touched us, the consultant was delighted. They got us for eight out of fifteen [possible points] . . . and they were for nothings'. Overall, the standard was estimated to have taken under a year to implement and cost £4,500 excluding registration. Nonetheless, the fee was seen by the respondents to be 'a lot of money'. But they agreed that implementation was less of a burden than expected and the biggest problem was said to be 'getting the manuals organised'.

MAINTAINING BS 5750

The financial director is almost completely responsible for maintaining the quality system, though he does not see this as a burden: 'it's in place, it's how we work. If we change our work procedure we will have to change our manual'. Most staff simply carry on their jobs as usual in his view. If there is a problem, the financial director goes and talks to the relevant staff about it and quality is maintained. The cost of maintaining the system he estimated is about £1,000 a year for two half yearly assessment visits from BVQI.

OPINIONS ON THE QUALITY SYSTEM

Paperco implemented BS 5750 primarily as a reaction to external market conditions in the paper trade. Suppliers were insisting that merchants maintain a sufficiently high level of quality in distributing their products. Registration had been implemented to meet this insistence but efforts were made to ensure the internal operations of the business were not disrupted. However, the respondents believed that the firm has made operational improvements as a result of registration, for example, by improving its customers' complaints procedures. The standard was also seen to provide a framework though which growth could be achieved more comfortably.

THE FUTURE

Since Paperco implemented BS 5750 more to counter market pressures, both respondents believed that they may have to implement further standards if, as they feel is inevitable, BS 5750 becomes 'old hat'. That is, if so many firms become registered that the standard no longer acts as a means of differentiating the firm from its competition, suppliers may insist on further changes in quality procedures. However, they stated that if this was a competitive necessity, then so be it, the firm would meet any new standards.

Notes

1 SMALL FIRMS AND QUALITY MANAGEMENT

1 The definition of what constitutes a 'small firm' is a matter of considerable discussion with no single definition accepted as authoritative or suitable for all purposes. Here the definition adopted, an independent firm with at least one but under 50 employees, is a commonly used one. For further discussion of what constitutes a 'small firm' see Chapter 3. The DTI data quoted here is for the end of 1994 and is the most up to date available. Compiling accurate data on the small business population is very difficult for a number of reasons discussed in DTI (1996a).

2 There is a good deal of confusion over the name of BS 5750. The standard was originally introduced in 1979 as BS 5750. In 1987, international (ISO 9000) and European (EN 23000) equivalents were introduced. It should be stressed that BS 5750, ISO 9000 and EN 23000 are exactly the same apart from nominally representing the different national and international status of the standard. In 1994, the confusion led the British Standards Institute (BSI) to rename BS 5750, BS EN ISO 9000, its current official label. Once again it should be stressed that differences between BS 5750 and BS EN ISO 9000 are nominal. Though many people currently use an abbreviated form ISO 9000, dropping BS EN, to talk about the standard in both a British and international context, we are sticking with the label BS 5750 throughout the book. This reflects the fact that when the research on which the book is based was undertaken the standard was generally known as BS 5750. The standard is also much better known and understood in Britain as BS 5750 and the development of the BS 5750 standard has historically been a British phenomenon. Therefore, to talk about BS EN ISO 9000 when discussing the development and introduction of the standard in Britain, especially before 1987, would, in our view, be misleading.

3 A feature of the Enterprise Initiative, a major support programme introduced to help small businesses in the late 1980s and early 1990s, was funded consultancy which provided advice on key business areas, including quality (DTI, 1991). Firms using the scheme were provided with consultancy advice lasting between 5 and 15 days with DTI providing 50 per cent of the costs (two thirds in assisted areas). According to a report by *Pera International* (1992), by mid-1991 around 13,000 firms had already used the scheme, almost all of which sought assistance with the introduction of BS

5750. Indeed, it was predicted that it could eventually result in 40,000 registrations. However, the DTI announced that the scheme was to be withdrawn from December 1993 and the total number of firms who registered as a result of the scheme is not known.

4 The text may appear to imply that what is referred to as BS 5750 is one standard. In fact, it is contained in a series of separate published documents, Part 0 to Part 13. The parts of the standard fall into two groups. Firstly, there are the quality system requirements themselves, Parts 1, 2 and 3. A business seeking registration under the standard opts to be assessed under only one of these parts dependent upon the firm's range of products and services (Callan, 1992: 20). Success or failure depends on demonstrating that the quality requirements set out in these parts have been met. The second group of parts (parts 0, 4, 8 and 13) provide guidance notes. The equivalent documents are now available for ISO 9000, BS EN ISO 9000 and the like.

5 Once the business is operating to BS 5750 procedures as documented in the manual, it can apply to become 'assessed'. This is carried out by one of a number of third party certification bodies (for a list see North *et al.*, 1993: 29). In the UK, the majority are accredited by the National Accreditation Council For Certification Bodies (NACCB), established by the DTI, to assess their technical competence and integrity. However, much media attention has focused on the fact that, technically, anyone can implement the standard (Batchelor, 1993; Halliday, 1993). This has given scope for so-called 'cowboy' third party bodies to emerge, with what have been seen as worrying implications for the misuse of registration.

6 Information supplied to the Small Business Research Centre, Kingston University by The Stationery Office, Norwich. This is now a privatised section of HMSO given responsibility for collecting data on registration from the DTI. The information supplied was correct on 13 December 1996.

7 Summaries of the ideas of these exponents of quality strategies abound and there is no need to go into detail for the purposes of this discussion of the quality strategies of small business owner-managers. Useful introductions are, however, provided by Barad (1996) and Tuckman (1995). The latter is particularly interesting in offering an introduction which puts the ideas into their social and political contexts.

8 This notion echoes a main theme in one of the most influential books published in the quality literature, *Quality Is Free* by Crosby (1979). Crosby argued that quality is always 'free' in the sense that prevention costs are always likely to be lower than the costs of detection (of defective items) and correction (scrap, replacement, restoring reputation among customers etc.). This led to the 'zero defect' approach in quality strategies.

9 This information is in BSI's promotional material collected by the Kingston University Small Business Research Centre as part of the research project.

10 The notion of the 'internal market' made up of purchasers and providers has become a key motif in changes introduced into the public sector in the UK in the 1990s, most notably in the National Health Service.

11 For a brief discussion of why large firms and government organisations are adopting this position and the effects on small firms see North *et al.* (1993: 5) and Curran and Blackburn (1994).

12 There are, however, other quality guides in the hotel sector such as the

'crown' system or those used by hotel and food guides. These do not resemble BS 5750 because they are either based on whether the business has certain characteristics (all rooms *en suite* or with tea/coffee making facilities, for example) and/or the subjective judgements of the guides' inspectors.

2 QUALITY: DEFINITIONS AND CONCEPTUALISATIONS

1 This is, of course, an over-simplification since a high price is itself sometimes used as a signifier of high quality, that is, a high price is a component of the notion of quality under certain conditions. It may even be the key signifier of quality. However, this does not necessarily detract from a conceptualisation of quality in an absolutist sense, since the good or service in question may still be regarded as the best, in the sense of 'the best money can buy'.

2 In the public sector, it is sometimes alleged, no doubt anecdotally, that fewer babies are born over weekends or public holidays because medical staff are tempted to induce to ensure births take place in normal working hours rather than when staff would normally be off duty. Again, the 'customer' is not likely to be in a position to be able to accurately assess the need for inducing a birth and other official minimum standards of care may be met.

3 At first sight these schemes resemble the second party schemes discussed earlier. The difference, however, is that in the second party controlled version, a single firm provides the external assessment and accreditation. In these third party schemes the standard is applied across the whole sector and is operated by some body such as a trade association, to which a proportion of the firms in the sector can belong or have links with.

4 For those who doubt the commitment of the latter two groups, try subscribing to the 'Quality List' on the internet. This is supposed to be a forum – mainly used by US academics and staff of large organisations – for critically discussing the philosophy of, and developments in, TQM. In reality, critical debate is at a minimum. Rather, participants tend to unreservedly support TQM choosing instead the continuous near evangelical delivery of prescriptive messages.

3 RESEARCHING QUALITY IN SMALL FIRMS: THE METHODOLOGICAL ISSUES

1 The other obvious quantitative measure upon which definitions of the small firm are based is turnover. The DTI Small Firms Statistics Unit provides estimates of turnover for firms in various size categories measured by numbers of employees. In practice, however, turnover measures are difficult to use in research because small firm owners are often reluctant to provide accurate financial information on their businesses.

2 During the course of the research one business was involved in a merger which increased its employment to 80. However, because this is an occasional occurrence among small businesses and since this was only a single case, this firm was retained in the study.

3　The definition is described as 'close' because the European Union definition of a small firm is 'under 50 employees' whereas for the purposes of the present research a firm had to have at least one employee or full-time equivalent. As pointed out earlier, it was felt that the discussion of quality management strategies in small firms would be more meaningful if the sample was confined to firms with employees rather than 'one person businesses', that is, the self-employed without employees.

4　The proportion is in fact likely to be at the upper end of this estimate since Jenning's estimate was made before the increases in the registration threshold since 1991 which have more than matched increases in inflation over the same period.

5　The problems this creates in estimating the total number of businesses at any one time is well illustrated by the DTI's Small Firms Statistics Unit's attempts, most recently for the end of 1994 (DTI, 1996a).

6　For example, it might be thought that in a sector such as 'electricity, gas and water supply' (a category used by the DTI in its small business statistics, based on the official Standard Industrial Classification categorisation) there would be few small firms and that the sector would be dominated by large undertakings. In fact, 316 (83.2 per cent) of the 380 businesses in the sector which employ at least one person would be classified as 'small' using the definition adopted for this research, that is, businesses with at least one but under 50 employees.

7　This sampling frame was constructed as part of a £250,000 research programme supported by the Economic and Social Research Council, Barclays Bank, the then Department of Employment, the Rural Development Commission and the European Commission. One result of this generous level of funding was that the centre was able to very carefully construct a set of locality-based sampling frames for small businesses in the services sector in 1990. Since then the sampling frame has been used for a number of projects and regularly updated to take account of firms ceasing to trade, being taken over or moving.

8　The project was an analysis of large firm–small firm relations in two local economies sponsored by the Midland Bank.

9　The centre receives a good deal of press coverage for its research and frequently ensures that respondents who have helped in particular research projects receive feedback on the results.

10　The current research utilised three separate interview schedules. One telephone interview schedule and two face-to-face case study schedules, one for small firm owners who were operating formal methods and one for owners who were operating informal methods. These are available on request from Julian North at the Small Business Research Centre, Kingston University.

11　Though printing firms are classified by SIC code as 'manufacturing' firms, they are sometimes seen as providing a business service so it is not always easy to classify printing. In our sample, 16 printing firms were interviewed. Fourteen of the firms were in general printing and the remaining 2 were paper merchants, that is, supplying manufactured materials to printers. For the study, the conventional SIC classification which puts printing in the manufacturing sector was retained. In noting this difference, none of the 14 printing firms used formalised methods of quality control, and the 2 paper merchants had either implemented or registered BS 5750. An interesting finding in itself.

12 For a breakdown of UK BS 5750 registrations by locality see Pera (1992). This supports the approach adopted by the research design. This is not to assert that spatial considerations never have any influence on quality management strategies. There might, for example, be agglomeration effects in particular localities where groups of firms copy each other in relation to quality management but the size of the sample selected for the present research would not be able to offer sufficient detail to show such effects.

4 SMALL FIRMS AND QUALITY: A QUANTITATIVE APPROACH

1 The above data was gathered through a multiple response question in which respondents were reminded of each institution as a possible source. This makes it less likely that the respondents failed to recall any such sources.

2 TECs have been replaced to some extent by Business Links as the key source of local support for small businesses but at the time the interviews were conducted, Business Links were not fully operational while TECs have been in place since 1990–1991.

3 The high use of formal methods in this instance probably reflects a definitional difference between the current study and SBRT (1994b). Formal methods might mean, for example, that the business claims it operates with a quality manual of some kind but this may not be externally accredited or monitored. The extent of the application of these procedures may also vary greatly and, in practice, in some firms may be virtually indistinguishable from the informal methods relied upon by other firms.

4 One of the authors has recently been a member of a national judging panel to select a 'small business of the year' in which entrants' quality policies and strategies were the main criteria upon which they were assessed. Some of the quality statements and information on procedures submitted could be technically described as formal but were actually minimal. This did not mean the owners were not committed to quality but that their formal procedures did not appear important in achieving quality: the statement was often simply a proclamation of their commitment rather than an instrument by which it was achieved.

5 The obvious example of this simultaneous occurrence is the serving of a meal in a restaurant. The serving of the meal is itself part of the 'consumption' of the meal as a service or what may be termed 'the eating out experience'. However, it is not always the case that services are produced and consumed in this way. For instance, a cinema film converts a combined writing/directing/acting 'service' into a manufactured product which is then converted back into a 'service' in the cinema or when the video cassette is viewed. Delayed delivery of services in this way produces its own quality problems of course.

6 'Sector' here is shorthand for a wide range of possible influences (which will vary depending on the sector) some of which are detailed in the sector discussions below: customer influences are only one of the possible influences.

7 The Federation of Recruitment and Employment Services (1989) reported a 23 per cent growth of the number of firms in the industry between 1988

and 1989, a growth that occurred as trade was slowing down as a result of the onset of recession, thus increasing competition in the industry.

8 For example, *The Interviewer*, an employment agency trade magazine, has published a number of articles and advertisements uncritically promoting BS 5750 as a means of attaining competitive success.

9 These external sources are supported by training provided by equipment suppliers in the industry who provide semi-formal training to operatives when firms purchase equipment with, again, an emphasis on achieving high quality from the equipment (Curran *et al.*, 1996a).

10 This overstates to some extent since often the customer does not really want something too original but a variation on what has been generated for other customers. Equally, the advertising, marketing and design firms themselves may have a limited repertoire of ideas and designs upon which they ring variations aimed to suit the customer's particular needs. But the customer wants some semblance of originality and freshness of approach and this produces the essential non-routine character of the operations of firms in this sector.

5 SMALL FIRMS AND QUALITY OWNER-MANAGERS' STRATEGIES

1 We use the term 'logic' here in a special sense to refer to the ways in which actors (in this case owner-managers) reason in arriving at decisions governing their actions. It comprises assumptions, beliefs, values, knowledge (which may be accurate or inaccurate as assessed by some other person) and the links (particularly causal links) between these which they make in analysing situations and formulating decisions and actions. 'Logics' may vary greatly between individuals even when the situation appears to be the same to outsiders. For instance, in deciding on who to employ, owner-managers may make assumptions and hold values about the suitability of younger or older workers, about different genders and races etc. which when linked with, for example, assessments of skills, can produce very different employment decisions. In this study the attempt is to tease out the varying logics of owners in relation to quality management strategies.

2 As Table 3 in the previous chapter reported, only just over 5 per cent of owner-managers said they were unaware of BS 5750.

3 This assumption ascribing such positive management skills to small business owners in relation to quality management could, of course, be proved wrong, but we believe the data from the study shows that it is more plausible than the more usual assumptions of small business owner ignorance and poor management skills.

4 By 'limited way' here, we refer to the practice adopted by a number of small business owners in the study of adopting some elements of a BS 5750 type approach to quality management without proceeding to full registration.

5 These are, of course, invented business names to preserve the anonymity of the case study firms. The quotes are taken from the tape recorded interviews with owner-managers. Rendering spoken English into printed quotations is always problematic since spoken and written English are different: few people speak in a way which translates to the printed page as perfectly formed, entirely grammatical English. Here we have punctuated to reproduce as closely as possible what respondents said. Further detailed accounts

of all 10 of the case study firms discussed in Chapters 5 and 6 can be found in the Appendix.

6 The belief by those living in a particular time period that change is very rapid and more rapid than in the past might be more psychological than real. For instance, the period from, say, 1890 to 1920, arguably experienced at least as rapid a rate of technological change as the period from 1970 to 1990.

7 Another example is the adoption of computers and IT by small businesses. PCs especially, but also other IT applications, are often now seen as the norm with an assumption that no business can function without them. Yet surveys (Curran *et al.*, 1994; Hepworth, 1994, *Financial Times*, 1996) have reported that perhaps, at most, 85 per cent of small firms have a PC. In some sectors the proportion could be as low as a third. More recent surveys (for example, Curran *et al.*, 1996b) suggest PC use and IT-based business support is now increasing in small firms. The slow take-up among small firms might be seen as another example of the 'backwardness' of small firm owners in adopting up to date management practices. But it might also be the result of a rational assessment of what IT can contribute to their businesses. We suspect it is the latter. Only recently has the cost of IT hardware and software become suited to the budgets and needs of small enterprises. Small business owners adopt IT when they see a positive contribution to the business's bottom line and this might only now be occurring for a substantial proportion of small firms.

8 Because this was an open question, it needs to be kept in mind that respondents mentioned those quality control strategies they thought were important. This does not mean that strategies not mentioned were not important since a respondent might not mention what to them were 'obvious' strategies or what they took as given for their type of business. Respondents were much more likely to mention what they personally concentrated on or thought was especially important in managing quality in their business.

9 An example of how quality controls in services can be formalised occurs in the provision of advice on financial services products. Many insurance companies, unit and investment trusts now record telephone conversations between staff and the public to monitor the quality of advice being given. Other businesses such as airlines time telephone calls between staff and callers to ensure acceptable productivity levels by staff.

10 We reproduce here what the respondent said. It does not mean that we agree with his assessment of the quality of employees: what is important is not whether the assessment is accurate but that the owner-manager in question bases the firm's quality management strategies in part on his beliefs about the quality of labour available to the firm. We doubt that the owner-manager would be willing to make this statement in public but it adds to the confidence which can be placed in the findings from the research that he is so willing to offer a candid view in the interview.

11 Although skill levels and trust may be positively correlated (higher skilled employees are more likely to work in a high trust environment) there is no necessary link here, that is, employers may choose to create low or high trust environments regardless of the skill levels of employees.

12 The use of training as a reward has been found in previous research on

small firms (Curran *et al.*, 1996a: 29) with other gains from training such as improved work skills sometimes even seen as secondary.

13 One of the most publicised examples is at Nissan UK's Sunderland plant where production line workers are expected to be able to do all the tasks on their section of the 'line' to maximise the efficient use of labour. For an account by a representative of Nissan see Wickens (1987).

14 Here is yet another example of owner-manager practice which echoes a more formal programme with much the same aim. The Skills for Small Business initiative announced in 1994 by the government provided £63m to train key workers in small firms who then become skills 'champions' in their firms passing on skills to other employees (DTI, 1996b: 52–53).

15 Not all the respondents mention the use of informal methods of quality control as Table 7, Chapter 4, reported but it is difficult to imagine any economic enterprise where informal quality controls are not used. Even where great reliance is placed on formal controls some informal methods will still be used. Those responsible for administering formal controls will still rely to some extent on informal inspection and their experience to ensure standards are being met.

16 As recorded earlier in the chapter, some owner-managers who decide not to adopt BS 5750 still incorporate some of the elements of the standard in their operations which they believe will have positive benefits.

6 SMALL FIRMS AND FORMAL METHODS OF QUALITY CONTROL

1 A list of the main organisations offering third party certification of BS 5750 or equivalent standards, is given in North *et al.* (1993).

2 Customer imposed formal quality systems should be seen as separate from 'vendor assessment' exercises which involve customers inspecting rather than dictating suppliers' operating procedures and practices. The latter are common but no precise data appears to be available on their overall incidence in the UK.

3 It should be kept in mind, however, that 'popular' is relative here: the 18 firms implementing or already registered for BS 5750 were out of 150 firms in the study.

4 In the public sector other motives may be important. For example, it has been suggested that local authorities may use it as a means of keeping contracts in house for their Direct Service Organisations thus avoiding the object of compulsory competitive tendering (CCT), that is, of opening up the market for local authority services to the private sector (Davis-Coleman in Rock, 1992: 42). Since BS 5750 is still relatively rare in the private sector, insisting on possession of BS 5750 as a condition of being able to submit a tender prevents potential suppliers from participating in the CCT process, it is alleged. See the evidence below in the text on the importance of local authority's insistence on BS 5750 accreditation among suppliers and Abbott *et al.* (1996).

5 These are immediate costs: the costs of retaining registration after it has been achieved are discussed later.

6 The figures given in the table need to be treated with caution. Some respondents may not have been providing an accurate estimate of all costs, direct and especially indirect, resulting from implementation/registration.

For example, owner-manager and employee time costs are often not fully recorded or difficult to estimate. It is likely, therefore, that there is an element of understatement in the totals recorded.

7 Some would argue that small firms always have advantages of this kind because they are small. Small firms, it is alleged, always have good communication and strong team spirit, making change easier. However, this is another example of a size reductionist explanation. Small size does not automatically produce such effects. A small firm can be managed in a highly centralised, autocratic way with poor communication and poor involvement of employees so that change may be just as difficult to manage as in larger firms.

8 The phrase 'reduced scrap' and the size of the proportion reporting this effect suggests that the sample contained a high proportion of manufacturing firms. Service firms are unlikely to report such effects.

9 As for all of the data on the 20 firms discussed in this chapter, they also need to be treated with caution because of the small size of the sub-samples being discussed in relation to some of the issues.

References

Abbott, B. (1993) 'Training Strategies in Small Service Sector Firms: Employer and Employee Perspectives', *Human Resource Management Journal*, vol. 4, no. 2, pp 70–78.

Abbott, B., Blackburn, R. A. and Curran, J. (1996) 'Local Authority Privatisation and Markets for Small Businesses', *Local Government Studies*, vol. 23, no. 3, pp 72–89.

Ajimal, K. S. (1987) 'Small Enterprise Development for Job Creation: Training and Development Implications', *Training and Development*, vol. 6, no. 8, pp 13–16.

Ashton, P. and Jackson, D. (1993) *Implementing Quality Through BS 5750*, London, Kogan Page.

Bailey, E. (1992) 'How a Paper Kite Is Giving Nightmares to Plumber Tim', *Daily Telegraph*, 15 December.

Bannock, G. (1991) 'Opinion – BS 5750: No Rush to Register', *Small Business Perspective*, pp 15–16, Jan.–Feb.

Barad, M. (1996) 'Total Quality Management', *International Encyclopedia of Business and Management*, vol. 5, London, Routledge.

Barkham, R., Hart, M. and Hanvey, E. (1996) 'The Role of Established SMEs in Regional and Local Economic Development' in Blackburn, R. and Jennings, P. (eds.) *Small Firms: Contributions to Economic Regeneration*, London, Paul Chapman.

Batchelor, C. (1992) 'Badge of Quality', *Financial Times*, 4 September.

Batchelor, C. (1993) 'Need a Quality Certificate: Ask Tom, Dick or Harry', *Financial Times*, 8 March.

Bethell, J. (1993) 'Small Firms Head Revolt Against Quality Standard', *Sunday Times*, 12 September.

Bethell, J. (1994) 'Cheap Ways to Acquire BS 5750', *Sunday Times*, 17 July.

Blackburn, R. A. (1996) 'The Future of the Small Firm in the UK Economy', the Third Midland Bank Lecture, delivered at Kingston University, July.

Blackham, A. (1992) 'The Value of ISO 9000 Registration – Conclusions Of International Survey', paper presented at 'The UK Quality Management Exhibition', November.

Bolton Report (1971) *Small Firms, Report of the Committee of Inquiry on Small Firms*, London, HMSO, Cmnd 4811.

Bowbrick, P. (1992) *The Economics of Quality, Grades and Brands*, London, Routledge.

British Standards Institute (1987) *BS 4778: Terms and Definitions*, London, BSI.

British Standards Institute (1987) *BS 5750 Part 1, Specification for Design Development, Production, Installation and Servicing*, London, BSI.

Brown, R. K. (1992) *Understanding Industrial Organisations: Theoretical Perspectives in Industrial Sociology*, Routledge, London.

Bryson, J., Wood, P. and Keeble, D. (1993) 'Business Networks, Small Firm Flexibility and Regional Development in UK Business Services', *Entrepreneurship & Regional Development*, vol. 5, pp 265–267.

Burns, T. and Stalker, G. M. (1966) *The Management of Innovation*, London, Tavistock.

Burrows, R. and Curran, J. (1989) 'Sociological Research in Service Sector Small Businesses: Some Conceptual Considerations', *Work, Employment and Society*, vol. 3, no. 4, pp 527–539.

Callan, R. J. (1992) 'Quality Control at Avant Hotels – The Debut of BS 5750', *The Service Industries Journal*, vol. 12, no. 1, pp 17–33, January.

Chittenden, F., Masooda Mukhtar, S. and Poutziouris, P. (1996) 'BS 5750 and Quality Management in SMEs' in Blackburn, R and Jennings, P (eds.) *Small Firms: Contributions to Economic Regeneration*, London, Paul Chapman.

Churchill, N. C. and Lewis, V. L. (1983) 'The Five Stages of Small Business Growth', *Harvard Business Review*, vol. 6, no. 3, pp 43–54.

Coote, A. and Pfeffer, N. (1991) *Is Quality Good For You? A Critical Review Of Quality Assurance in Welfare Services*, London, Institute for Public Policy Research.

Crosby, P. B. (1979) *Quality Is Free*, New York, McGraw-Hill.

Curran, J. (1987) *Small Firms and Their Environments: A Report*, Kingston upon Thames, Small Business Research Centre, Kingston University.

Curran, J. (1996) *The Role of the Small Firm in the UK Economy*, Midland Bank Small Business Lecture, Kingston upon Thames, Small Business Research Centre, Kingston University, June.

Curran, J. and Burrows, R. (1988) *Enterprise in Britain: A National Profile of Small Business Owners and the Self Employed*, London, Small Business Research Trust.

Curran, J. and Blackburn, R. A. (1992) *Small Firms and Local Economic Networks: Relations Between Small and Large Firms in Two Localities*, Kingston upon Thames, Small Business Research Centre, Kingston University, March.

Curran, J. and Blackburn, R. A. (1994) *Small Firms and Local Economic Networks: The Death of the Local Economy?*, London, Paul Chapman.

Curran, J., Blackburn, R. A. and Woods, A. (1991) *Profiles of the Small Enterprise in the Service Sector*, Kingston upon Thames, ESRC Centre for Research on Small Service Sector Enterprises, Kingston University.

Curran, J., Blackburn, R. A. and Woods, A. (1993) *A Longitudinal Study of Small Enterprises in the Service Sector 1993 Survey Report*, Kingston upon Thames, Small Business Research Centre, Kingston University.

Curran, J., Blackburn, R. A. and Klett, M. (1994) *Small Firms in Services – The 1994 Survey*, Kingston upon Thames, Small Business Research Centre, Kingston University, May.

Curran, J., Blackburn, R. A., Kitching, J., North, J. and Blizzard, D. (1995)

Small Firms in Services – The 1995 Survey, Kingston upon Thames, Small Business Research Centre, Kingston University, November.

Curran, J., Blackburn, R. A., Kitching, J. and North, J. (1996a) *Establishing Small Firms' Training Practices, Needs and Difficulties and Use of Industry Training Organisations*, London, Department of Education and Employment Research Studies 17, HMSO.

Curran, J., Blackburn, R. A. and Fitchew, S. (1996b) *Small Firms in Services – The 1996 Survey*, Kingston upon Thames, Small Business Research Centre, Kingston University.

Dale, B. G., Lascelles, D. M. and Plunkett, J. J. (1990) 'The Process of Total Quality Management', in Dale, B. G. and Plunkett, J. J. (eds.) *Managing Quality*, Hemel Hempstead, Phillip Alan.

Davies, P. (1990) 'TQM in Small Firms', *Total Quality Management Magazine*, vol. 2, no. 5, pp 251–252.

Deming, W. E. (1986) *Out of the Crisis*, Cambridge, Mass., MIT Press.

Dewhurst, J. and Burns, P. (1993) *Small Business Management* (3rd edn), London, Macmillan.

Drummond, H. (1992) *The Quality Movement*, London, McGraw-Hill.

DTI (1991) *Introducing the Enterprise Initiative*, London, Department of Trade and Industry, August.

DTI (1992) *BS 5750/ISO 9000: 1987 A Positive Contribution to Better Business*, London, Department of Trade and Industry, January.

DTI (1994) Information Provided to the Small Business Research Centre, Kingston University.

DTI (1995) *Small Firms in Britain Report 1995,* London, Department of Trade and Industry.

DTI (1996a) *Small and Medium Sized Enterprise (SME) Statistics for the United Kingdom, 1994*, Sheffield, Small Firms Statistics Unit, Department of Trade and Industry, July.

DTI (1996b) *Small Firms in Britain Report 1996*, London, Department of Trade and Industry.

ESRC (1994) *Building Partnerships: Enhancing the Quality of Management Research*, Swindon, Economic and Social Research Council, January.

European Commission (1996) *The Week in Europe*, WE 6/96, 15 February.

FEI (1995) *The FEI Review 1994/95*, London, Federation of the Electronics Industry.

Feigenbaum, A. V. (1972) *Total Quality Control*, New York, McGraw-Hill.

Felstead, A. (1991) 'Facing Up to the Fragility of "Minding Your Own Business" as a Franchisee' in Curran, J. and Blackburn, R. A. (eds.) *Paths of Enterprise: The Future of the Small Business*, London, Routledge.

Felstead, A. and Green, F. (1993) *Cycles of Training? Evidence from the British Recession of the Early 1990s*, Discussion Paper 93/3, Leicester, Department of Economics, University of Leicester, April.

Fennel, E. (1991) 'Kite Marks Call for Legal Eagles', *Times*, 23 April.

Financial Times (1996) 'Britain in Focus: 55% of Business Still PC-Free', 22 April.

Fox, M. J. (1991) *Ensuring Your Business Achieves and Profits from BS 5750 Registration*, Letchworth, Technical Communications (Publishing) Ltd.

Goss, D. (1994) *Principles of Human Resource Management*, London, Routledge.

Gouldner, A. (1954) *Patterns of Industrial Bureaucracy*, London, Macmillan.

Gronroos, C. (1994) 'From Marketing Mix to Relationship Marketing: Towards a Paradigm Shift in Marketing', *Management Decision*, vol. 32, no. 2, pp 4–20.

Halliday, S. (1993) 'Small Firms and BS 5750', *Journal of European Business Education*, vol. 2, no. 2, pp 95–99, May.

Harbourne, D. (1993) 'The Forgotten Role of the Industry Training Organisation', *Paper Presented to the 16th National Small Firms Policy and Research Conference*, Nottingham, November.

Harris, D. (1991) 'Standards Needed to Tender for Contracts', *Times*, 14 June.

Hepworth, M. (1994) *Engineering Industries and Business Services in Croydon*, London, London Borough of Croydon Economic and Strategic Development Unit, September.

Hill, S. (1991) 'How Do You Manage a Flexible Firm? The Total Quality Model', *Work, Employment and Society*, vol. 5, no. 3, pp 397–415.

Hodgart, A. and Temporal, D. (1991) 'Building a Quality Approach to Legal Services', *Bulletin 4*, London, Hodgart and Temporal & Co, Consultants.

Holliday, R. (1994) *'Double Standards: BS 5750 and Quality Management in Two Small Companies'*, paper presented to a Quality Workshop at Kingston Business School, Kingston University, Kingston upon Thames, February.

Holliday, R. (1995) *Investigating Small Firms: Nice Work?*, Routledge, London.

Huczynski, A. and Buchanan, D. (1991) *Organisational Behaviour: An Introductory Text* (2nd edn), London, Prentice-Hall.

Jack, A. (1991) 'Setting Standards To Keep Customers Loyal', *Times*, 27 September.

Jackson, M. C. (1993) *Beyond The Fads: Systems Thinking For Managers*, University of Hull Working Paper, no. 3.

Jackson, P. and Ashton, D. (1995) *Managing a Quality System Using BS EN ISO 9000*, London, Kogan Page.

Jay Communications, (1991) *Attitudes within British Business to Quality Management Systems*, Burnham, Buckinghamshire, The CMC Partnership Ltd.

Jennings, K. (1991) 'How to Make Your Start-Up Stay Up', *Observer*, 17 March.

Juran, J. M. (1991) 'Strategies for World Class Quality', *Quality Progress*, vol. 24, no. 3, pp. 81–85, March.

Keeble, D., Bryson, J. and Wood, P. (1992) 'Small Firms, Business Services Growth and Regional Development in the United Kingdom: Some Empirical Findings', *Regional Studies*, vol. 25, no. 5, pp 439–457.

Kelly, A. (1991) 'The Enterprise Culture and the Welfare State' in Burrows, R. (ed.) *Deciphering the Enterprise Culture: Entrepreneurship Petty Capitalism and the Restructuring of Britain*, London, Routledge.

Kerfoot, D. and Knights, D. (1995) 'Empowering the "Quality Worker"?: The Seduction and Contradiction of the Total Quality Phenomenon' in Wilkinson, A. and Willmott, H. (eds.) *Making Quality Critical, New Perspectives and Organizational Change*, London, Routledge.

Keynote (1993) *Computer Services*, London, Keynote.

Kirkpatrick, I. and Martinez Lucio, M. (1995) *The Politics of Quality in the Public Sector*, London, Routledge.

Kuusisto, J. (1997) 'The Determinants of Service Capability in Small

Manufacturing Enterprises', unpublished Ph.D., Kingston upon Thames, Kingston University.

Macdonald, J. (1993) *TQM: Does It Always Work?*, TQM Practitioner Series, Letchworth, Technical Communications (Publishing) Ltd.

Macmillan, K., Curran, J. and Downing, S. (1990) 'Government Consultations with Small Business Owners: Empirically Evaluating Communication Strategies', *International Small Business Journal*, vol. 8, no. 4, pp 14–32.

Manpower Services Commission (1986) *Small Firms Survey*, Sheffield, Manpower Services Commission.

Meadows, P. (1996) (ed.) *Work Out – Or Work In? Contributions to the Debate on the Future of Work*, York, Rowntree Foundation.

Murphy, P. E. and Laczniak, G. R. (1981) 'Marketing Ethics: A Review With Implications for Managers, Educators and Researchers' in Enis, B. M. and Roering, K. J. (eds.) *Review of Marketing*, Chicago, American Marketing Association.

North, J., Curran, J. and Blackburn, R. A. (1993) *Quality Standards and Small Firms: A Position Paper*, Small Business Research Centre, Kingston University, September.

North, J., Curran, J. and Blackburn, R. A. (1995) 'Quality and Small Firms: A Policy Mismatch and its Impact on Small Enterprise', paper presented to the 18th National Small Firms Policy and Research Conference, Paisley, November.

North, J., Blackburn, R. A. and Curran, J. (1996) 'Reaching Small Businesses? Delivering Advice and Support to Small Businesses Through Trade Bodies', paper presented to the 19th *National Small Firms Policy and Research Conference*, Birmingham, November.

Nuttal, N. (1991) 'Marker for the Future', *The Times*, 14th November.

Oakey, R. (1991) 'Government Policy Towards High Technology: Small Firms Beyond 2000' in Curran, J. and Blackburn, R. A. (eds.) *Paths of Enterprise, The Future of the Small Business*, London, Routledge.

Oakey, R. (1995) *High Technology New Firms: Variable Barriers to Growth*, London, Paul Chapman.

Oliver, G. B. M. (1990) *Quality Management in Construction Interpretations of BS 5750 (1987) – 'Quality Systems' for the Construction Industry*, Special Publication 74, Construction Industry Research and Information Association.

O'Rourke, P. (1993) 'Making Quality Pay', *Interviewer*, vol. 7, no. 11, pp 12–13, June.

Øvretveit, J. (1993) *Measuring Service Quality: Practical Guidelines*, TQM Practitioner Series, Letchworth, Technical Communications Ltd.

Payne, A. (1996) 'Relationship Marketing', *International Encyclopedia of Business and Management*, London, Routledge.

PERA International and Salford University Business Services Limited (1992) *A Survey of Quality Consultancy Scheme Clients 1988–1990*, Melton Mowbray, PERA International.

Peters, T. and Waterman, R. (1982) *In Search of Excellence, Lessons From America's Best Run Companies*, New York, Harper and Row.

Rainnie, A. (1989) *Industrial Relations in Small Firms: Small Isn't Beautiful*, London, Routledge.

Rees, C. (1996) 'Employee Autonomy and Management Control in the Quality

Organisation', Paper presented at 14th Annual International Labour Process Conference, Aston University, Birmingham, March.

Reeves, C. and Hoy, F. (1993) 'Employee Perceptions of Management Commitment and Customer Evaluations of Quality Service in Independent Firms', *Journal of Small Business Management*, vol. 31, no. 4, pp 52–59.

Robinson, R. and Le Grand, J. (1993) *Evaluating the NHS Reforms*, Poole, BEBC.

Rock, M. (1992) 'Twist and Turns on Quality Street', *The Director*, vol. 46, no. 5, pp 41–43.

Rutherfoord, R. (1996) 'Small Business and Community: Whose Community, Which Small Business?', paper presented to the 19th National Small Firms Policy and Research Conference, Birmingham, November.

Sadgrove, K. (1994) *ISO 9000/BS 5750 Made Easy*, London, Kogan Page.

Scase, R. and Goffee, R. (1989) *The Real World of the Small Business Owner* (3rd edn), London, Croom Helm.

Scott, M., Robert, I., Holroyd, G. and Sawbridge, D. (1989) *Management and Industrial Relations in Small Firms*, Research Paper no. 70, London, Department of Employment.

Shaw, E. (1995) 'Small Firm Networks That Really Matter', paper presented to the 18th National Small Firms Policy and Research Conference, Paisley, November.

Sherwood, K. F. (1986) *A Guide To Quality*, London, Institution of Production Engineers.

Small Business Research Trust (1992) 'Quality Procedures: BS 5750', *NatWest Quarterly Survey of Small Business*, vol. 8, no. 3, pp 18–22.

Small Business Research Trust (1994a) *Small Businesses and BS 5750*, Small Business Research Trust, October.

Small Business Research Trust (1994b) *Quarterly Small Business Management Report*, vol. 2, no. 2.

Smith, I. T. (1985) 'Employment Laws and the Small Firm', *Industrial Law Journal*, vol. 14, no. 1, pp 18–32.

Stanworth, J. and Gray, C. (1991) (eds.) *Bolton 20 Years On: The Small Firm in the 1990s*, London, Paul Chapman.

Stanworth, J., Curran, J. and Hough, J. (1984) 'The Franchised Small Enterprise: Formal and Operational Dimensions of Independence' in Lewis, J. *et al.* (eds.) *Success and Failure in Small Business*, Aldershot, Gower.

Stebbing, L. and Pengelly, R. J. (1994) *Quality Management for the Smaller Business*, London, Ellis Horwood.

Stokes, D. (1994) *Discovering Marketing: An Active Learning Approach*, London, DP Publications.

Storey, D. (1994) *Understanding the Small Business Sector*, London, Routledge.

Storey, D. and Westhead, P. (1994) *Management Training and Small Firm Performance: A Critical Review*, Coventry, Centre for Small and Medium Enterprises, Warwick University.

Taylor, F. W. (1911) *The Principles of Scientific Management*, New York, W. W. Norton.

Taylor, P. (1992) 'Faith in the Religion of Quality is Starting to Waver', *Financial Times*, 21 October.

Thompson, H. (1994) 'Putting Training Within Reach', *The Interviewer*, vol. 8, no. 19, p 9, 15–29 September.

Thorburn, J. T. and Takashima, M. (1992) *Industrial Subcontracting in the UK and Japan*, Avebury, Aldershot.

Tickit (1992) *Guide to Software Quality Management System Construction and Certification using EN 29001*, Department of Trade and Industry, February.

Tisdall, P. (1990) 'National Council Gets Its Big Break', *Times*, 25 October.

Tisdall, P. (1991) 'How the System Began', *Times*, 14 November.

Tomes, A. (1989) 'Time for Quality?: Implementing BS 5750 in Small Companies Has Its Problems', *OR Insight*, vol. 2, no. 1, pp 4–6.

Tuckman, A. (1995) 'Ideology, Quality and TQM' in Wilkinson, A and Willmott, H (eds.) *Making Quality Critical, New Perspectives and Organizational Change*, London, Routledge.

Webb, J. (1995) 'Quality Management and the Management of Quality', in Wilkinson, A. and Willmott, A (eds.) *Making Quality Critical, New Perspectives and Organizational Change*, London, Routledge.

Wickens, P. (1987) *The Road to Nissan: Flexibility, Quality and Teamwork*, Basingstoke, Macmillan.

Wilkinson, A. and Willmott, H. (1995) 'Introduction' in Wilkinson, A. and Willmott, A. (eds.) *Making Quality Critical, New Perspectives and Organizational Change*, London, Routledge.

Wilkinson, A., Marchington, M. and Ackers, P. (1992) 'Total Quality Management and Employee Involvement', *Human Resource Management Journal*, vol. 2, no. 4, pp 1–20.

Woodcock, C. (1992) 'The Cost of Keeping up to Standard', *Guardian*, 31 August.

Zajonc, R. B. (1960) 'Balance Congruity and Dissonance', *Public Opinion Quarterly*, vol. 24, no. 2, pp 280–296.

Author Index

Subject Index